THE CHINESE IN MEXICO
1882–1940

THE CHINESE
IN MEXICO
1882–1940

ROBERT CHAO ROMERO

THE UNIVERSITY OF ARIZONA PRESS
TUCSON

THE UNIVERSITY OF ARIZONA PRESS

© 2010 The Arizona Board of Regents

First issued as a paperback edition 2011

www.uapress.arizona.edu

Library of Congress Cataloging-in-Publication Data
Romero, Robert Chao, 1972–
The Chinese in Mexico, 1882–1940 / Robert Chao Romero.
p. cm.
Includes bibliographical references and index.
ISBN 978-0-8165-2772-4 (cloth : alk. paper)
ISBN 978-0-8165-1460-1 (pbk. : alk. paper)
1. Chinese—Mexico—History. 2. Mexico—Race relations.
3. Race discrimination—Mexico—History. 4. Mexico—
Emigration and immigration—Government policy.
5. Immigrants—Mexico—History. I. Title.
F1392.C45R65   2010
972'.004951—dc22   2010007909

Manufactured in the United States of America on acid-free, archival-quality paper and processed chlorine free.

16   15   14   13   12   11   8   7   6   5   4   3

To Erica

Contents

Illustrations

Figures

Tables

Acknowledgments

I am deeply grateful for the many people who have helped make this book possible. They have journeyed with me not only through the development and completion of this manuscript but also through my adventure-filled transformation over the past ten years from law student at Boalt Hall to historian and Assistant Professor of Chicana/o Studies at UCLA.

I had the great privilege of conducting my graduate studies under the mentorship and direction of José C. Moya. His wise counsel and guidance played a very important role in the successful completion of the dissertation upon which this book is based. I am also thankful for the encouragement and support provided by Kevin Terraciano, Henry Yu, Laura Gomez, and Juan Gomez-Quiñones, all of whom served on my doctoral committee. I wish to thank Evelyn Hu-DeHart of Brown University for her pioneering scholarship in the study of the Chinese in Latin America and for her support since my early days as a graduate student.

I am also grateful for the strong support of my colleagues at the Chavez Department of Chicana/o Studies at UCLA. This book project pushes the academic boundaries of our discipline, and my colleagues have believed in my nontraditional "Asian-Latino Studies" project from the get-go. Special thanks to past and current chairs Reynaldo Macias, Abel Valenzuela, Eric Avila, and Alicia Gaspar de Alba, who have sacrificed much to establish our department as one of the best of its kind. Special thanks also to Alessandro Duranti, Dean of the Social Sciences Division at UCLA, who provided generous subvention funding for this manuscript.

I have enjoyed the privilege of devoting my full energies to the research and writing of this book thanks to generous funding provided by the Ford Foundation and the University of California Office of the President. I am deeply grateful for their support, which took the form of a University of California President's Postdoctoral Fellowship from 2003–2005 and a Ford Foundation Diversity Fellowship for the 2008–2009 academic year. I would not be where I am today apart from my participation in these outstanding programs. Thanks also to Bill Deverell of the Huntington–USC

Institute on California and the West and Chon Noriega of the UCLA Chicano Studies Research Center for hosting me during my postdoctoral fellowship years with the UCOP and the Ford Foundation. Early support for my research project was also provided by the Ford Foundation in the form of a Predoctoral Fellowship.

A special thanks is owed to senior acquisitions editor Patti Hartmann and the rest of the staff of the University of Arizona Press. Thank you for believing in my project and for publishing my first book. A warm note of thanks is also owed to manuscript editor Lisa Williams. Her thoughtful revisions were critical to the successful completion of this manuscript.

A portion of chapter 3 was previously published as an article titled, "Transnational Chinese Immigrant Smuggling to the United States via Mexico and Cuba, 1882–191," *Amerasia Journal* 30 (2004–2005): 1–16. The analysis in chapter 4 of Chinese–Mexican intermarriage was previously published as an article titled, "El destierro de los chinos: Popular Perspectives on Chinese-Mexican Intermarriage in the Early Twentieth Century," *Aztlán: A Journal of Chicano Studies* 32, no. 1 (Spring 2007): 113–44. Parts of chapter 6 of this book also appeared in substantial part in this previous *Aztlán* article.

Thanks to Maura Dykstra, who assisted in the Chinese language translations used in this text. Thanks also to Leonard Melchor and Raul Sandoval, who both helped with the Spanish-language translations of this book. Leonard Melchor provided the Spanish-language translations included in chapter 4, and Raul Sandoval assisted with the translations found in chapters 5 and 6. Nicholas Bauch created the map found in chapter 3. Melissa Walker provided helpful assistance with the formatting of this manuscript.

Finally, I wish to thank my family for their unwavering love and support. Without them, I would not be where I am today. Much love and special thanks to my parents, Drs. David Torres Romero and Ruth Chao Romero. They formed the original Asian-Latino family years before it became fashionable to study the topic, and their support is what sustained me through the grueling years of graduate school and my years as a post-doctoral fellow. Thanks also to my brothers, James, Michael, and Richard.

For my wife, Erica, and my children, Robertito and Elena, I am most grateful. This book is dedicated to them. D.O.M.

Robert Chao Romero

Note on Transliteration of Chinese Names

Most names in this book have been transliterated into pinyin, the system of romanization endorsed by the People's Republic of China and most commonly used by historians of China. Some notable exceptions/complications occur.

Organizational names: While the name of the Nationalist Party (Guo Min Dang) has been changed to pinyin, the Chee Kung Tong (Zhi Gong Tang) has been kept in its original Spanish-language spelling. The main reason for this is that the Guo Min Dang is a widely recognized party whose name can be found in many Chinese language contexts as well as in English writings, whereas the Chee Kung Tong appears to have been an organization dedicated primarily to the interests of Chinese from the southern provinces. To reflect the southern identities of its members and retain the regional feel of the name, as well as to keep the name of the group consistent with the way that it appears in most Mexican historical materials, the non-pinyin spelling *Chee Kung Tong* has been used in this book.

Canton/Guangdong/Guangzhou: Canton is the name used for both the entire Guangdong province and its capital city of Guangzhou. *Canton* has been changed in most cases for the appropriate city/province name. The adjective *Cantonese,* common today, has been retained. In proper names (such as Canton Bank of Hong Kong in chapter 2), the original spelling has been retained. The spelling of *Hong Kong* has also been retained, due to its wide recognition. The spelling of *tong wars* and *tong* has also been retained, because of its use in contemporary scholarship. Names of businesses have also been retained, since the absence of Chinese characters leads to an insufficient amount of evidence for conversion to pinyin.

Because of the difficulty of tracing their exact historical and linguistic origins, village names are presented consistent with the way they appear in primary source documents. Cities and provinces have been updated into pinyin whenever possible, given the constraints of the sources.

THE CHINESE IN MEXICO
1882–1940

1

Introduction

*Chinese Immigration to Mexico and the
Transnational Commercial Orbit*

Pablo Chee (see fig. 1.1) immigrated to Chiapas, Mexico, from Guangdong, China, in November 1901. Less than a decade later, after establishing himself as a successful merchant, Pablo married a Mexican woman, Adelina Palomegus. In 1910, the couple gave birth to their first son, Manuel Jesús Chee. Together with his Mexican wife and son Manuel, Pablo traveled to China in 1914 to visit family members in his home village of Jiu Jang. In 1915, he returned to Mexico, leaving Adelina and Manuel behind to live with their newfound Chinese relatives. As the privileged son of a successful overseas merchant, Manuel subsequently began his educational career as a student in a British school in Guangdong. Following Pablo's return to Mexico, he increased his fortune as a successful businessman in Baja California. He made a large fortune as the owner of a grocery and general merchandise firm, as proprietor of a hotel and saloon, and, allegedly, as an opium dealer. Capitalizing upon his extensive licit commercial successes and based upon his merchant status, Pablo eventually gained the right to immigrate to the United States. In 1924, he applied for permission from the U.S. Immigration and Naturalization Service to bring his wife and son from China to live with him in Imperial Valley, California.[1]

Pablo Chee's immigration to Mexico was part of a larger migration of more than 60,000 Chinese immigrants to Mexico during the late nineteenth and early twentieth centuries.[2] Following the passage of the Chinese Exclusion Act of 1882 barring the legal immigration of Chinese male laborers to the United States, Chinese immigrants flocked to Mexico in search of economic opportunity.[3] By 1910, Chinese immigrants had come to settle in every state and territory of Mexico except for the central state of Tlaxcala, and by 1926, at a size of more than 24,000, the Chinese comprised the second-largest immigrant group in all of Mexico.[4]

As evidenced by the example of Pablo Chee, the Chinese of Mexico also achieved a high degree of economic success. Although the Chinese were initially recruited to Mexico to serve as agricultural contract laborers,

Figure 1.1. Pablo Chee.
Source: Laguna Niguel,
California, National Archives,
Pablo Chee, Chinese Exclu-
sion Act Case File no. 2295/7.

many Chinese transitioned into employment as merchants involved in the grocery and dry goods trade. Chinese shops were ubiquitous and dotted the streets and neighborhoods of Sonora, Chihuahua, and Baja California. Much like 7-Eleven convenience stores in the United States today, Chinese grocery and dry goods stores were found on virtually every street corner in places like Sonora during the early twentieth century.

By the 1920s, Chinese merchants developed a monopoly over the grocery and dry goods trade in northern Mexico. Their great success engendered organized anti-Chinese protests and campaigns replete with lootings, boycotts, massacres, and racist legislation. Sonoran anti-Chinese laws banned Chinese-Mexican intermarriage and ordered the segregation of Chinese into racially restricted neighborhoods. Tragically, anti-Chinese sentiment also expressed itself violently. The most horrendous act of violence perpetrated against the Chinese community occurred on May 15, 1911, during the massacre of Torreón. As part of the massacre of Torreón, 303 Chinese immigrants were murdered by revolutionary soldiers in a single day. The organized anti-Chinese movement in Mexico culminated in the expulsion of virtually the entire Chinese population of the state of Sonora in 1931.[5]

In response to the immigration restrictions placed upon them by the Chinese Exclusion Act of 1882, Chinese immigrants flocked to Mexico not only in search of employment opportunities as agricultural laborers and merchants but also to get smuggled into the United States. Unknown to most people, the Chinese were the first "undocumented immigrants" from Mexico, and they created the first organized system of human smuggling from Mexico to the United States. As part of their efforts to circumvent the U.S. Chinese Exclusion Laws, Chinese immigrants created a vast, "transnational" smuggling business that involved agents and collaborators in China, Mexico, Cuba, and various cities throughout the United States. The Chinese also developed a variety of schemes and techniques to smuggle immigrants into the United States via train, boat, and "coyote," or guide.

Chinese Immigrant Transnationalism

As reflected by the historical phenomenon of immigrant smuggling, Chinese migration and settlement in Mexico was characterized by transnationalism. "Transnationalism" has been defined as: "[T]he emergence of a social process in which migrants establish social fields that cross geographic, cultural, and political borders. Immigrants are understood to be transmigrants when they develop and maintain multiple relations— familial, economic, social, organizational, religious, and political—that spans borders. . . . The multiplicity of migrants' involvements in both the home and host societies is a central element of transnationalism."[6]

Chinese immigrant smuggling represents a compelling historical example of transnationalism because it involved a multinational socio-economic network spanning China, Latin America, and the United States. As a way of circumventing the Chinese exclusion laws of the United States, enterprising Chinese merchants and capitalists created a highly sophisticated transnational immigrant smuggling network involving representatives in China, Mexico, Cuba, and various cities throughout the United States, including Tucson, San Diego, El Paso, New York, Boston, New Orleans, and San Francisco. The Chinese Six Companies, a transnational immigrant fraternal organization based out of San Francisco, was reportedly the chief sponsor of the illicit traffic of Chinese immigrants. During the late nineteenth century, Havana, Cuba, was reportedly the geographic headquarters for the Chinese immigrant smuggling business. The smuggling business was coordinated from Havana because the city was home to a key official of the Chinese Six Companies who possessed strategic insider connections to important transportation companies such as the Pacific Railroad Company, the Morgan Steamship Line, and the Ward Steamship Company. Building upon these important institutional connections, the Six Companies developed a variety of schemes and techniques to smuggle Chinese immigrants into the United States. It is estimated that as many as 2,000 Chinese illegally entered the United States annually between 1876 and 1911.[7]

This global smuggling network established by Chinese businessmen formed the basis for a broader Chinese "transnational commercial orbit" during the late nineteenth and early twentieth centuries.[8] This transnational economic orbit encompassed China, Latin America, Canada, and the Caribbean, and it was shaped by entrepreneurial Chinese who pursued commercial opportunities not only in human smuggling but also in labor contracting, wholesale merchandising, and small-scale trade. In addition to immigrant smuggling, one important activity of this commercial orbit involved the recruitment of contract laborers for mining and agriculture in northern Mexico. Ironically, the passage of the Chinese exclusion laws in the United States coincided with efforts of the Mexican government to attract Chinese immigrants as laborers for its developing economy. In the early twentieth century, Mexican businessmen developed an organized system of Chinese contract labor recruitment in direct collaboration with prominent Chinese merchants of San Francisco.

Two other important aspects of the transnational commercial orbit involved the practices of transnational capital investment based upon familial ties and the provision of wholesale supplies and goods for sale in Mexican shops. One of the most important means by which Chinese entrepreneurs in Mexico gained access to business capital was through the pooling of transnational capital from family members residing in the United States and China.[9] Although the financial resources of any individual Chinese immigrant might be insufficient to launch a business, this strategy of transnational economic investment enabled Chinese entrepreneurs to become partners in well-capitalized commercial ventures. Chinese borderland merchants of Mexico also purchased much of their store inventory from Chinese and Anglo wholesale suppliers of the United States.[10] U.S.–based Chinese wholesale suppliers traveled regularly into Mexico to sell their products to Chinese grocery and dry goods merchants, and Chinese shop owners in Mexico ordered goods from transnational suppliers located in Calexico, Los Angeles, San Francisco, Canada, and

Hong Kong. Commercial collaboration between Chinese merchants of Mexico and family members and wholesale suppliers of the United States, Canada, and China therefore represents another important feature of the transnational economic orbit.

My central argument in this book is that the Chinese created a transnational commercial orbit in resistance, and adaptation, to the Chinese exclusion laws. One unintended consequence of the closure of the United States to Chinese immigration was the diversion of Chinese migration streams to Mexico. As previously discussed, in response to legal restrictions against them in the United States, Chinese immigrants journeyed to Mexico for two main reasons: first, to be smuggled into the United States; and, second, in search of employment opportunities within Mexico's developing economy. The transnational commercial orbit was developed by entrepreneurial Chinese as a means of facilitating the big business of immigrant smuggling and contract labor recruitment. Both immigrant smuggling and contract labor recruitment operated within the same transnational economic network and likely involved many of the same key financial business interests and players. In both instances, prominent Chinese merchants of San Francisco played central roles in the development and ultimate success of these commercial activities. In addition, the economic success of Chinese merchants in Mexico was made possible in large part by access to transnational capital and wholesale supplies of the transnational commercial orbit.

A "Diasporic Transnational" Approach

The formation of the Chinese economic orbit led to the development of unique transnational socioeconomic and political relationships between the Chinese diasporic communities of Mexico and those of the United States. One important aim of this book is to examine these complex transnational relationships, as well as to understand Chinese immigration to Mexico within the context of the broader global Chinese diaspora of the mid-nineteenth through the early twentieth century.

The term *diaspora* has traditionally been defined as "the scattering and migration of . . . minority groups who have a common ancestral homeland, reside in several foreign areas, share a common culture, hold similar aspirations and beliefs, and maintain some kind of linkage with a homeland."[11] As will be discussed in greater detail in chapter 2, Chinese immigrant communities of Mexico and the United States fit this definition of diaspora and figured uniquely within the much larger global Chinese diaspora of the late nineteenth and early twentieth centuries. As part of the Chinese diaspora of this era, more than eight million Chinese immigrated throughout the world to foreign destinations such as Africa, Southeast Asia, Australia, and the Americas.[12] This study analyzes the significant historical connections between Chinese immigration and settlement in two specific diasporic destinations—Mexico and the United States.

Utilizing a "diasporic transnational approach," this book examines Chinese immigration to Mexico within the context of the global Chinese diaspora of the mid-nineteenth through the early twentieth century. In addition, it illuminates many of the transnational socioeconomic and political linkages that members of the Chinese colony of Mexico shared with both their home villages and the Chinese diasporic communities of the United States and Cuba. This book examines Chinese transnationalism in the forms of merchant networks, transnational capital investment and wholesaling, contract labor recruitment, human trafficking, transnational families, transpacific interracial marriages, and political organizing. Based upon these examples, the Chinese of Mexico provide a unique and overlooked historical case study of transnationalism.

In addition to being a study of Chinese transnationalism, this book is primarily a social history of the Chinese of Mexico. It provides a comprehensive social history of the Chinese colony of Mexico during the late nineteenth and early twentieth centuries and examines such varied themes as: Chinese immigration and settlement patterns; Chinese migrant smuggling networks; gender, family, and racial intermarriage; residential and employment patterns; the development of Chinese community organizations; the "tong wars"[13]; and the anti-Chinese campaigns and strategies of Chinese-immigrant resistance.

Despite the rich and controversial history of the Chinese of Mexico, their story has been largely overlooked and forgotten in the popular imagination. One reason for this lapse of historical memory relates to the minimal visible presence of Chinese immigrants and their descendants in Mexico today. Aside from the Chinese community of Mexicali in Baja California, which numbers approximately five thousand, and apart from the well-known "cafés chinos" in Mexico City, individuals of Chinese descent are rarely visible in other Mexican cities and states. As a result, few people realize that there was once a large and flourishing Chinese community in Mexico. Another reason why the story of the Chinese of Mexico is lost from public memory is its exclusion from official histories of Mexico. Because the organized anti-Chinese campaigns and the massacre of Torreón represent a dark chapter in the history of modern Mexico, the story of the Chinese community of Mexico has been largely omitted from official Mexican history texts.

Review of the Literature

Although lost to popular memory, the story of the Chinese in Mexico has been preserved over the years by a handful of Mexican and U.S. historians. This study has benefited greatly from the solid foundation of research that has been laid by these scholars over the past several decades. José Jorge Gómez Izquierdo, Juan Puig, Maria Elena Ota Mishima, Maricela Gonzales Félix, and José Luis Trueba Lara have published important foundational studies in Mexico.[14] Evelyn Hu-DeHart has pioneered the study of the Chinese of Mexico in the United States, and Gerardo Renique, Grace Delgado, and Julia Schiavone Camacho have also published seminal works on the topic in recent years.[15] With some exception, much of the previous literature on the Chinese of Mexico focuses on the topic of Mexican xenophobia and the anti-Chinese campaigns. Previous works tend to fetishize xenophobia and place secondary emphasis upon a detailed examination of Chinese socioeconomic adaptation patterns. In addition, because most prior studies are based upon Mexican governmental records and sources generated by proponents of the anti-Chinese movement, the Chinese immigrant voice and perspective have been largely overlooked and omitted. Prior studies paint Chinese immigrants as passive victims of the sinophobic campaigns, and Mexicans from the north are depicted as being monolithically racist. One of the important aims of this book is to move past this dominant paradigm by providing a social history that humanizes Chinese immigrants.

In addition to building upon the historiography related to Chinese immigration and settlement in Mexico, this book also contributes to the substantial anthropological and historical literatures of transnationalism.[16] Most directly, it builds upon the historiography of Chinese American transnationalism pioneered by scholars such as Sucheng Chan, Madeline Hsu, Erika Lee, Adam McKeown, and Yong Chen.[17]

Although many of the most prominent theorists of transnationalism assert that transnationalism is a postmodern phenomenon and a by-product of global capitalism and modern technologies, these scholars have published important historical studies of Chinese transnationalism in the early twentieth century.[18] Building upon the work of these scholars, *The Chinese in Mexico* contributes a unique example of historical Chinese transnationalism in Mexico during this same time period. In addition, with the notable exception of McKeown's *Chinese Migrant Networks and Cultural Change,* most prior studies of Chinese transnationalism focus on an examination of the rich transnational ties that existed between the overseas Chinese community of the United States and China, and place secondary emphasis upon the historical interactions between Chinese diasporic communities in the Americas. Through its analysis of Chinese transnational ties in Mexico, Cuba, and the United States, this book offers a unique contribution to this new direction of research.

Finally, this study also builds upon the growing body of historical and anthropological literature that seeks to uncover the forgotten history of Latin America's Asian population, or *cuarta raíz.*[19] Despite the historic and contemporary presence of millions of Asians in Latin America, Latin American culture has traditionally been viewed as resulting from the racial mixture, or "mestizaje," of three races—European, indigenous, and African. As a consequence, the fields of Latin American studies and Chicano/Latino studies have been slow to incorporate Asians within their discussions of racial theory and mestizaje. In recent years, a growing number of scholars have begun to challenge this trichotomous view of race in Latin America and have published important studies on the historic and contemporary Asian populations of the region. In addition to the previously mentioned historians of the Chinese in Mexico, Adam McKeown, Humberto Rodriguez Pastor, Juan Jiménez Pastrana, Chikako Yamawaki, Evelyn Hu-DeHart, Kathleen Lopez, Walton Look Lai, and Armando Choy have published important studies on the Chinese of Peru, Cuba, and the broader Caribbean.[20] Jeffrey Lesser, Daniel Masterson, and Steven Masami-Ropp have authored seminal publications on the Japanese of Brazil, Mexico, and Peru.[21] As the first English-language monograph on the Chinese of Mexico, *The Chinese in Mexico* contributes significantly to this developing historiographical wave of Asians in Latin America and the re-envisioning of traditional notions of Mexican mestizaje.

Methodology

Methodologically, this study is based upon a wide array of Mexican and U.S. archival sources. It culls from various quantitative and qualitative sources, including Mexican census records and municipal manuscripts, interviews of Chinese immigrants conducted by the U.S. Immigration Service in the early twentieth century, U.S. consular and Treasury Department reports and correspondence, Mexican periodicals, immigration reports issued by the Mexican federal government related to the Chinese presence in Mexico, and oral histories.

Of these various sources utilized in this study, two merit special elaboration: (1) the Chinese Exclusion Act case files of the Immigration and Naturalization Service, and (2) the 1930 Mexican municipal census manuscripts. The former records have been scarcely used by scholars of Chinese immigration to Mexico; the latter have never been utilized by prior studies of Chinese migration and settlement in Mexico. Together, these two sources provide a comprehensive sociological and historical window into the lives of Chinese immigrants in Mexico during the early twentieth century.

Drawn from the holdings of the U.S. National Archives, the Chinese Exclusion Act case files offer tremendous amounts of qualitative data from the perspective of Chinese immigrants themselves. In addition, they shed great insight into the transnational socioeconomic and political linkages shared by the Chinese diasporic communities of Mexico, Cuba, and the United States. They provide a wealth of qualitative data related to Chinese patterns of immigration, employment, family, marriage, gender, and residential settlement. Individual case files contain a variety of records, including in-depth interviews of Chinese immigrants conducted by U.S. immigration officials, photos, partnership lists, visa documentation, and Immigration Service correspondence. Life stories sifted from these materials are included throughout the book, as a means of providing personal immigrant perspectives on macrohistorical processes.

The vast amount of qualitative data culled from Chinese Exclusion Act case files was, moreover, corroborated and confirmed by quantitative data drawn from Mexican municipal census manuscripts. Municipal census data were gathered from the Sonoran municipalities of Hermosillo, Magdalena, Guaymas, Arizpe, Moctezuma, and Nogales, and the Chihuahua state capital of Chihuahua City. The states of Sonora and Chihuahua were selected for analysis because both possessed large Chinese populations during the early twentieth century. The six chosen Sonoran municipalities provide a geographically diverse sampling of large, medium, and small Sonoran cities. In addition to these six Sonoran municipalities, Chihuahua City was selected for comparative analysis because it represents another large city that was a focus of Chinese settlement in northern

Mexico during the early twentieth century. Samples were obtained through the review of municipal manuscript records and the selection of individuals categorized as Chinese nationals, together with members of their households.

Like the Immigration Service case files, these census manuscripts provided a wealth of information related to the social history of the Chinese in Mexico. They yielded data related to age, gender, marital status, literacy, employment, place of birth, citizenship, religion, and property ownership. Taken together, the quantitative data supplied by these census manuscripts and the qualitative information contained within the Chinese Exclusion Act case files provide a veritable snapshot of life within the Chinese community of northern Mexico during the early twentieth century.

Overview of Chapter Contents

Chapter 2 of this book situates Chinese immigration and settlement in Mexico within the broader context of the global Chinese diaspora and analyzes the origins of the Chinese transnational commercial orbit. It examines the socioeconomic and political circumstances in China, the United States, and Mexico that led to the development of this transnational commercial orbit and the wide-scale migration of Chinese to Mexico. The following chapter traces the multinational journeys traveled by Chinese immigrants along the transnational commercial orbit and asks the basic question: What were the different ways and means by which Chinese immigrated to Mexico? This chapter examines the three migration mechanisms of transnational immigrant smuggling, transnational contract labor recruitment, and familial chain migration.

Whereas chapters 2 and 3 focus on an analysis of Chinese immigration patterns, chapters 4 and 5 examine the adaptation experiences and transnational lives lived by Chinese immigrants in Mexico. Once the Chinese made their way to Mexico, what was their experience like of adapting to this new land? Whom did they marry, where did they live, what kinds of jobs did they take, and what types of organizations did they form? Chapter 4 discusses gender, family, and marriage patterns and pays particular attention to the cross-cultural marriages formed by Chinese immigrant men and Mexican women and the transnational families that Chinese men maintained with both Mexican and Chinese spouses across the Pacific. Chapter 5 examines the transnational economic lives lived by Chinese merchants in Mexico and the profitable commercial relationships they maintained with their diasporic counterparts in the

United States and their kinsmen who remained in China. Through an examination of Chinese borderland merchants and their strategies of transnational commercial investment and wholesaling, this chapter also provides a more detailed glimpse into the inner, day-to-day workings of the transnational commercial orbit. In addition, this chapter analyzes the vocational diversity and stratified socioeconomic nature of the Chinese immigrant community in Mexico more broadly. Chapter 5 concludes with an examination of some of the transnational community organizations formed by the Chinese in Mexico and describes the "tong wars" that were fought by the Guo Min Dang and Chee Kung Tong over the control of the opium trade.

Chapter 6 examines the broad array of Mexican responses to the Chinese presence in Mexico and the perceived economic prosperity of the Chinese immigrant community. Particular attention is given to the massacre of Torreón, the organized anti-Chinese movement, and the historical events leading up to the ultimate expulsion of the Chinese from Sonora in 1931. Although the sinophobic campaigns represent the major focus of this chapter, it also analyzes strategies of Chinese resistance to racial persecution and explores the Chinese immigrant community's use of the Mexican judicial system as a means of protecting its political and commercial interests.

By way of conclusion, chapter 7 summarizes the major findings of this study and discusses some of its important theoretical implications for the academic disciplines of Latin American, Chicano/Latino, and Asian American studies. This chapter proposes the development of a new intellectual space within these fields—that of Asian-Latino, or more playfully, Chino-Chicano, studies. This new field of study would explore the historical and contemporary interactions between Asians and Latinos in Latin America and the United States as well as analyze the historical and sociological experiences of the large population of Asian-Latinos currently living in the United States.

2
The Dragon in Big Lusong
Chinese Immigration to Mexico and the Global Chinese Diaspora

My family was poor, so I was going to Lusong. Who would have known this would be a prison even for those just passing through?

One cannot bear to ask about the loneliness in the wooden building. It is all because of a militarily weak nation with an empty national treasury.

I leave word with you gentlemen that you should all endeavor together.
Do not forget the national humiliations; arouse yourselves to be heroic.[1]

Unknown to most people, Chinese migration to Mexico dates back to the 1600s as part of the Spanish Manila galleon trade. As part of this vibrant colonial transcontinental trade, Spanish merchants purchased large quantities of Chinese luxury items, such as silks and porcelain, from Chinese merchants stationed in the Philippines.[2] From the port of Manila, Spanish merchants transported their cargoes of exotic eastern goods to the port of Acapulco, Mexico, on board large Spanish galleons. From Acapulco, these luxury items were then distributed throughout Mexico and the rest of Latin America. As part of this transpacific trade, small numbers of Chinese immigrants entered colonial Mexico as personal servants of Spanish merchants from the Philippines.[3] Following their initial arrival, many Chinese immigrants of colonial Mexico earned their living as tradesmen, barbers, and shopkeepers, and often resided in segregated quarters in the periphery of the city. During the period of the Manila galleon trade, Chinese referred to the Philippines as "Xiao Lusong," or "Little Luzon," and Mexico came to be known as "Da Lusong," or "Big Luzon."[4] Though the Manila galleon trade ended in 1815, as evidenced by the poem introducing this chapter, Chinese immigrants of the early twentieth century continued to refer to Mexico as "Lusong" or "Luzon."[5]

Although Chinese immigration to Mexico began nearly four hundred years ago, wide-scale Chinese migration to Big Lusong did not occur until the late nineteenth and early twentieth centuries. Chinese immigration to Mexico during these years was part of a much larger international Chinese diaspora and was connected in important ways to patterns of Chinese migration and settlement in the United States. Following the passage of the Chinese Exclusion Act of 1882, which barred the immigration of Chinese laborers to the United States, Chinese emigrants set their sights on Mexico as a new land of economic opportunity and a gateway to the United States. Understanding this diasporic context of Chinese immigration to Mexico is important because it sheds light on three interrelated historical phenomena: (1) the shift of Chinese migration flows from the United States to Mexico during the late nineteenth and early twentieth centuries, (2) the creation of a Chinese transnational commercial orbit in the Americas during these years, and (3) the development of rich transnational socioeconomic and political ties between the Chinese diasporic communities of Mexico and the United States. This chapter situates Chinese immigration to Mexico within the context of the global Chinese diaspora and examines the socioeconomic and political circumstances in China, the United States, and Mexico that engendered wide-scale migration to Mexico and the development of these three historical phenomena.

Lee Kwong Lun and the Global Chinese Diaspora

Lee Kwong Lun emigrated from his native Guangdong to Cuba during the second half of the nineteenth century.[6] Cuba became a major hub of Chinese immigration and settlement during these years because of the "coolie" trade occurring between the years of 1847 and 1874, and later because it further became a popular destination for Chinese immigrants seeking employment as merchants in the Cuban commercial sector. Following a brief sojourn in Cuba, where he developed proficiency in Spanish and acquired the skill of cigar-making, Lee immigrated to San Francisco, where he began a family and settled as a merchant. During the first decade of the twentieth century, following preparation of the documentation necessary to maintain and secure U.S. residency privileges for himself and his family under the merchant clause of the Chinese Exclusion Act, Lee gathered his wife and children together and migrated south of the border to Sonora, Mexico. In Sonora, Lee earned a living by serving as economic middleman between Chinese merchants of Mexico and Chinese wholesale suppliers of San Francisco. Capitalizing upon his multilingual proficiency in Spanish, English, and Chinese, which he acquired as part of his global travels, Lee served as transnational commercial broker and merchant, writing letters to California merchandise suppliers who delivered goods to Mexico by train for sale in Chinese shops. Following a decade-long tenure in Sonora, the Lee family returned to the United States and settled in Tucson, Arizona.[7]

Lee Kwong Lun's flight from the South China province of Guangdong and his multinational travels throughout Cuba, Mexico, and the United States occurred within the broader context of the international Chinese diaspora of the nineteenth and early twentieth centuries. As discussed in chapter 1, *diaspora* may be been defined as "the scattering and migration of . . . minority groups who have a common ancestral homeland, reside in several foreign areas, share a common culture, hold similar aspirations and beliefs, and maintain some kind of linkage with a homeland."[8]

As part of the Chinese diaspora, more than eight million Chinese emigrants like Lee Kwong Lun scattered throughout every continent on the globe and settled in diverse places such as the United States, Mexico, Cuba, Peru, Australia, South Africa, Thailand, and the Philippines. Most Chinese emigrants of the diaspora were from two provinces of southern China known as Fujian and Guangdong. Like Lee Kwong Lun, most Chinese emigrants who eventually settled in the United States and Mexico were from Guangdong. Cantonese and Fujianese emigrants journeyed abroad in search of economic opportunity and a better life for their family members who stayed behind in China. In addition, as will be discussed in detail in this and subsequent chapters, overseas Chinese maintained rich transnational socioeconomic and political connections to their patria and home villages.

Between the years of 1848 and 1888 alone, more than two million Chinese immigrated to California, Hawaii, Australia, the West Indies, the Philippines, Java, Indochina, Sumatra, and the Malay peninsula.[9] During the nineteenth and early twentieth centuries, large numbers of Chinese also immigrated to Brazil, Cuba, Peru, and other parts of Latin America.[10] By the turn of the twentieth century, more than five million Chinese were scattered internationally, and by 1922, this number had increased to

8,190,815.[11] Emigrants like Lee Kwong Lun journeyed overseas through a handful of major seaports located primarily in South China.[12] Xiamen, Macao, Warupu, Caming, Shantou, and Hong Kong were popular ports in the province of Guangdong. Some also emigrated through the Portuguese port of Macao and the northern port of Gongzhou. Hong Kong, Xiamen, Shantou, and Gongzhou served as ports of embarkation for immigrants settling in continental destinations such as Penang, Singapore, French Indo-China, and the Philippines. In addition to being a major port of embarkation for continental destinations in the continental Straits Settlements, Hong Kong was also the principal port of departure for immigrants headed for various intercontinental destinations such as the United States, Canada, and Latin America. The Portuguese seaport of Macao was also utilized by immigrants traveling to intercontinental destinations such as Peru (see table 2.1).

Several historical factors conspired to create a "migration-prone" situation in Guangdong during these years. Overpopulation, the commercialization of agriculture, trends of nascent industrialization, western imperialism, peasant rebellions, and natural disasters served as "push" factors that encouraged wide-scale migration.[13]

Between the years of 1787 and 1850, the population of Guangdong grew from sixteen million to twenty-eight million. This population boom of the nineteenth century resulted largely from the long period of sociopolitical peace that followed the squelching of the Three Feudatories Revolt in 1681.[14] This demographic explosion in the province of Guangdong, moreover, took place within the context of a larger national population boom. Between the years of 1741 and 1851, the overall population of China increased from 143 million to 432 million. This explosion of the Chinese population during the eighteenth and nineteenth centuries may be attributed to an increase in the food supply, internal sociopolitical peace under Manchu rule during the 1700s, an increase in foreign commerce, public health disease control, and transportation improvements allowing for greater facility of movement within the kingdom.[15] Despite such marked demographic growth, this boom of new births was not accompanied by any increase in agricultural productivity or natural resources, and the Qing government initiated no new agrarian or land reform policy measures designed to counter the negative impact of Chinese population pressures.[16] In Guangdong, demographic pressures engendered land shortages, reduced standards of living, increased indebtedness, and peasant socioeconomic displacement.[17]

Table 2.1. Numbers of overseas Chinese in 1922 by country, continent, and region.

Country	Chinese population
Annam (Vietnam)	197,300
Australia	35,000
Brazil	20,000
Burma	134,600
Canada	12,000
Cuba	90,000
East Indies	1,023,500
Europe	1,760
Formosa (Taiwan)	2,258,650
Hawaii	23,507
Hong Kong	314,000
Japan	17,700
Java	1,825,700
Korea	11,300
Macao	74,560
Mexico	14,233
Peru	45,000
Philippines	55,212
Siam (Thailand)	1,500,000
Siberia	37,000
Straits Settlements	432,764
South Africa	5,000
Continental United States	61,639
Total	8,190,815

Sources: Based upon data compiled from Walter F. Wilcox, ed., *International Migrations*, vol. 1, *Statistics, Compiled on Behalf of the International Labour Office, Geneva*, (New York: National Bureau of Economic Research, Inc., 1929), 149; Mexico, Secretría de la Economía Nacional, *Quinto censo de población 1930, resúmen general* (Mexico, D.F.: Dirección General de Estadística); Mexico, Secretaría de la Economía Nacional, *Anuário estadístico de la República Mexicana 1930* (Mexico, D.F.: Dirección General de Estadística).

In addition to overpopulation, economic changes involving the development of commercial agriculture and incipient industrialization also contributed to peasant socioeconomic displacement in Guangdong during the late nineteenth century.[18] The growing agricultural shift from subsistence farming to the production of commercial cash crops, and the development of nascent industry, forced many Cantonese peasants to sell off their land holdings. Moreover, in response to such displacement from their traditional agricultural lands, many sought employment as tenant farmers, city workers, or hired hands.

Western imperialism, peasant rebellion, ethnic land disputes, and natural disasters further contributed to the socioeconomic deterioration set in motion by trends of demographic overpopulation, industrialization, and the commercialization of agriculture. Following the Chinese defeat by the British in the Opium War of 1839–1842, in accordance with the Treaty of Nanjing, China was required to open up five commercial seaports at Guangdong, Shanghai, Fuzhou, Xiamen, and Ningbo. In addition, according to the terms of this treaty, the port city of Hong Kong was ceded to the British.[19] In 1860, moreover, China was required to open up eleven new treaty ports as prescribed by the Conventions of Beijing.[20] Inexpensive European textile imports forced upon Chinese domestic markets through western treaty ports drove many Cantonese cloth merchants and others involved with local textile production out of business. In addition, many Guangdong porters, warehouse employees, boatmen, and shroffs lost their jobs with the opening of Shanghai and Ningbo as treaty ports for the export of Chinese teas and silks.[21] It is estimated that more than one hundred thousand porters and boatmen of northern Guangdong lost employment following the diversion of Zhejiang and Anhui export teas from Canton to the port cities of Shanghai and Ningbo after 1842. Because of its strategic geographic location near the national centers of Chinese silk production, moreover, Shanghai became the principal silk trade port, causing many Cantonese compradors, porters, and shroffs to lose their jobs.

In addition to western imperialism, civil war, and peasant rebellion, domestic ethnic conflict further stirred the waters of Cantonese social instability during the mid-nineteenth century. Beginning in 1851 in Guangxi province, the Taiping Rebellion spread throughout southern China and claimed approximately twenty million lives by the time of its conclusion in 1864.[22] Attempting to establish an egalitarian "Heavenly Kingdom of Great Peace," the founder of the movement, Hong Xiuquan, a Hakka school teacher from Guangxi, claimed to be the younger brother of Jesus Christ and sought to overthrow Qing dynastic rule. During the years of this bloody civil war, the province of Guangdong became the site of brutal military confrontations between dynastic and rebel forces, and such conflict further eroded the social harmony of South China.

Although Guangdong was a central theater of military conflict during the years of the Taiping Rebellion, the port city of Guangzhou was spared from participation in the worst of the fighting. Nonetheless, local governmental authority in Guangdong became sufficiently weakened as a consequence of the civil war as to inspire further peasant rebellion in the form of the Red Turban Rebellion of 1854. In the spring of 1854, sporting their signature red turbans, antidynastic secret societies known as the Triads launched an assault upon the city of Guangzhou and its surrounding vicinity. Following the suppression of the civil uprising, imperial authorities executed more than seventy thousand suspected sympathizers and participants of Guangzhou; upward of one million persons throughout the entire province of Guangdong lost their lives, moreover, as part of the revolt.

Shortly after the conclusion of the Red Turban Rebellion, Cantonese social harmony was further disrupted by the outbreak of ethnic conflict in the Siyi region of Guangdong between Punti "locals" and members of the "Hakka" minority group. Beginning in 1856, locals and Hakka residents of Chixi County entered into a period of twelve years of bloody skirmishing over arable farm lands in Siyi and the counties of Yangjiang and Xiangshan. Hakka–Punti land disputes claimed the lives of thousands of residents of Guangdong, and it was reported that one to two thousand persons might have lost their lives in any single battle. As an example of the tremendous human casualties suffered as a consequence of the Hakka wars, more than three thousand lives were lost in the Xinning District in one month of bloody skirmishing in 1856. Together with the Taiping Rebellion and the Red Turban revolt, therefore, the Hakka–Punti wars contributed significantly to Cantonese socioeconomic instability and dislocation during the mid-nineteenth century.[23]

During these years of Cantonese civil unrest, the destructive effects of common natural disasters such as droughts and floods became exacerbated. With its efforts focused upon the suppression of subaltern rebellion and the containment of western imperialistic aggression, the Qing government failed to implement necessary disaster relief measures to assist the Cantonese peasantry. In addition, constant military conflict prevented peasants from properly maintaining their agricultural lands and resulted in problems such as flooding. As a consequence of the incessant fighting, for example, almost annual flooding occurred in the Sanyi region after 1844, because peasants were unable to properly maintain their agricultural lands and water channels. The threat of starvation and famine, moreover, was not uncommon in South China in the mid-nineteenth century, because of the difficulty of transporting and importing necessary foodstuffs during these years of civil unrest.

In sum, overpopulation, the commercialization of agriculture, trends of nascent industrialization, western imperialism, peasant rebellions, and natural disasters served to create a "migration-prone" situation in the province of Guangdong during the nineteenth century. Dislocated and displaced by great forces of social, political, and economic change that swept across China during this time period, along with Lee Kwong Lun, millions turned to emigration as a means of securing their personal and familial economic livelihoods.

Pushed from their homelands by conditions of socioeconomic and political deterioration, Chinese emigrants like Lee Kwong Lun were pulled abroad by perceived economic opportunities. Chinese immigrants were recruited to fill labor shortages in British, Spanish, Portuguese, and Dutch colonial possessions as part of nineteenth-century western imperialistic expansion.[24] The demand for Chinese labor, moreover, was especially high in the mid-nineteenth century, as a consequence of the abolition of African slavery between the years of 1838 and 1850. In addition, Chinese emigrants were attracted to economic opportunities within mining and agriculture in places such as California, Hawaii, British Columbia, and Latin America. Scattered internationally, Chinese immigrants took up employment in a variety of positions such as agricultural laborers, independent farmers, skilled workers, merchants, and shopkeepers.

Although push factors such as overpopulation, western imperialism, and civil unrest, and pull factors such as overseas economic opportunities, served to encourage emigration, changes in Chinese immigration law and policy were of signal importance in facilitating Chinese diasporic movement during the nineteenth and early twentieth centuries. Prior to the arrival of European economic colonialism, Chinese emigration was officially banned according to a governmental legislative decree of 1718. In addition to prohibiting emigration, this law of 1718 commanded all emigrant Chinese to return to their patria. In 1728, all Chinese still residing abroad were issued an official sentence of banishment, and returning emigrants, moreover, were charged with the commission of a capital violation.[25]

Contrary to the policy aims of eighteenth-century Chinese emigration laws, Chinese emigration erupted in the nineteenth and early twentieth centuries following the opening of western treaty ports and the legalization of Chinese immigration as a consequence of European diplomatic pressures. Chinese emigration greatly increased after the opening of the southern Port of Xiamen in 1842 as part of the terms of the Treaty of Nanjing. The first steps toward the legalization of emigration and the official reversal of the 1718 restrictions barring emigration were taken in 1859 when Pehkwei, the governor of Guangdong, allowed for the recruitment of contract laborers by British and French governmental representatives. The floodgates of Chinese emigration were legally opened on a national level one year later when China and Britain signed the Treaty of 1860, which by its terms cancelled prior legislative emigration restrictions and legalized emigration from all parts of China. Seeking to regulate the employment of Chinese immigrant laborers, moreover, China, Great Britain, and France negotiated a diplomatic Convention at Beijing in 1865. Although this agreement did not receive official ratification by Great Britain and France, the terms of the convention were nonetheless subsequently recognized by China. However, in 1877 China and Spain entered into a subsequent treaty that banned the immigration of Chinese contract laborers to all Spanish territories. This treaty prohibition was later extended by Chinese governmental authorities to apply to all countries of Chinese immigrant destination.[26] Notwithstanding such efforts at the regulation of emigration by the Qing government, the emigration of indentured laborers continued after 1877 as a consequence of protest by western colonial powers.

Changes in Chinese emigration law and policy in response to European diplomatic pressures were therefore of signal importance in facilitating Chinese diasporic movement during the nineteenth and early twentieth centuries. In response to western colonialist pressures, the Chinese government reversed its centuries-old prohibition against emigration and legally sanctioned the recruitment of immigrant laborers for overseas western territories and possessions. One of the most important effects of European colonialism upon trends of Chinese emigration, therefore, was not only to encourage emigration through the creation of socioeconomic dislocation in South China but also to promote wide-scale diasporic movement through the legalization of emigration and the opening of transpacific networks of migration and labor recruitment.

Lee Kwong Lun's immigration to Cuba therefore took place within the larger context of the international Chinese diaspora of the late nineteenth and early twentieth centuries during which millions of dispossessed rural Cantonese and Fujianese emigrants scattered themselves throughout Southeast Asia, Australia, the Caribbean, and the Americas in search of economic opportunities and respite from oppressive socioeconomic and political conditions caused by western imperialism, civil war, natural disasters, and demographic pressures.

Although the global Chinese diaspora grew out of a common set of socioeconomic and political conditions in South China that made emigration an attractive option, what led thousands of Chinese emigrants to journey specifically to Mexico during these years? The genesis of broad Chinese immigration to Mexico is directly linked to patterns of Chinese migration to the United States and shifts in Mexican and U.S. immigration law and policy in the late nineteenth century.

The Dragon at Gold Mountain: Chinese Immigration to California, 1848–1882

Lee Kwong Lun's immigration to California was part of a larger movement of more than 335,000 Chinese immigrants who entered the United States between the years of 1848 and 1882.[27] Attracted by the gold rush and the hope of instant wealth, most Chinese immigrants to the United States chose to settle in California, and in the year of 1852 alone, 20,000 Chinese entered the United States through the port of San Francisco.[28] Along with gold seekers, a small but significant number of Cantonese merchants also arrived during this first wave of Chinese immigration to California. These merchants amassed substantial fortunes by serving as passage brokers and labor contractors for aspiring Cantonese immigrants and by selling food and supplies to Anglo and Chinese miners. The commercial infrastructure they laid, moreover, would later serve as the basis for a transnational commercial orbit spanning the United States, Mexico, Cuba, and China. As discussed later in this chapter, Mexican business interests would later look to these same Cantonese merchants of San Francisco to create a system of recruiting Chinese contract laborers to Mexico. Using their own financial capital brought from China, many opened restaurants geared toward Anglo taste buds, as well as stores that sold Chinese groceries and luxury items like silk and lacquerwares. As part of the "credit ticket system," merchant passage brokers advanced funds to cover immigration expenses for emigrant laborers. On their part, contracted laborers agreed to sell their services to designated labor contractors and to pay back passage loans at a monthly interest rate ranging from 4 to 8 percent.[29]

The second wave of Chinese immigration to California took place in 1867 as part of the construction of the Central Pacific Railroad. Between 1867 and 1870, approximately 40,000 Chinese immigrated to the United States from Guangdong as part of recruitment efforts for the transcontinental railroad. By 1877, the Chinese population of California had grown to 148,000.[30]

Most Chinese immigrants were from ten counties in the southern Chinese province of Guangdong: Taishan/Toisan, Xinhui, Kaiping, Enping, Zhongshan/Chungshan, Chixi, Shenzhen, Panyu, Nanhai, and Shunde. Of these ten counties, Taishan, Xinhui, Kaiping, and Enping—known collectively as Siyi (literally, "the four towns/districts")—generated the largest number of emigrants. In addition, although most Cantonese merchants of the early wave of Chinese migration originated from the vicinity of the port city of Guangzhou, most emigrant laborers came from more outlying counties of the Guangdong province.[31]

Although the two large waves of Cantonese migration to California were precipitated by the gold rush and labor recruitment for the construction of the transcontinental railroad, Chinese immigrants eventually came to participate in a wide range of laboring activities.[32] They worked as agricultural laborers, domestics, launderers, miners, and manufacturing plant workers, and by the 1870s and early 1880s they comprised up to one-fourth of all laborers in the state. Because they were willing to work for low wages and had a reputation for being industrious and reliable, Chinese immigrants were initially praised and welcomed by state officials.[33]

Notwithstanding their official welcoming, Cantonese immigrants were the targets of popular racism almost from the time of their initial arrival in the 1840s. By the early 1850s, anti-Chinese sentiment expressed itself in the forms of "anti-coolie" clubs, bigoted newspaper editorials, and boycotts of Chinese commercial products. In reaction to the Chinese presence in mining, anti-Chinese activists successfully lobbied in 1852 for an invidious tax targeting Cantonese miners. By the 1860s and 1870s, the Chinese immigrant community became the focus of both a broad political smear campaign by the Democratic Party and racist protests by white labor union organizers.[34] Because of the willingness of Chinese immigrants to work for low wages, white workers condemned the Chinese as unfair competition. Moreover, according to Alexander Saxton, the Democratic Party scapegoated Chinese immigrants and manipulated popular anti-Chinese sentiment to gain political advantage at the polls. Crippled by their political defeat over the issue of slavery during the Civil War, the Democratic Party successfully resuscitated itself during the 1860s in California through the harnessing of popular racism against the Chinese. Appealing to supporters of the xenophobic movement, the Democratic Party led the charge against Chinese immigrants by supporting a full slate of sinophobic candidates in the 1867 fall state elections. This political strategy proved successful as Democrats swept the 1867 elections, winning the governorship, a large majority in the state assembly, and two out of three federal congressional seats. In his gubernatorial victory speech, Henry Haight underscored the sinophobic position of the Democratic Party that carried him and his fellow Democratic candidates to political success in the fall elections of 1867:

> I will simply say that in this result we protest against corruption and extravagance in our State affairs—against populating this fair State with a race of Asiatics—against sharing with inferior races the Government of the country . . . and this protest of ours, echoing the voice of Connecticut and Kentucky, will be re-echoed in thunder tones by the great central states until the Southern States are emancipated from negro domination, and restored to their proper places as equals and sisters in the great Federal family.[35]

Like the Democratic Party, trade union officials during the late nineteenth and early twentieth centuries also harnessed popular sinophobia for their own advantage. Isolated from the craft union strongholds of the East Coast, California trade union organizers by necessity reached out to unskilled workers to strengthen their West Coast numerical power base. Craft union officials attracted the support of unskilled white workers through the manipulation of anti-Chinese rhetoric. This recruitment strategy proved extremely successful, and by the second decade of the twentieth century San Francisco had become a trade union bastion due in large measure to the scapegoating of Chinese immigrant laborers.

One consequence of the scapegoating of Chinese immigrants by labor unions and the Democratic Party was the nationalization of the Chinese question and the promulgation of various types of discriminatory legislation targeting both the resident Chinese overseas community and potential Chinese immigrants.[36] In 1870, Congress denied Chinese immigrants residing in the United States the legal right to become naturalized citizens through their exclusion from amendments made that year to the Nationality Act of 1790. The Page Law, passed through the federal legislature in 1875, although intended to target the immigration of Chinese female prostitutes, had the effect of precluding the movement of Chinese women in general to the United States. However damaging the Page Law was upon the development of the Chinese American community, the most devastating assault upon Chinese immigrants occurred in 1882 as a consequence of the passage of the Chinese Exclusion Act in May of that year. The Chinese Exclusion Act of May 6, 1882, barred the immigration of Chinese laborers to the United States for a period of ten years. However, according to certain exceptions built into the federal legislation, merchants, students, and teachers were allowed to enter the United States in small numbers upon governmental issuance of special "Section Six" identification certificates. Like the Page legislation of 1875, the Chinese Exclusion Act, moreover, targeted Chinese women and therefore further impaired the balanced development of the Chinese immigrant community of the United States. Under the federal statute, only a few Chinese women were allowed to immigrate to America, as the wives of merchants or as the spouses of Chinese born in the United States. Outside of these limited exceptions, Chinese females were defined as laborers and therefore barred from entrance to the country.

In the Scott Act of 1888, the Geary Act of 1892, and federal legislation of 1904, Congress further tightened the reins against Chinese immigration. Expanding the restrictions of the Chinese Exclusion Act of 1882, the Scott Act barred not only the entrance of Chinese emigrant laborers but also the re-entry of immigrant laborers who had returned to visit China with valid return certificates in their possession. In response to the illicit Chinese immigrant smuggling trade, which had begun to develop after the passage of the exclusionary legislation of 1882, the Geary Act required the official registration of all Chinese laborers residing in the United States and allowed for the deportation of all those failing to comply with the registration requirement. In addition, this act also extended the various other invidious immigration laws targeting the Chinese for ten years. As a final death blow to Chinese immigration to the United States, in 1904 Congress permanently barred Chinese immigration through the indefinite extension of the Chinese exclusion laws.

With the option of legal immigration to the United States closed to them, in the decades to come, many Chinese turned their sights to Mexico as a land of economic opportunity and a surreptitious gateway to "Gold Mountain."[37] The exclusion laws of the United States had the effect of diverting Chinese migration streams to Mexico and resulted in the creation of a new and thriving Chinese diasporic community in North America. Chinese immigrants to Mexico were met, at least initially, with open arms.

The Dragon in Big Lusong: Chinese Immigration and Settlement in Mexico

Ironically, the movement to bar Chinese immigrants from the United States during the late nineteenth century coincided with efforts by the Mexican government to recruit Chinese emigrants as part of President Porfirio Diaz's program of economic modernization. Inspired by the positivist writings of Auguste Comte and Herbert Spencer, Diaz and his "científico" cabinet advisors sought to remedy their country's socioeconomic and political underdevelopment through a modernization program consisting of four major components: (1) the establishment of political order and stability; (2) the recruitment of foreign capital and investment; (3) the creation of an extensive transportation network; and (4) the promotion of European immigration.[38] According to Porfirian policy makers and liberal theorists of the late nineteenth century, European immigrants would facilitate Mexican modernization and development by filling labor shortages in places like the frontier farming and mining territories of the northern sierras, by colonizing remote, unpopulated regions, and by introducing modern production methods to the Mexican populace.[39] In addition, wide-scale European immigration would also serve to westernize and culturally homogenize Mexican society. Despite numerous efforts to recruit European immigrants through means such as land grant incentives, the Mexican government was ultimately unsuccessful in promoting large-scale European migration.[40] According to historian Kennett Cott, Mexican efforts to recruit Europeans as laborers and colonists failed because of a shortage of governmental funds, the absence of a national transportation system, and the preference of European immigrants to reside near population centers where their settlement was not required. In addition, Cott argues that Mexico was unsuccessful at promoting substantial immigration because European immigrants rejected the modest lifestyle of the Mexican laborer.[41]

As a consequence of the failure to attract significant numbers of European immigrants as part of its Porfirian modernization plan, the Mexican government turned to Chinese immigration in an attempt to fill its labor shortage demands. Although extensive diplomatic efforts to promote Chinese immigration to Mexico occurred only after 1880, Chinese emigrants were recruited to Mexico as railroad laborers as early as 1864.[42] In addition, far-sighted Mexican capitalists sought to recruit Chinese laborers as part of a royal concession granted by Emperor Maximilian in 1865.[43] In 1865, Emperor Maximilian granted one D. Manuel B. da Cunha Reis the exclusive privilege of recruiting both East Asian and Egyptian emigrants as contract laborers for agriculture, mining, and public works. According to the ten-year royal concession, Cunha Reis and his Compañía de Colonización Asiática were given the rights to import immigrant laborers for single contract periods of between five and 10 years, to transfer labor contracts to third persons with priority given to company stock holders, and the right to conduct an initial experiment involving the recruitment of five hundred Egyptians as laborers for certain Veracruz haciendas.

Despite these early attempts at recruiting Chinese emigrants, extensive diplomatic negotiations for the promotion of wide-scale Chinese immigration occurred only after 1880 at the insistence of Mexican finance minister Matias Romero.[44] In 1875 and 1876, Romero publicly advocated for the recruitment of Chinese laborers in two articles published in the Mexico City newspapers, the *Revista Universal* and *El Correo del Comercio*. In his 1875 article from the *Revista Universal,* Romero extolled Chinese immigration as the solution for labor shortages experienced by the coastal haciendas of the "tierra caliente": "It seems to me that the only colonists who could establish themselves or work on our coasts are Asians, coming from climates similar to ours, primarily China. The great population of that vast empire, the fact that many of them are agriculturalists, the relatively low wages they earn, and the proximity of our coast to Asia mean that Chinese immigration would be the easiest and most convenient for both our coasts." In the later article from *El Correo del Comercio,* in addition to arguing for the benefits of Chinese immigration, Romero also highlighted the economic benefits that Mexico would receive from increased trade relations with China and Japan. Beyond these public calls for Chinese labor recruitment, Romero likely also advocated for the promotion of Chinese immigration in private sessions with his colleagues of the Mexican government.

Between 1880 and 1889, toward the ends of recruiting Chinese immigrants en masse and increasing foreign trade as part of the Porfirian plan of economic modernization, the Mexican government unsuccessfully sought to establish official diplomatic ties with China.[45] In 1882, the year of the passage of the Chinese Exclusion Act, Romero proposed the idea of promoting Chinese immigration to Mexico to the Chinese minister in Washington, D.C., and in 1884, the foreign ministry appointed a commercial agent to represent Mexican interests in the port of Hong Kong. Moreover, that same year, as part of an initial attempt to stimulate trade relations with China, the Mexican government supervised the organization of the Mexican Pacific Navigation Company. The Mexican Development Ministry granted the steamship company the right to transport goods and immigrants between Mexico and Asian ports and provided government subsidies for each worker brought to Mexico and for each successful round-trip voyage. In addition, between the years 1885 and 1889, Romero attempted to negotiate a commercial treaty with the Chinese government from his post at the Mexican embassy in Washington but was ultimately unsuccessful, in part because of the frequent absence of Chinese diplomatic officials. Despite these numerous efforts, the Mexican government was unable to establish significant diplomatic and trade relations with the Qing imperial regime during the decade of the 1880s; it was only at the instigation of the Chinese government in the 1890s that negotiations were reestablished and a treaty of amity and commerce was finally agreed upon by the two nations. In 1891, Chinese diplomatic representatives called upon Romero to establish a commercial treaty, and, following a decade more of sporadic negotiations, China and Mexico signed a treaty of amity and commerce in 1899. The treaty opened wide the floodgates of Chinese immigration to Mexico as it allowed for "free and voluntary" movement between the two countries. Together with the U.S. Chinese exclusion laws, this treaty had the effect of diverting Chinese migration streams to Mexico and led to the formation of a new Chinese diasporic community in Latin America during the early twentieth century.

With the diplomatic stage set, the Mexican government turned to Chinese merchants of San Francisco to assist in the recruitment of Chinese immigrant laborers. Together, they created a profitable and effective scheme of transnational immigrant labor contracting. Ramón Corral, future vice president of Mexico, led both the negotiations of the Treaty of Amity and Commerce and these efforts to organize the recruitment of Chinese immigrant laborers. According to one Mexican source, Corral collaborated with Chinese "mafia" tong leaders of San Francisco to develop a plan for the systematic recruitment of Chinese contract laborers.[46] As part of their deal, Chinese merchants of California promised to solicit Chinese emigrant laborers under contract at Chinese port cities like Hong Kong and Shanghai. As part of these contracts, tong agents covered immigration costs for emigrant laborers in exchange for repayment at steep rates of interest. In addition, as part of this arrangement between Chinese merchants and Corral, the latter and other influential Mexican officials were paid a monetary sum for each Chinese contract laborer who reached Mexican shores. In many ways, this scheme resembled the "credit ticket system" practiced in California just a few decades before, and it is likely that some Chinese merchants may have served as passage brokers and labor contractors for the recruitment of Chinese laborers in both California and Mexico.[47]

This system of transnational labor contracting established by Mexican business interests and Chinese merchants of San Francisco helped to lay the foundations for a broader Chinese "transnational commercial orbit" that lasted well into the twentieth century. This transnational economic orbit encompassed China, Latin America, Canada, and the Caribbean, and it was developed and traveled by entrepreneurial Chinese capitalists who pursued commercial opportunities not only in labor contracting but also in human smuggling, wholesale merchandising, and small-scale trade. This transnational commercial orbit facilitated the licit, and illicit, movement of people and goods among China, Mexico, Cuba, and the United States, and it is what makes the case study of the Chinese in Mexico a unique example of Chinese transnationalism in the global Chinese diaspora during the late nineteenth and early twentieth centuries.

Conclusion

Together with Lee Kwong Lun, more than eight million Chinese immigrants scattered themselves internationally between the years of 1840 and 1940 as part of a global Chinese diaspora. An apocalyptic-like concurrence of historical factors such as overpopulation, civil rebellion, famine, and European colonialism conspired to create great socioeconomic and political instability in Southern China during these years and served as push factors that encouraged international Chinese migration. Drawn by the allure of the California gold rush and employment opportunities in railroad construction, industry, and agriculture, one important stream of more than 300,000 Cantonese immigrants journeyed to the United States between the years of 1848 and 1882. Following the passage of the Chinese Exclusion Act of 1882, which severely restricted Chinese immigration to the United States, many Chinese emigrants set their sights on Mexico as a new land of economic opportunity.

The wide-scale migration of Chinese to Mexico was made possible largely by the Treaty of Amity and Commerce that was signed by representatives of Mexico and China in 1899. This treaty opened the floodgates of Chinese immigration to Mexico, because it allowed for the "free and voluntary" movement of Chinese and Mexican citizens between the two countries. Whereas the Chinese population of Mexico consisted of a scant 1,023 persons in 1895,[48] by 1910, just ten years after the promulgation of the diplomatic agreement, the Chinese community of Mexico increased to more than 13,000.[49] By 1926, the Chinese population of Mexico had grown to become the second-largest immigrant community in all of Mexico, at a size of 24,218 persons.[50]

Many Chinese immigrants were attracted to Mexico as part of a system of transnational contract labor recruitment organized by the Mexican government in collaboration with Chinese merchants of California. The creation of this organized system of contract labor recruitment laid important foundations for the development of a transnational Chinese commercial network and "orbit" spanning Mexico, China, Cuba, and the United States. This commercial orbit opened up transnational financial opportunities for enterprising Chinese merchants, not only in labor contracting but also in wholesale merchandising and small-scale trade.

Drawing upon the commercial networks of the economic orbit, moreover, Chinese immigrants developed an important means of circumventing the Chinese exclusion laws. In resistance to these laws that sought to exclude them, Chinese immigrants "invented" undocumented immigration from Mexico to the United States. They created a highly sophisticated transnational immigrant smuggling network involving representatives in China, Mexico, Cuba, and various port and borderland cities of the United States. As a consequence, for thousands of aspiring Chinese immigrants, Mexico became not only a land of financial opportunity but also a strategic gateway into the United States.

3
Transnational Journeys
Transnational Contract Labor Recruitment, Smuggling, and Familial Chain Migration

On the first of July, 1911, Chinese immigrants Hom Hing, Ah Fong, Lee Lock, Sam Seu, and Leu Lin, accompanied by their Chinese-Mexican compatriot Joaquin Mon, drove by wagon from Ensenada to Carise, Lower California. Hom Hing, Ah Fong, Lee Lock, Sam Seu, and Leu Lin were received at the vicinity of the border by two Mexicans, Francisco Rios and Antonio Solis, who were contracted to take them safely across into the United States. Hom Hing promised to pay the Mexican guides $120 for their services, Lee Lock agreed to pay $405 in gold for safe transport to the United States, and Sam Seu contracted to pay $300 for his delivery to the "land of the flowery flag." On the third of July, the five Chinese immigrants, together with Rios and Solis, entered the United States through San Ysidro, Lower California. Following their illegal crossing at San Ysidro, the group proceeded to the city of El Cajon in San Diego, where they were hidden by their Mexican guides in a straw stack on a hill located close to Riverview Station. Five days later, while en route to Anaheim, California, Hom Hing, Ah Fong, Lee Lock, Sam Seu, Leu Lin, Rios, and Solis were spotted by Immigration Service inspector-in-charge Harry H. Weddle near San Marcos, California, at about three o'clock in the morning on the tracks of the Santa Fe Railroad. Following an escape attempt, the group was arrested and subsequently interrogated by Weddle and his partner, Chinese Inspector Ralph L. Conklin. Upon their inspection and interrogation of Rios and Solis, Weddle and Conklin learned that the five captured contraband immigrants were consigned to Chinese individuals residing in Anaheim, California. Moreover, according to the smuggling arrangement, Rios was contracted to receive $150 for each contraband Chinese after safe delivery to Anaheim and upon the presentation of a special letter of identification given to him by Joaquin Mon of Ensenada written in the Chinese language.

Following the successful apprehension of Hom Hing, Ah Fong, Lee Lock, Sam Seu, Leu Lin, Rios, and Solis, Inspectors Weddle and Conklin proceeded north to Anaheim, California, in pursuit of the Chinese agents to whom the five smuggled immigrants had been consigned. As part of their plan, Weddle and Conklin stopped first in Santa Ana, California, where they recruited sheriff employee George Placencia to pose as Francisco Rios. On July 15, 1911, Weddle, Conklin, and Rios traveled to Anaheim seeking to locate the intended recipient of the smuggling letter. Posing as Rios, Placencia learned from an elderly man, Ngan Fook, that the correspondence was addressed to the "big boss man," Chin Tung Yin, who resided in Los Angeles. Fook further explained to Placencia that Chin would meet with him the next evening in Anaheim to discuss the arrangement. On the evening of July 16, 1911, Placencia met with Fook and the big boss man in the Anaheim Chinatown, and they worked out a plan for the delivery of the contraband Chinese described in the secret letter. Following an initial miscommunication as to the designated place of meeting, Placencia, together with Inspectors Weddle and Conklin, drove to meet Chin Tung Yin and Ngan Fook at a small Chinese garden located approximately one mile east of the city of Anaheim. Upon arrival at the garden, Weddle and Conklin parked their car on a side road and hid themselves behind a blackberry bush. Placencia proceeded to meet the big boss man, who was waiting for him in a house located in the Chinese garden. At the meeting, Chin paid Placencia $10 for expense costs and promised to pay Placencia the balance of the amount owed after the delivery of the Chinese immigrants. Moreover, Placencia was instructed to meet Chin at the railroad station the following morning and travel to Los Angeles Chinatown, where he would receive remuneration for services rendered. After their discussion, Placencia led Chin and Fook outside to the blackberry hedge, where they were arrested by Inspectors Conklin and Weddle. The U.S. Attorney subsequently dismissed charges against Ngan Fook for conspiracy to violate immigration laws related to Chinese exclusion; Francisco Rios and the big boss man Chin Tung Yin were also acquitted.[1]

This case study provides an intimate glimpse into the inner workings of the transnational smuggling business that developed in response to the Chinese Exclusion Act of 1882. As a means of resisting and circumventing the Chinese exclusion laws, entrepreneurial Chinese invented undocumented emigration from Latin America and created a vast transnational smuggling network that encompassed China, Mexico, Cuba, and various cities throughout the United States. As with transnational contract labor recruitment, Chinese immigrant smuggling played a key role in the development of the broader Chinese transnational commercial orbit.

Although in the present day undocumented immigration is closely correlated in the minds of many to the movement of native Mexicans and Latin Americans to the United States, ethnic Chinese were the first illegal aliens from Mexico. This chapter uncovers the largely unknown history of Chinese immigrant smuggling to the United States. It also looks at other "migration mechanisms," or means by which the Chinese immigrated to Mexico. In addition to undocumented immigration, this chapter takes a closer look at the migration mechanism of transnational contract labor recruitment and also examines the topics of "coolie smuggling" and familial chain migration. As final topics of consideration, this chapter examines Chinese population trends and patterns of geographic distribution.

Smuggling to Gold Mountain

As suggested by the opening vignette, the smuggling of Chinese immigrants into the United States during the late nineteenth and early twentieth centuries was a sophisticated business, involving an elaborate transnational network of Chinese agents and non-Chinese collaborators. The organized smuggling of Chinese into the United States through Mexico began in the late nineteenth century as a response to the Chinese Exclusion Act of 1882 and thrived as a lucrative business until 1916 when the trade came to a screeching halt as a consequence of the interruption of transpacific steamship passenger service during World War I.

The Chinese Six Companies, a transnational Chinese immigrant fraternal organization headquartered in San Francisco, directed the illicit smuggling traffic from Havana, Cuba.[2] The Chinese Six Companies was first established during the mid-nineteenth century as an immigrant fraternal organization comprised of representatives of the major Cantonese district of origin associations of San Francisco, and was charged with the defense and representation of the collective socioeconomic and political interests of the Chinese immigrant community.[3] Although this organization was initially created to provide a unified collective voice for the Chinese of San Francisco, its members eventually developed an international economic network or "transnational commercial orbit," which allowed them to branch out into various types of import-export ventures and profit-making activities. This transnational commercial orbit encompassed China, Mexico, Cuba, Canada, and the United States, and allegedly involved both licit activities such as wholesaling, labor recruitment, and small-scale retail trade, and illicit ones such as immigrant smuggling, opium importation, and the white slave trade.

According to U.S. Treasury Department special agent reports from the late nineteenth century, Havana was both the headquarters and distribution point of the Chinese immigrant smuggling business organized by the Chinese Six Companies of San Francisco.[4] Moreover, the Six Companies possessed a strategic insider connection in Havana that allowed for the flowering of the illegal immigrant trade during the late nineteenth century. In 1896, Chin Pinoy, chief representative of the Six Companies, directed and managed the Chinese smuggling business from his office in Havana.

As previously discussed in chapter 2, Cuba was an important hub of the Chinese diaspora during the mid-nineteenth through mid-twentieth centuries. Between the years of 1847 and 1874, some 125,000 Chinese immigrated to Cuba as plantation contract laborers. Chinese immigrant coolies were recruited to fill labor shortages in Cuban sugar plantations engendered by the abolition of African slavery.[5] Following the demise of the coolie trade, many former contract laborers transitioned into employment as small-scale merchants. In the late nineteenth and early twentieth centuries, thousands of Chinese immigrated to Cuba to take advantage of commercial and employment opportunities occasioned by national independence and trends of economic modernization prompted by the growth of sugar production. During these years many Chinese also traveled to Cuba as part of the transnational immigrant smuggling trade. As we will see, the Chinese diasporic communities of Cuba and Mexico shared deep transnational socioeconomic connections during the late nineteenth and early twentieth centuries because of the immigrant smuggling trade. The two diasporic communities were closely linked as important geographic nodes along the Chinese transnational commercial orbit and the immigrant smuggling network of the Americas. In 1922, the Chinese population of Cuba was estimated to be 90,000 and was larger than that of the Chinese diasporic community of the continental United States.[6]

In addition to his role as eastern chief of the Chinese Six Companies in Havana, Chin Pinoy concurrently held the position of Chinese agent for the Southern Pacific Railroad Company, the Morgan Steamship Line, and a line of the Ward Steamship Company sailing from Tampico, Mexico, to New York.[7] Chin's strategic transnational socioeconomic connections allowed for the flowering of the Chinese immigrant smuggling trade under his leadership and direction.[8] Treasury Department agents estimated that these three transportation companies for which Chin served as Chinese agent carried approximately four-fifths of the Chinese immigrants who eventually illicitly entered the United States during much of the 1890s. Leveraging and building upon this key insider connection, the Chinese Six Companies developed not only a flourishing immigrant smuggling business but also an impressive transnational smuggling network involving representatives in China, Mexico, Cuba, and various cities of the United States, including El Paso, Tucson, San Diego, New York, Boston, and New Orleans. In addition, the Chinese Six Companies devised a multiplicity of schemes, procedures, and techniques to maximize smuggling efficiency through these various U.S. ports of entry.

The smuggling procedure described in the example of the big boss man Chin Tung Yin and his partner in crime, Ngan Fook, for example, closely resembles a popular scheme devised by the Six Companies to illegally transport Chinese nationals into the United States via Sonora and Baja California during the early twentieth century.[9] According to this scheme, Chinese residents of the United States would make smuggling arrangements for friends or relatives desirous of immigrating to the United States through the Six Companies representative of their local town. As part of this procedure, the local U.S. agent would proceed to contact a Chinese agent in a port city such as Shanghai, and the emigrant friend or relative would be instructed to travel to that city. Upon arrival at the port city, the emigrant would receive basic training in both the English language and American cultural etiquette and then would be transported to Mazatlán, Manzanillo, or Guaymas, Mexico, via Chinese steamer. Chinese immigrants were met at Mexican ports by Six Company representatives who distributed them temporarily into various jobs related to their future employment in the United States. Following further inculcation in American culture and preliminary job training, emigrants traveled by train to Nogales, Sonora, and then from Nogales they were transported to border cities such as Mexicali, Naco, or Agua Prieta, where they would be delivered across the U.S. line by a Mexican guide to a Six Companies agent waiting for them in a local city. Upon arrival in the United States, illegal Chinese newcomers were assigned new identities—according to this common scheme, the identity of citizens born in the United States. Chinese immigrants appropriated entire falsified biographies that established their legal claims to be in the country, and, in the event that they were taken to court by immigration officials on suspicion of entrance into the United States in violation of the Chinese exclusion laws, Six Company representatives hired false witnesses to corroborate their fabricated identities. The absence of official municipal birth records as a consequence of the 1906 San Francisco earthquake and fire made it even more difficult for immigration authorities to disprove the false identities of Chinese immigrants who claimed to be born in San Francisco, which contributed to the popularity of this smuggling procedure. Immigration Service official Clifford Alan Perkins claimed that this strategy of assigning false identities became so effective and common that, over time, government officials ceased to challenge suspected illegal aliens on these grounds, and "that if all of those who claimed to have been born in San Francisco had actually been born there, each Chinese woman then in the United States would have had to produce something like 150 children."

In addition to this popular scheme of smuggling Chinese immigrants into the United States through the use of Mexican guides and the assignment of fictitious identities, the Six Companies also devised various illicit "substitution" procedures based upon the abuse of the "in transit" privilege. Although Chinese laborers were not allowed to legally immigrate to the United States after 1882, according to this privilege many Chinese emigrants were allowed to land at American seaports and travel in transit through the United States en route to Mexico. In addition, according to the in transit privilege, Chinese laborers were also allowed to travel through U.S. territory in transit from Mexico or Cuba en route to China via American seaports such as New York City.

Many Chinese immigrants destined for Mexico traveled to San Francisco by steamship and then journeyed to Mexico by train, entering Mexico at various southwestern border ports such as El Paso, Texas, and Calexico, California.[10] Upon entrance in the United States, the collector of customs required Chinese laborers traveling in transit to Mexico to produce a through-ticket that verified their travels across U.S. territory and into Mexico. In addition, as part of the in transit requirements, the collector of customs also demanded a penal bond of at least $200 to be posted by either the transportation company providing the through-ticket or by "some responsible person on behalf of the laborer" to guarantee the timely arrival of Chinese immigrants at Mexican ports and to guard against illegal Chinese immigration schemes.[11] Upon arrival of immigrants at the Mexican port of destination within twenty days from the date of entrance at U.S. ports and verification of in transit passenger identities, the bond was canceled; upon failure of timely arrival, the penal bond was paid by the transportation company or individual who originally posted the bond. The Chinese Six Companies developed a multiplicity of substitution methods to circumvent U.S. immigration law through the creative manipulation of the in transit policy loophole.

The Joseph Lam case provides an example of one such successful substitution method devised to beat the Chinese exclusion laws.[12] In mid-May of 1891, forty Chinese immigrants arrived in New Orleans aboard the Southern Pacific Railroad traveling in transit to Havana, Cuba. The forty passengers landed originally at the port of San Francisco, and, following a stay of about one week in New Orleans, were scheduled to depart to Havana from nearby Algiers, Louisiana, on board the SS *Arkansas,* a Morgan steamship owned by the Southern Pacific Company. During their weeklong layover in New Orleans, the forty Chinese immigrants vacationed and visited freely with their compatriots residing in New Orleans while under the supervision of Joseph Lam, Southern Pacific Chinese agent at this Cajun port. Sometime during their one-week stay in New Orleans, passengers Fong H. and Leong Y., along with three other of their immigrant countrymen, made deals with five residents of the New Orleans Chinese community to be substituted in their stead. According to this arrangement, the five New Orleans residents switched places with their five countrymen traveling in transit to Havana for a fee somewhere in the range of $100 to $125. As legal residents of New Orleans, the hired substitutes, in addition to the handsome fees, received a free trip to Havana and, because of their legal entitlement to be in the United States, could return to New Orleans whenever they desired. Two of the contracted substitutes were, in fact, citizens of the United States and "professional" substitutes. Following the swapping of identities, the five Chinese laborers originally destined for Havana slipped away illegally into the United States, presumably blending themselves into the local Chinese community of New Orleans to avoid detection by immigration authorities. The Six Companies also utilized a similar strategy to substitute Chinese merchants for Chinese immigrant laborers traveling in transit through U.S. territory by train to Chihuahua, Mexico, from the seaport of San Francisco.[13]

In addition to this practice of substitution en route to Cuba and Mexico, the Chinese Six Companies also developed a creative scheme of circumventing the Chinese exclusion laws by substituting Chinese laborers from Mexico and Cuba traveling in transit through the United States to China via the port of New York City.[14] According to further legal loopholes in U.S. immigration policy, Chinese immigrants from Mexico and Cuba, although not entitled to immigrate to the United States, were allowed to travel through U.S. territory via railroad to seaports such as New York, and from these ports to depart to China by steamship. Upon arrival at seaport, lists of in transit passengers were created by immigration officials that included descriptions of age, physical appearance, and last place of residence of each immigrant. Following the construction of descriptive lists and the posting of bonds for each passenger, Chinese immigrants en route to China, like their compatriots traveling in transit through the United States to Latin America and the Caribbean, were allowed to visit freely in the port city under supervision of other Chinese agents while they awaited departure. According to Treasury Department agents, some Chinese laborers abused the in transit privilege by swapping places with Chinese merchants during their port city layover. As part of this substitution scheme, Chinese laborers gained illegal residence in the United States, and their compatriot merchants received, ostensibly, a free trip back to China as well as likely remuneration for their services. Moreover, in addition to earning a free visit to their homeland, because of their legal exemption from the exclusion laws, merchants were allowed to return to the United States whenever they desired. This technique of substitution highlights the deep interconnectedness of the Chinese diasporic communities of Mexico, Cuba, and the United States. As a successful method of evading restrictive U.S. immigration policy, it required the sophisticated coordination of efforts by smuggling agents and participants in at least three distant, disparate transnational locations in Mexico, the Caribbean, and the northeastern United States. In a day and age that did not possess the technological innovations of the Internet, airplanes, cell phones, and fax machines, this was quite a feat. Far from being disconnected immigrant hubs, the Chinese diasporic communities of Mexico, Cuba, and the United States were intimately interwoven as part of the big business of Chinese transnational immigrant smuggling.

An incident involving the detention and investigation of seven Chinese immigrants at the New York port of Malone on February 24, 1896, clearly illustrates this in transit to China substitution scheme. In February of 1896, Land Ah Hop, Chong Ah You, Chong C. Tuck, Chong Kung Foon, Lie Ah Long, Lam Ah Lin, Loy Kong Tin, and four other Chinese immigrants from Mérida, Mexico, and Havana, Cuba, arrived at the port of New York aboard the Canadian Pacific Railway, traveling in transit through the United States to China. Prior to their scheduled departure to China, and following a layover in New York City, nine of the original eleven in transit passengers appeared before Deputy Collector N. W. Porter and Chinese Inspector H. E. Tippett in Malone on the twenty-fourth. Discrepancies between the descriptive lists and the physical appearances of passengers appearing that day, as well as faulty responses to governmental queries made by Chinese passengers, convinced Porter and Tippett that seven illegal substitutions had taken place during the layover stay in New York City. In addition, substitution suspicions were also raised by Tippett's observation that most of the Chinese interrogated spoke English, although they purportedly arrived in the United States from Spanish-speaking host countries. Porter and Tippett based their assessment largely upon the following specific descriptive list inconsistencies:

Land Ah Hop: According to the descriptive list created upon the initial arrival of the in transit passengers in New York City, Land was 5 feet 6 inches tall, possessed a distinctive scar on his forehead, and had his left ear pierced. Upon inspection on February 24, the person purporting to be Land was only 5 feet 3½ inches tall, had no scar on his forehead, and no piercing in his left ear.

Chong Ah You: Although listed as 5 feet 6 inches tall with last place of residence being Havana, Cuba, on February 24 appeared to be only 5 feet tall and cited his last place of residence as Mérida, Mexico.

Chong C. Tuck: According to the descriptive list, Chong was a teenager of 15 years of age, 5 feet 1½ inches tall, and last lived in Havana. Upon inspection prior to departure, appeared to be 25 to 30 years old, was 5 feet 3½ inches tall, and stated Mérida was his last place of residence.

Chong Kung Foon: During interrogation Chong stated he was 35 years old instead of 25 years old as recorded in descriptive list and was not the same height as listed in the government list.

Lie Ah Long: Like Chong Ah and Chong C., cited incorrect last place of residence and was of different height than that described in list.

Lam Ah Lin: Upon governmental query, said last place of residence was Mexico instead of Cuba. Also, Lam was shorter than detailed in description and lacked facial discoloration described in list.

Loy Kong Tin: Stated he last lived in Mérida, instead of Havana, as recorded in descriptive list.

Based upon these many conspicuous discrepancies, Porter and Tippett denied cancellation of the penal bonds posted by the Canadian Pacific Railway on behalf of Land, Chong Ah, Chong C., Chong Kung, Lie Ah, Lam, and Loy.

In addition to these substitution schemes involving the swapping of Chinese passengers en route to Cuba and China via the ports of New Orleans and New York City, convicted illegal Chinese immigrants of Los Angeles and San Diego devised an ingenious "deportation substitution" procedure involving the collusion of U.S. immigration officials.[15] According to governmental deportation policy, Chinese nationals convicted in Los Angeles and San Diego of entering the United States in violation of the exclusion laws were transported by train from these southern California locations to the Alameda County Jail in Oakland and then from Oakland were taken to steamers in the port of San Francisco and deported to China. According to the deportation substitution scheme, Chinese detainees paid bribes to immigration officials while en route to the Bay Area and were allowed to swap places with other Chinese immigrants desirous of returning to China. Vouching for the efficacy of this substitution technique, Treasury Department agent officials during the late nineteenth century reported the sightings of many convicted and purportedly deported Chinese immigrants in the city of San Francisco. Intrigued and stirred to action by rumors of this illegal immigration scheme, Datus E. Coon, Chinese Inspector at the port of San Diego, conducted an interesting investigational experiment in August of 1890, which proved conclusively the reality of the rumors. As part of his plan, Coon, in secret cooperation with the U.S. commissioner and jailor, photographed seventeen Chinese immigrants convicted and scheduled to be transferred and deported from San Diego. Two sets of prints were delivered to the collector of the San Francisco port, one by Coon through registered mail, and another by the San Diego collector, and it was requested that the identification of deportees be verified prior to admission at the Alameda County Jail through comparison with the mailed photographs. If the prints matched, then this would indicate that Chinese deportees were substituted somewhere in the Bay Area; if the photos did not correspond correctly, then this would constitute strong circumstantial evidence that the substitutions took place sometime during the lengthy sally from southern California to Oakland. Coon's curious experiment proved the existence of the insider immigrant trading scheme, but not through the tests he had devised. Although the two sets of photographs arrived safely at the San Francisco collector's office according to plan, thirty-three of the thirty-four prints were stolen from the collector's desk before they could be used.

As a final abuse of the in transit privilege, many Chinese immigrants during the late nineteenth century landed at American seaports and traveled to Mexico and Cuba through U.S. territory only to surreptitiously reenter the United States after an ephemeral stay in their supposed Latin American countries of destination. According to one common procedure developed by the Six Companies, Chinese immigrants arriving by steamship in San Francisco traveled in transit by train to the city of Torreón in the northern Mexican state of Coahuila. In Coahuila, they were received by Six Companies agent Mar Chark, alias "Bum," who distributed them to strategic smuggling points along the three-thousand-mile U.S.–Mexico border.[16] For his services as distribution agent, Mar Chark, described as a "middle aged, good looking, shrewed [sic] Chinaman," received a monthly salary of $100 from the San Francisco Six Companies headquarters. Laredo, Texas, served as one such strategic site for smuggling into the United States utilized by Mar and the Six Companies. Many Chinese immigrants passed in transit through Eagle Pass, Texas, into Mexico, and reentered the United States furtively in the vicinity of Laredo. From Laredo, they were transported to a location near San Antonio aboard freight trains of the International and Great Northern Railroad companies. In addition to Laredo, the border city of Juarez in Chihuahua, Mexico, also served as a popular surreptitious gateway of reentrance into the United States for Chinese in transit passengers.[17] By the late 1890s, this abuse of the in transit privilege by Chinese immigrants had become so egregious that, according to W. P. Hudgins, special agent of the U.S. Treasury Department, at most 20 percent of all Chinese laborers entering Mexico between the years of 1894 (the date of the signing of the U.S.–China treaty that legally established the in transit privilege) and 1897, still resided in Mexico in 1897. The remaining 80 percent "mysteriously disappeared," presumably smuggled into the United States in flagrant abuse of the treaty privilege. Immigration officials such as Hudgins, in response to these rampant in transit smuggling abuses, advocated for amendments to the 1894 treaty that would limit passage in bond to Chinese nationals traveling through U.S. territory en route to transatlantic port destinations.[18]

To facilitate the smuggling of illegal Chinese immigrants into the United States, both in transit passengers to Mexico and those arriving directly at Mexican and Cuban ports, the Chinese Six Companies developed an elaborate underground market for the illicit sale of forged and fraudulent merchant, laborer, naturalization, and habeas corpus certificates. Chinese laborers desirous of entering the United States purchased forged and fraudulent merchant and laborer certificates through agents in China and the diasporic communities of Mexico, Cuba, and the United States.[19] Moreover, Chinese immigrant smugglers devised an ingenious variety of methods to both procure and create bogus immigration documents. In the late nineteenth century, Havana served as a central market for the purchase of both naturalization and merchant certificates.[20] Chinese laborers in Havana purchased fraudulent merchant papers acquired through the collusion of Chinese agents in New York City and the Chinese consul of Havana, as well as old U.S. certificates of citizenship naturalization originally procured in New Orleans and delivered to Cuban Chinese agents. According to one popular procedure, Chinese laborers in Cuba who wanted to immigrate to New York City sent photographs fastened to large blank pieces of paper to Chinese agents in the Big Apple, who transformed the photos and leaves of paper into fabricated merchant certificates complete with official seals, signatures, and notarization. In further circumvention of the Chinese exclusion laws, the Chinese consular general of Havana also colluded with laborers desirous of immigrating to the United States, through the issuance of merchant passports that falsely alleged merchant status.[21] In New Orleans, conniving entrepreneurs of the bogus immigration certificate racket even secured illegal copies of naturalization papers belonging to dead people and distributed them to willing buyers who attempted to use them to gain entrance through various U.S. ports, such as Eagle Pass, Laredo, and Key West, Florida.[22] Not to be left out of the lucrative document forgery bonanza, San Franciscan West Coast labor certificate counterfeiters and Bostonian East Coast passport brokers also abetted the illegal immigration of Chinese laborers through the illicit commercial provision of false documentation.[23]

In sum, utilizing a variety of creative certificate procurement schemes such as these, Chinese smuggling agents in China, Mexico, Cuba, New York, New Orleans, and San Francisco developed a sophisticated and elaborate black market for the sale of bogus immigration papers that facilitated the illegal entry of thousands of Chinese laborers into the United States during the late nineteenth and early twentieth centuries. These methods, moreover, which required the collusion of transnational agents in Havana, Cuba, Mexico, and various cities throughout the United States such as New York City, New Orleans, Eagle Pass, and Key West, demonstrate the interconnectedness of the Chinese diasporic communities of Latin America and the United States, as well as the practical functioning of the Chinese transnational commercial orbit of the Americas.

"Impersonally Organized Migration": Transnational Contract Labor Recruitment and Illegal "Coolie" Smuggling

The Chinese transnational commercial orbit developed not only as a means of smuggling aspiring immigrants into the United States but also as a way of bringing Chinese contract laborers to work in Mexico. Although thousands of Chinese used Mexico as a temporary layover destination en route to being smuggled into the United States, many were also recruited to Mexico to serve as agricultural contract laborers for haciendas and ranchos. These agricultural laborers journeyed to Mexico as part of systems of "impersonally organized migration." Impersonally organized migration can be defined as immigration that occurs based upon "impersonal recruitment and assistance."[24] Examples of impersonally organized migration include immigration coordinated by foreign national governments, shipping businesses, and employers of the host country.

Following this pattern, and as discussed in chapter 2, thousands of Chinese immigrated to Mexico during the late nineteenth and early twentieth centuries as part of the organized efforts of Chinese capitalists, the Mexican and Chinese governments, Chinese immigrant fraternal societies, and Mexican industrial interests. The wide-scale organized movement of Chinese to Mexico began after 1899 under the protection of the Treaty of Amity, Commerce, and Navigation between Mexico and China. Because of the inability to attract sufficient numbers of native Mexican laborers and European immigrants to areas of rapid industrial expansion in the lower coastal regions and underpopulated frontier zones located far from the capital of Mexico City, Porfirian economic interests successfully lobbied the federal government to negotiate a treaty of amity and commerce with China as part of a plan to recruit Chinese immigrants as laborers for their various mining, agricultural, and manufacturing commercial ventures. Following several decades of extensive diplomatic negotiations between Mexico and China, the two nations, on June 3, 1900, signed the Treaty of Amity, Commerce, and Navigation.[25] This treaty accorded

China most-favored-nation status, and, under terms of the agreement, Chinese immigrants in Mexico became entitled to all the special rights and privileges owed subjects of a "most-favored nation."

Ramon Corral, future vice president of the Mexican Republic, spearheaded the Porfirian government's efforts both to negotiate the Treaty of Amity between the two countries and to organize the recruitment of Chinese laborers.[26] As governmental representative and capitalist entrepreneur, Corral collaborated with Chinese business leaders of San Francisco to arrange for the recruitment and movement of immigrant laborers from China to Mexico. According to the agreement made between Corral and the San Francisco Chinese leaders, Corral was to guarantee the inclusion of a clause in the Treaty of Amity that guaranteed the favorable treatment of Chinese immigrants as subjects of a most-favored nation; on their part, the representatives of the Chinese tongs of California promised to cover the immigration costs of Chinese laborers and to pay Corral and other influential Mexican officials a monetary sum for each Chinese immigrant destined for Mexican shores. San Francisco tong agents recruited Chinese immigrants under contract at Chinese port cities such as Hong Kong and Shanghai. According to the terms of these reportedly onerous contracts, agents paid the immigration costs in exchange for repayment in regular, timely installments from recruits. Presumably, repayment included steep rates of interest and various fees that covered the salaries of agents and ensured a hefty profit for the Chinese business leaders who organized the immigration ring. Moreover, factored into the necessary immigration costs were also specific sums destined for the coffers of unscrupulous high-level Mexican government officials such as Corral and his cronies, as well as fees for the bribery of port health inspectors.[27]

Arriving at Mexican ports such as Mazatlán, Manzanillo, and Salina Cruz in groups of four hundred to eight hundred, Chinese newcomers were met by representatives of the Chinese tongs.[28] Tong agents received the recent immigrants, taught them basic Spanish, and familiarized them with the fundamentals of Mexican culture. As part of this system of impersonally organized recruitment, tong representatives also distributed recent arrivals throughout various towns, haciendas, and cities, where they found employment as launderers, cooks, servants, and gardeners. Moreover, wealthy Chinese merchants from California residing in northwestern Mexico also sometimes assisted Chinese immigrants by extending them credit to start up basic commercial ventures as street vendors.

Although the movement of Chinese immigrant laborers to Mexico occurred largely as a part of official diplomatic and commercial negotiations between entrepreneurial Chinese and Mexican government officials and businessmen, Chinese labor migration also took place as part of another, illicit, system of impersonally organized migration— transnational coolie smuggling. Transnational coolie smuggling involved the illegal distribution of Chinese immigrant laborers throughout Latin America and was organized by a myriad of multinational participants, including Chinese investors in Hong Kong and San Francisco, plantation owners of Mexico, Cuba, Peru, and Chile, and Chinese, Filipino, and Spanish officers and crew.

The "New China" incident, which occurred in Mexico during the years of 1921–1922, gives specific insight into the inner workings of the transnational coolie smuggling business of the early twentieth century. It also highlights the broad geographic scope of the Chinese transnational commercial orbit. This transnational commercial orbit was developed and maintained by multicultural and multinational businessmen and participants in China, the United States, Latin America, Spain, the Caribbean, and the Philippines. This economic orbit, moreover, linked together Chinese diasporic communities not only in Mexico, Cuba, and the United States but also in South American countries such as Peru and Chile.

The steamship *New China* illegally departed from Lantau Island near Hong Kong on July 6, 1921, carrying more than three hundred Chinese passengers destined for various plantations of Mexico, Peru, Chile, and Cuba.[29] Despite the existence of international agreements and immigration laws prohibiting the traffic of Chinese emigrant coolie laborers into these countries of Latin America, the Spain and China Navigation Company contracted with the more than three hundred Chinese immigrants aboard the *New China* to transport them to Mexico, Peru, and Cuba.[30] Moreover, adding to the illegality of the arrangement, although each Chinese passenger on board the *New China* possessed a Cantonese passport, none of the passports contained proper visa authorization from the appropriate consular representatives in China. In addition to improper documentation, Chinese passengers on board the *New China* also carried with them separate contracts with specific plantations or companies in Mexico, Peru, and Cuba.[31] Although the crew of the vessel, like its passenger list, was comprised of Chinese nationals, the majority of the ship's officers were citizens of the Philippines. One American, two

Spaniards, and an Englishman also ranked among the vessel's officers for the anticipated three months' journey to Mexico and South America.

The illegal immigration venture was directed by the ship's owner, Chinese national B. C. Wong, and Spaniard Secundino Mendezona, manager of the Spain and China Navigation Company.[32] Wong was a high-roller transnational investor who served as submanager of the Canton Bank of Hong Kong, which maintained a branch bank in the city of San Francisco, and which also held the mortgage to the steamship *New China*.[33] As manager of the Spain and China Navigation Company, a business venture involved in the illegal trafficking of Chinese emigrant laborers, Mendezona was responsible for ensuring the safe arrival of Chinese immigrants to their respective destinations, either through their direct shipment on board the *New China* or through their subcontracted transshipment via other ships at various Mexican ports.

The *New China* arrived with 306 Chinese passengers on September 5, 1921, at the Oaxacan port of Salina Cruz. Upon arrival, however, the *New China* was detained based upon libel charges filed by Spanish creditor Francisco Echeguren of Mazatlán.[34] Following the embargo of the vessel in Salina Cruz, the ship's owners sent word from China promising to remit the funds necessary to cover the debt, and Mendezona journeyed to Mexico City for six weeks to negotiate a contract for the transshipment of the Chinese immigrants headed for Cuba.[35] By November 28, 1921, neither the funds from China nor the transshipment arrangement materialized, and as a direct consequence, numerous Chinese passengers died on board the steamer as a result of unsanitary health conditions and insufficient supplies of food.[36] Eventually, the Mexican government intervened in the debacle by feeding the crew and passengers, advancing funds for the return of stranded immigrants and crew members back to Asia, and by paying the accumulated wages owed the officers and crew of the *New China*.[37] On September 18, 1922, a full year after the initial arrival of the SS *New China*, the Mexican government auctioned the vessel to recover the sums it had advanced and would further pay as part of its intervention in the botched immigration venture.[38]

The *New China* debacle highlights both the sophistication and the transnational nature of the illegal-coolie-smuggling business of the early twentieth century. It also provides further illustration of the broad geographic reach of the Chinese transnational commercial orbit of this era. Wealthy Chinese investors such as B. C. Wong, with access to transnational

Chinese banking capital in places such as Hong Kong and San Francisco, financed and directed the illicit immigrant trade. Moreover, wealthy transnational investors like Wong formed shipping companies such as the Spain and China Navigation Company which worked in conjunction with various Latin American plantations and companies in Mexico, Peru, Cuba, and even Chile, to recruit Chinese immigrant laborers.[39] From the *New China* incident, we also learn that Chinese investors in the coolie trade sometimes hired non-Chinese to supervise operation of the smuggling trade itself. Providing the funds necessary to finance the shipment of Chinese emigrants, Chinese capitalists such as Wong and his Canton Bank of Hong Kong appear to have relied upon experienced non-Chinese such as Secundino Mendezona to manage the outfitting of ship crews and the actual transportation of immigrants, as well as to cut the necessary political and business deals to allow for the landing and transshipment of illegal Chinese passengers at various Latin American ports. The hiring of Mendezona and his motley crew of officers further demonstrates the broad geographic scope of the Chinese transnational commercial orbit and its participants. Mendezona was himself a Spaniard, his officers hailed from the United States, England, and the Philippines, and his deckhand crew was comprised entirely of Chinese nationals!

In sum, from the *New China* incident we learn that the Chinese coolie trade to the Latin America of the early twentieth century was a well-organized, sophisticated, and transnational affair, financed and directed by wealthy transnational Cantonese capitalists, managed by experienced and politically savvy non-Chinese seamen, and fueled by the demand for cheap labor in plantations and companies of Mexico, Cuba, and South America. Insofar as the transnational coolie trade functioned to distribute Chinese immigrants throughout Latin America, it played an important role in helping to establish new Chinese diasporic communities. These diasporic communities were all linked together by the big business of coolie recruitment and the Chinese transnational commercial orbit.

Familial Chain Migration

Although thousands of Chinese immigrant laborers traveled to Mexico as part of the impersonally organized migration systems of transnational contract labor recruitment and illegal-coolie smuggling, smaller numbers of privileged Chinese immigrants came to Mexico with the financial assistance of family members already residing in Mexico. This migration mechanism is known as "familial chain migration." Chain migration is defined "as that movement in which prospective migrants learn of opportunities, are provided with transportation, and have initial accommodation and employment arranged *by means of primary social relationships with previous migrants*."[40] Emigration based upon "chain" relationships of kinship is called familial chain migration.

The vignettes of Ricardo Cuan and José Chong demonstrate the migration mechanism of familial chain migration and highlight the important role played by family relationships in the immigration and settlement of Chinese in Mexico. Born in the Kiukon Village of Guangdong's Nanhai District on May 5, 1900, Ricardo Cuan immigrated to Guaymas, Mexico, at the age of twelve, accompanied by his brother-in-law Manuel Ung.[41] The latter owned a grocery business in Guaymas and had returned to China to bring Ricardo to Mexico. They traveled by steamer to San Francisco and then passed in transit over land to Nogales, Arizona, where they entered Sonora and proceeded to Guaymas. For his first three years in Big Lusong, Ricardo, being of grammar school age, attended the Colegio Guaymense in Guaymas. Following his brief stint in the Mexican school system, Ricardo Cuan moved to Mérida, Yucatán, and became a partner in a perfume shop with his nephew Pablo Cuan. In 1927, Ricardo traveled north to Ensenada, Baja California, where he joined the seven-man business partnership of Rafael Chan y Cia., which operated a general merchandise store in the city. Besides Ricardo, the partners were Rafael Chan, Roberto Chan, Rafael Leon, Yua Chan, Juan (Cuan) Chim, and Pablo Chong.

Like Ricardo Cuan, José Chong first traveled to Mexico while still of grammar school age and attended a Mexican colegio for a time before entering the workforce.[42] Also like Ricardo Cuan, José Chong depended upon familial support from the time of his first arrival in Mexico. Entering Mexicali at the age of fifteen in transit from San Francisco in 1915, the young José depended largely upon his older brother José Chong Cuy for economic livelihood during the first ten years of his stay in Mexico and even into his adulthood. In an interview with Immigration and Naturalization Service officer Marshall E. Kidder from November 30, 1938, Jose Chong admitted this dependency:

[Before 1931] I worked at the Yew Kee Co., tailors, Reforma Ave., Mexicali, Mexico, as a tailor, for about two years or a little over. Before that I wasn't doing anything steady in particular. I went to a Mexican school for a while. My first real job was at the tailor's, and I really don't recall exactly how I spent all my time before that, but I know I wasn't working. I didn't know the tailoring business and had to learn it. My older brother, José Chong Cuy, has always taken care of me.[43]

In 1931, the younger José Chong invested $1,000 in the Las Quince Letras Company of Mexicali, where he served as salesman and partner, together with his brothers Chong Cuy and Lung Chong, selling Mexican and American groceries, Chinese herbs, and dry goods.[44]

These vignettes of Ricardo Cuan and José Chong illustrate the important role of kinship in the immigration and settlement of Chinese immigrants in Mexico. In Cuan's life story we observe the phenomenon of familial chain migration, and we see the important influence of kinship connections in the selection of geographic residence.[45] Consistent with the model of familial chain migration, Manuel Ung first immigrated to Mexico himself in search of economic opportunities. After establishing himself financially as the owner of a grocery store in Guaymas, he then returned to China to bring his wife's younger brother, Ricardo, to Mexico. Brought to Sonora at a young age, Ricardo, for the first three years of his tenure in Mexico, was also dependent upon his brother-in-law for his economic livelihood. Ricardo's subsequent travels to the Yucatán and Baja California, like his initial settlement in Guaymas, were also shaped by familial considerations. Based upon his interviews with U.S. immigration officials, it appears that Ricardo Cuan made his decisions to resettle in these two places because of the availability of new business opportunities made possible by kinship connections. In Mérida, he formed a perfume business together with his nephew Pablo Cuan; in Ensenada he joined the Rafael Chan y Cia. firm which had one Juan (Cuan) Chin, ostensibly a relative of Ricardo, as one of its seven partners.

Through José Chong's life story we also see the important influence of kinship connections in the choice of geographical residence. Whereas Ricardo Cuan's example highlights the significant role played by extended family members such as brothers-in-law and nephews in Chinese immigrant settlement patterns, in José Chong's case, however, we observe the importance of immediate kinship ties in the influence of decisions to reside in particular localities. Like Cuan, Chong immigrated to Mexico at a young age and depended upon family for his economic livelihood during the initial period of his stay in Mexico as he attended school. Whereas Cuan ostensibly received his early sustenance and support from his brother-in-law, Chong however, relied upon his older brother Chong Cuy. Chong's economic dependence upon his older brother, moreover, is seen to have continued well into his adulthood and appears to have been a major factor in his decision to remain in Mexicali from the time of his arrival in 1915 until at least the late 1930s. Taking his first real job as a tailor in about 1928, Chong seems to have relied upon Chong Cuy for financial assistance for the first thirteen years of his stay in Mexicali. Moreover, Chong's 1931 investment in the partnership of Las Quince Letras was also made possible because of his older brother. On October 1, 1931, the elder Chong Cuy reorganized a firm formerly known as El Cielo Azul Company, bringing his brothers José Chong and Lung Chong into the partnership to form Las Quince Letras Company. Upon first entering the partnership in 1931, José Chong acted as salesman and also conducted manual labor in the store, such as unloading stock and maintaining the stock in neat piles; by 1938, following a subsequent reorganization of the company in 1937, José was elevated to the position of buyer for the company.

The life stories of José Chong and Ricardo Cuan therefore highlight a third important means by which Chinese immigrants journeyed to Mexico—as part of systems of familial chain migration. According to this migration mechanism, successful immigrant merchants financed immigration costs and secured initial housing accommodations for their emigrant kin. In addition, they hired newly arrived relatives as employees, brought them on as business partners, or arranged for alternative employment. As exemplified by the vignettes of José Chong and Ricardo Cuan, familial chain migration was a preferred mechanism of migration enjoyed by only the most privileged and fortunate of Chinese immigrants in Mexico.

Finally, it is worth noting that familial chain migration was made possible by, and functioned as a part of, the broader Chinese transnational commercial orbit. The same steamship lines, railroad pathways, and in transit mechanisms that were developed as part of the transnational commercial orbit to transport contract laborers and would-be undocumented immigrants were also used by chain migrants to travel to Mexico. Because of their privileged financial position, however, chain migrants possessed the economic resources that allowed them to travel first class on the same steamers, boats, and trains that transported their less privileged compatriots to bitter fields of labor in the haciendas and ranches of Mexico and to illicit, danger-ridden passageways across the U.S.–Mexico border.

Having examined the different ways in which Chinese immigrated to Mexico, this chapter now turns to three related questions. What historical factors account for the steady increase of the Chinese population of Mexico during the first decades of the twentieth century and its precipitous decline after 1930? Where did Chinese immigrants choose to settle and what historical factors shaped their selection of geographic residence? What role did the transnational commercial orbit play in determining patterns of Chinese geographic distribution?

Population Trends and Geographic Distribution

Born in the Guangdong county of Taishan on September 11, 1888, Santiago Wong Chao landed in the Mexican Pacific port of Mazatlán in 1907.[46] Following a brief, one month's stay in Mazatlán, Wong migrated to the southwestern Mexican border state of Sonora, where he spent one year in the port city of Guaymas working in a grocery store owned by his compatriot Wah Chong, before settling in the mining town of Cananea for fifteen years. Before purchasing a 3,000-peso interest in the Quong Lung Hing Grocery store in 1919, Wong worked for twelve years in various places in and around Cananea as an employee of a Mexican grocer, a laborer on a Chinese ranch, a waiter in the Chinese café of a French hotel, and as an employee in a Chinese ice cream parlor. In January 1922, he sold his interest in the Quong Lung Hing firm of Cananea and relocated to Juárez, Mexico, where he remained for one year while working as an employee for one Antonio Chew before moving to Mexico City in search of promising business opportunities. Following his failure to find any lucrative commercial investments in the capital, Wong briefly returned to Juárez and then relocated to the Baja California border city of Mexicali in 1924. He remained in Mexicali for three years, working as a laborer on various Chinese cotton ranches and seeking out potential business opportunities. Spurred by his lack of commercial success in Mexicali, Wong migrated west to the border city of Tijuana, where, on January 1, 1929, he opened La Oriental grocery store, together with three other partners of the Yeon Ton and Company firm.

Santiago Wong Chao's diverse travels followed common Chinese migration routes and took him to many of the hubs of the Chinese immigrant community and of the transnational commercial orbit. Like Wong, most Chinese who traveled to Mexico by steamship in the early twentieth century entered through Mexican Pacific ports such as Mazatlán, Manzanillo, and Salina Cruz. Although in the late nineteenth century larger numbers of Chinese landed in Gulf ports such as Progreso, Tampico, and Veracruz, rather than in the Pacific ports, by the turn of the century, this trend had reversed. In 1895, 77 Chinese immigrants arrived at the Pacific ports of Guaymas, Mazatlán, Salina Cruz, and Todos Santos, as compared with 271 Chinese who entered Mexico through the Gulf ports of Progreso, Tampico, and Veracruz.[47] In 1901, out of a total of 922 registered Chinese arrivals, 909 landed at Pacific ports, and only 13 at the Gulf port of Veracruz.[48] In the following years, with the explosion of Chinese immigration to Mexico, this trend toward Pacific port arrivals continued forcefully. In the year 1907, some 5,616 Chinese entered Mexico through the Pacific ports of Acapulco, Ensenada, Guaymas, Manzanillo, Mazatlán, Salina Cruz, San Benito, and San Blas. Salina Cruz received the overwhelming majority of Chinese immigrants that year, recording a total of 5,286 entries. That same year, only 247 Chinese arrived at Mexican Gulf ports, with 93 landing at Progreso, 6 at Tampico, and 148 at Veracruz.[49]

This shift toward Pacific port arrivals was the practical consequence of one of the central commercial activities of the Chinese transnational economic orbit during these years—the immigrant smuggling trade. As has been discussed, in the early twentieth century Chinese entrepreneurs developed an elaborate transnational smuggling network involving representatives in China, Mexico, Cuba, and the United States.[50] Pacific ports such as Mazatlán, Manzanillo, and Guaymas played strategic roles in the immigrant smuggling trade, serving as ports of entry for Chinese immigrants destined for illicit entrance into the United States. The trend toward Pacific port arrivals during the early twentieth century was, therefore, likely connected to the important role played by such ports as part of the immigrant smuggling trade and the transnational commercial orbit.

Chinese immigrants such as Santiago Wong Chao journeyed to Mexico on American, Japanese, and Chinese steamships. The Mexican government granted concessions to both Chinese and Japanese capitalists to operate passenger, mail, and freight steamship lines servicing the needs of Chinese immigrants.[51] Such steamship companies provided a central means by which Chinese immigrants were able to traverse the Chinese transnational commercial orbit of the Americas. The China Commercial Steamship Company, for example, under contract with the Mexican government between the dates of February 17, 1903, and February 16, 1908, ran steamer lines between the ports of Hong Kong, Moji, Kobe, Yokohama, Salina Cruz, San Francisco, and Mazatlán.[52] The first Chinese steamer under concession with the Mexican government landed in Mazatlán in April of 1903.

While many Chinese nationals, like Santiago Wong Chao, arrived in Mexico on American, Japanese, and Chinese steamers directly through Mexican Pacific and Gulf seaports, large numbers of Cantonese immigrants also entered Mexico at borderland ports in transit through the United States.[53] José Chong, for example, resident of Baja California during the 1930s and native of the Ung Sing village of the Kai Ping County in Guangdong, first entered Mexico through the land port of Mexicali, which borders Calexico, California. First arriving in San Francisco on steamship, José Chong traveled in transit by land to Mexicali, entering Mexico on August 15, 1915.[54]

Entering Mexico through Pacific and Gulf seaports or at border-city land ports in transit through the United States, Chinese immigrants began to settle in Mexico in small numbers as early as the 1870s. Chinese immigrants appear in Mexican governmental records for the Gulf port city of Veracruz as early as 1878, in which they are reported as comprising 82.14 percent of the Asians residing in the city that year.[55] In 1884, Chinese represented 1.27 percent of all foreign nationals entering at Mexican Gulf and Pacific seaports. Moreover, that same year, Chinese immigrants comprised .06 percent of all foreigners arriving at Gulf ports, and 6.74 percent of all non-natives calling at Mexican Pacific ports.[56] U.S. governmental documents confirm the existence of Chinese immigrants in Mexico in the 1880s. U.S. consular records from the year 1885 report the existence of a small Chinese population of about 125 persons residing within the territory of the Guaymas Consular District in Sonora and employed primarily in shoe and garment-tailoring factories.[57] Extant consular records for the year 1889 further detail the development of two small Chinese populations in Baja California and Mazatlán during the late nineteenth century. According to these consular sources, many Chinese from California were sent to work in a Baja California mining site located roughly two hundred miles south of San Diego as part of a mining venture organized by Chinese investors from San Francisco during the summer months of 1889. In addition, these consular records from the year 1889 also describe the existence of an established Chinese community in Mazatlán as well as the recent recruitment of some one hundred Chinese immigrants by the Yedras Mfg. Co.[58]

By 1895, the Chinese population of Mexico had grown to about 1,023, and by the turn of the century the Cantonese immigrant community in Mexico, within a period of five years, nearly tripled its numbers, with a total of 2,835 registered in the 1900 national census.[59] Between the years

1900 and 1910, the Chinese population of Mexico experienced a substantial growth spurt. Although only a small community of several thousand at the turn of the century, by 1910, the Chinese population of Mexico increased to 13,203.

The genesis of Chinese immigration to Mexico in the 1880s and the subsequent growth of Cantonese movement to Mexico during the first decade of the twentieth century correspond causally with shifts in U.S. immigration law and policy during these years. As discussed in chapter 2, the Chinese Exclusion Act of 1882 barred Chinese laborers from entrance and residence in the United States and resulted in the rerouting of the stream of Cantonese immigration, in part, from the United States to Mexico. Legally excluded from immigrating to the United States, many Chinese flocked to Big Lusong in order to take advantage of the many economic opportunities afforded by Porfirian modernization policy as well as to use Mexico as a surreptitious gateway for illegal border crossings into the United States.

Although Chinese movement to Mexico increased during the late nineteenth and early twentieth centuries in part as a response to the Chinese Exclusion Act of 1882, the 1905 U.S. Supreme Court ruling of *Ju Toy* prompted and encouraged the rapid growth of Chinese immigration to Mexico between the years of 1905 and 1910. Prior to the 1905 *Ju Toy* ruling, thousands of Chinese immigrants managed to successfully resist exclusion by Bureau of Immigration officials through habeas corpus judicial review proceedings in the federal courts.[60] The *Ju Toy* decision of 1905, however, which largely removed jurisdiction to review exclusion cases from the federal courts, effectively eliminated the habeas corpus proceeding as a viable method of circumventing the Chinese Exclusion Act. Insofar as the *Ju Toy* ruling eliminated the popular habeas corpus method of resisting exclusion, it blocked the entrance of many future Chinese immigrant laborers who would have otherwise entered through the use of this legal circumvention and thereby increased the attractiveness of Big Lusong as a country of economic opportunity and as a surreptitious gateway to the "land of the flowery flag."

Although the Chinese population of Mexico increased dramatically between the years of 1900 and 1910 in response to the Chinese Exclusion Act and the *Ju Toy* decision, between the years of 1910 and 1921, the Chinese population of Mexico grew insignificantly from 13,203 to 14,472 largely as a consequence of World War I. The outbreak of World War I in 1914 made movement to Mexico virtually impossible for the many Chinese desirous of immigrating to Mexico during the years of the international conflagration, as it resulted in the interruption of transnational commercial passenger steamship lines running between Asia and Mexico.[61] Whereas 4,910 Chinese immigrants entered Mexico in 1913, the year before the outbreak of World War I, in 1914, these numbers dropped dramatically to 1,491. In 1915, only 474 Chinese arrived at Mexican ports, and the following year, in which steamship passenger service to Mexico from Asia became completely shut off, this number decreased to 228.[62] Following the end of World War I, Chinese immigration to Mexico quickly rebounded, with 1,151 registered entrances in 1919, then 2,669 in 1920, and 1,320 for the year 1921.

Ironically, Chinese movement to Mexico appears to have been largely unaffected by the economic instability and hostile political circumstances engendered by the early years of the Mexican Revolution. Despite the reduction of traditional commercial opportunities for Chinese caused by the internecine strife and the fact that Chinese immigrants often found themselves the targets of Mexican nationalistic xenophobia in the Revolution, during several of the bloodiest early years of the Revolution, 1911–1913, Chinese movement to Mexico actually continued at near-peak levels. In 1911, some 3,370 Chinese arrived at Mexican ports. With the escalation of the conflagration during the next two years, the number of Chinese entering Mexico increased, with 4,973 registered entrances in 1912, and 4,910 in 1913. It was not until the onset of World War I in 1914 that Chinese movement to Mexico began its downward plummet, and it was not until the resolution of the international conflict in 1918 that the rate of Chinese immigration to Mexico began its strong resurgence.

Even though the rate of Chinese migration to Mexico seems to have been unaffected significantly by the onset of the Mexican Revolution, the question remains as to why Chinese immigrants continued to enter Mexico in such large numbers during the early years of the civil war despite the reduction of employment and commercial opportunities caused by the internecine strife and the ostensibly unwelcoming environment resulting from the xenophobic targeting of Chinese by revolutionary sympathizers. One possible explanation for continued Chinese movement to Mexico is that many of the thousands of Chinese landing at Mexican ports during these years did not arrive with the intention of permanently settling, but rather entered with the goal of using Mexico as an illicit passageway into the United States. As was discussed in the first part of this chapter, during the years following the passage of the Chinese Exclusion Act in 1882 and the pronouncement of the *Ju Toy* decision in 1905, the illegal smuggling of Chinese immigrants into the United States from Mexico became big business for certain entrepreneurial businessmen of the Chinese fraternal society known as the Six Companies, and a sophisticated transnational smuggling network developed that included colluding Chinese representatives in the United States, Mexico, and Cuba. This smuggling business, moreover, was one of the key commercial activities leading to the development of the Chinese economic orbit of the Americas. It is likely that many of the Chinese who immigrated to Mexico between the years 1910 and 1913 entered as participants of this smuggling ring and therefore were unconcerned with Mexican domestic socioeconomic and political conditions insofar as such circumstances did not affect the functioning of the illegal immigration network and their eventual entrance into U.S. territory.

Although Chinese movement to Mexico began a strong resurgence in the years following the resolution of World War I, the rate of Chinese immigration to Mexico never rebounded to its prewar levels during the second decade of the twentieth century. Whereas 12,114 Chinese entered Mexico between the years of 1911 and 1913 alone, only 10,062 called at Mexican ports during 1919–1928.[63]

The precipitous decrease of Chinese movement to Mexico during these years can be accounted for largely by the decline of the organized Chinese smuggling trade precipitated by World War I. Whereas prior to World War I thousands of Chinese flooded Mexican seaports with the intention of surreptitiously entering the United States as part of the organized smuggling network, following the interruption of commercial steamship passenger service lines as a consequence of the war, the big business of smuggling Chinese immigrants into the United States via Mexican seaports came to a screeching halt.[64] Although the rate of Chinese movement to Mexico made a slight resurgence in the years immediately following the denouement of the war, based upon the small numbers of Chinese immigrants entering Mexico between the years of 1919 and 1928, it appears that World War I dealt a lethal blow to the organized smuggling trade, from which it never fully recovered.

Based largely upon the steady, but relatively small yearly influx of Chinese immigrants during the second decade of the twentieth century, by 1926, the Chinese population of Mexico grew to become the second-largest resident foreign ethnic community in Mexico (see table 3.1).[65] While Spaniards formed the largest foreign ethnic minority group that year, with 48,558 persons, the Chinese, at a size of 24,218, outnumbered

Table 3.1. The Chinese
population of Mexico, 1895–1940.

Year	Chinese
1895	1,023
1900	2,835
1910	13,203
1921	14,472
1926	24,218
1940	4,856

Sources: Mexico, Secretaría de Gobernacíon, *El Servicio de Migración en México por Landa y Pina jefe del Departamento de Migración* (Mexico, D.F.: Talleres Gráficos de la Nación, 1930), Bancroft Library, University of California, Berkeley, 38–39; Mexico, Ministerio de Fomento, *Censo general de la República Mexicana verificado el 20 de octubre de 1895, resúmen del censo de la República* (Mexico, D.F.: Dirección General de Estadística); Mexico, Secretaría de la Economía Nacional, *Quinto censo de población 1930, resúmen general* (Mexico, D.F.: Dirección General de Estadística); Mexico, Secretaría de la Economía Nacional, *Sexto censo de población 1940, resúmen general* (Mexico, D.F.: Dirección General de Estadística, 1943), 9.

the American, Syro-Lebanese, German, and Canadian communities, which boasted populations of 15,219, 12,644, 6,962, and 6,447, respectively. These large numbers distinguish the Chinese of Mexico as one of the most important Chinese diasporic communities in the Americas during the early twentieth century.

By 1940, the number of registered Chinese nationals in Mexico plummeted to 4,856.[66] This precipitous decline in the Chinese population can be attributed largely to the organized anti-Chinese movement in Mexico, which, targeting the Chinese populations of various states such as Sonora, Sinaloa, Nayarit, and Tamaulipas, culminated in the expulsion of virtually the entire Chinese population from the state of Sonora in August of 1931.[67] As will be discussed in great detail in chapter 6, the Mexican anti-Chinese movement sought to destroy the Chinese commercial monopoly in northern Mexico through the passage of various types of labor and public health legislation specifically targeting Chinese merchants, as well as through the organization of boycotts.[68] In addition, anti-Chinese special interest groups successfully lobbied for the promulgation of various types of invidious legislation, including laws that prohibited marriages between Chinese men and Mexican women and which attempted to segregate Chinese residents into ethnic barrios.

Although the Chinese community of Mexico successfully resisted the barrage of xenophobic assaults thrust against it from the inception of the organized anti-Chinese movement in 1916 until the late 1920s, following the onset of the Great Depression in 1929, the pendulum of public opinion and state governmental sympathy reversed its course in such a way that the Chinese were unable to defend themselves against the chicanery of the leaders of the nativist movement utilizing the same legal and political strategies that had worked for them in the past. On August 25, 1931, the governor of Sonora issued a vacation order, forcing the Chinese merchants of that state to abandon their businesses because of noncompliance with state labor law and resulting in the mass exodus of the Chinese population. In the face of such systematic xenophobic persecution, during the 1930s thousands of Chinese fled Big Lusong and the state of Sonora. Some relocated from Sonora to other parts of Mexico, such as Chihuahua, Sinaloa, and Mexico City. Others were deported to the United States by Mexican government officials, presumably forced to illegally cross the international border into the custody of American immigration officers. Still others returned to China with their Hispanic wives and children, forming distinct Mexican communities on the outskirts of rural Cantonese villages.[69]

Geographical Distribution

Like Santiago Wong Chao, during the early years of Chinese movement to Mexico, Chinese immigrants concentrated their settlement in northern Mexico. Tracing a similar geographic route as Wong Chao, 465 Chinese immigrants in 1895 scattered themselves throughout the northern states of Sonora, Chihuahua, Coahuila, and Nuevo León, with the majority, however, residing in the state of Sonora.[70] The next-largest population of 282 Chinese foreign nationals settled in the Pacific states and territories of Michoacán, Sinaloa, Chiapas, Oaxaca, Tepic, and Baja California. Of these areas of Chinese residence, the state of Sinaloa and the territory of Baja California received the bulk of Chinese immigrants. Although the majority of Chinese newcomers chose to settle in the northern and Pacific states, small numbers did find their way into central Mexico and the Gulf port states during the late nineteenth century.

By 1910, Chinese immigrants were ubiquitous, expanding their settlement into every state and territory of Mexico, with the single exception of Tlaxcala.[71] As depicted in figure 3.1, regional Chinese settlement patterns remained similar to those of 1895, with the largest Chinese communities located in the northern and Pacific states, and smaller populations residing in the Gulf and central territories. The overwhelming majority of Chinese immigrants of northern Mexico—4,486—chose to reside in

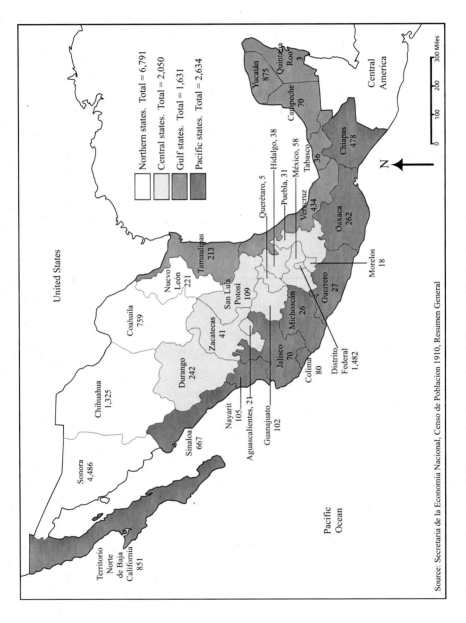

Figure 3.1. Number of Chinese foreign nationals living in Mexico, by region, 1910.

Source: Secretaria de la Economia Nacional, Censo de Poblacion 1910, Resumen General

Northern states. Total = 6,791
Central states. Total = 2,050
Gulf states. Total = 1,631
Pacific states. Total = 2,634

United States

Territorio Norte de Baja California 851

Sonora 4,486

Chihuahua 1,325

Sinaloa 667

Coahuila 759

Nuevo León 221

Durango 242

Zacatecas 41

San Luís Potosí 109

Tamaulipas 213

Nayarit 105

Aguascalientes, 21

Guanajuato 102

Jalisco 70

Colima 80

Michoacán 26

Distrito Federal 1,482

Querétaro, 5

Hidalgo, 38

Puebla, 31

México, 58

Guerrero 27

Morelos 18

Veracruz 434

Oaxaca 262

Tabasco 36

Chiapas 478

Campeche 70

Yucatán 875

Quintana Roo 3

Central America

Pacific Ocean

N

0 100 200 300 Miles

Sonora. Although they scattered themselves throughout all nine districts of the state, the majority concentrated in Hermosillo, Arizpe, Guaymas, Magdalena, and Moctezuma. The northern states of Chihuahua and Coahuila, moreover, boasted significant Chinese populations of 1,325 and 759, respectively. More than 2,600 Chinese made their home in the Pacific region of Mexico, with most choosing to settle in the territory of Baja California and the state of Sinaloa. A smaller Chinese Gulf community of 1,631 was concentrated primarily in the Yucatán, Veracruz, and Tamaulipas, and the Chinese of central Mexico focused their settlement upon the Federal District and Durango, with small numbers scattering themselves throughout the states of Aguascalientes, Guanajuato, Querétaro, Hidalgo, Mexico, Morelos, Puebla, and Zacatecas.

Geographical distribution patterns for the year 1910 suggest that Chinese immigrants chose to settle in particular localities based upon two factors related to the transnational commercial orbit—accessibility to the United States and occupational/commercial opportunities. The largest Chinese communities concentrated in the southwest border states of Sonora and Chihuahua, as well as in the California Pacific border territory of Baja California. These areas offered both direct access to U.S. territory and abundant employment and commercial opportunities as part of the Chinese transnational commercial orbit. As has already been discussed, Sonora, Chihuahua, and Baja California represented strategic gateways into the United States utilized by the organized immigrant smuggling ring. Thousands of Chinese illegally entered U.S. territory through the porous borders of Sonora, Chihuahua, and Baja California during the late nineteenth and early twentieth centuries, making these three places popular destinations for immigrants en route to the United States. Moreover, beyond their role as important passageways to the United States, Sonora, Chihuahua, and Baja California offered an abundance of economic opportunities for adventurous Chinese immigrants. As centers of developing economic modernization, sprouting urbanization, and the Chinese transnational commercial orbit, these three northern Mexican destinations provided many opportunities for employment as laborers in mining and agriculture, as well as a plethora of commercial opportunities in the petit bourgeois sector of the economy as grocers, dry goods and clothing retailers, shoe manufacturers, restaurant operators, and the like. Because the northern territories of Sonora, Chihuahua, and Baja California maximized both accessibility to the United States for purposes of the illegal immigrant smuggling network and economic opportunity as sites of incipient capitalist development, they became the logical centers of Chinese settlement in Mexico between the years 1895 and 1910.

For the purposes of drawing further attention to transnational history, it is important to emphasize the direct linkage between industrial-related employment opportunities in northern Mexico and Chinese migrant access to the United States. Chinese immigrants were drawn to Sonora, in particular, because of the abundant employment opportunities created by the expansive copper mining ventures of the American-owned Cananea Consolidated Copper Company (CCCC). As part of a series of complex negotiations between U.S. capitalists, Mexican politicians, and local Mexican elites, the CCCC helped spur the development of booming mining and railroad towns in Sonora such as Cananea, Nacozari, and Magdalena.[72] Chinese immigrants were drawn to these industrial towns because of the many commercial and job opportunities available. Chinese filled important commercial and employment niches in these towns, and over a short period of time came to dominate the grocery and vegetable trades. Their success, moreover, can be attributed in large part to their unique access to transnational capital and mercantile supplies, as part of the Chinese transnational commercial orbit. As will be discussed in detail in chapter 5, Chinese merchants of Sonora thrived above and beyond their Mexican counterparts because of their ability to garner transnational capital from family and friends in China and the United States, as well as because of strategic access to transnational wholesale suppliers. In addition to their role as small-scale merchants, Chinese immigrants also found steady employment as domestic cooks, houseboys, and handymen for American families of the CCCC.

Sonoran mining towns offered Chinese immigrants not only an abundance of job opportunities but also access to smuggling networks of the transnational commercial orbit that spanned the "copper borderlands" of southeastern Arizona and northeastern Sonora. As in Sonora, American capitalists in the late nineteenth century spearheaded mining and railroad development in the Arizona borderlands. Like their diasporic counterparts in Sonora, Chinese immigrants flocked to Arizona mining and railroad towns like Benson and Tombstone and found employment as launderers, cooks, farmers, merchants, and restaurant managers. In the early twentieth century, an underground railroad linked the Chinese copper borderland communities of Arizona and Sonora and helped facilitate the undocumented migration of Chinese. This transnational smuggling network was organized by a collaborative of Chinese merchants from both countries and literally followed the railroad lines that linked Sonora and Arizona. In 1913, one smuggling route traced the railroad lines from Cananea to Naco (Sonora) and up through the Arizona towns of Fairbank, Tombstone, Pearce, and Wilcox.[73]

Absent the motivating factor of close proximity to the United States for purposes of illegal entrance into U.S. territory, it appears that Chinese immigrants settled in other parts of Mexico according to the availability of economic opportunity. Mexico City, for example, although landlocked and hundreds of miles away from any port of entry into the United States, attracted the formation of the largest single community of Chinese outside of northern Mexico, ostensibly because of the many employment and commercial opportunities offered by the urban megalopolis. In addition, medium-sized numbers of Chinese clustered themselves in northern industrial centers such as Coahuila and Nuevo León, as well as in commercially vibrant Pacific and Gulf port cities such as Mazatlán and Veracruz, which, although not affording close geographical proximity to the United States, provided sufficient employment and business possibilities to draw hundreds of adventurous Chinese immigrants. Moreover, underscoring the ubiquitous character of Chinese settlement patterns and further supporting the claim that Chinese immigrants made their decision to reside in particular localities in large measure based upon the availability of economic opportunity, Chinese scattered themselves in small numbers throughout the most rural and commercially underdeveloped states and pueblos of central and southern Mexico such as Guerrero, Tabasco, Campeche, and Quintana Roo. Although not offering the veritable wealth of economic opportunities of northern developing industrial centers such as Sonora and Chihuahua, these rustic central and southern Mexican communities provided a sufficient number of jobs and business possibilities to attract at least a few adventurous Asian argonauts. This wide geographic distribution demonstrates the broad reach of the Chinese transnational commercial orbit in Mexico. Not limited to the borderland regions of the Southwest, the transnational commercial orbit reached even deep into central and southern Mexico because of adventurous Chinese immigrants who were quick to search out economic opportunity throughout all the states and territories of Mexico. This broad geographic distribution, moreover, also distinguishes the Chinese in Mexico from other diasporic destinations such as the United States, where Chinese immigrants tended to cluster in regional hubs such as the Southwest and Northeast.

By 1926, the Pacific and Gulf states eclipsed the northern states as hosts to the largest numbers of Chinese immigrants.[74] Whereas the Chinese population of the northern states of Coahuila, Chihuahua, Nuevo León, and Sonora in 1926 remained largely the size it had been in 1910, the numbers of Chinese in the Pacific states nearly quintupled during these years, growing from 2,050 in 1910 to 9,837 in 1926. Also increasing in popularity among Chinese immigrants during the second and third decades of the twentieth century, the Gulf states, while possessing a modest Chinese community of 1,631 in 1910, became the home of 6,727 Chinese by 1926. Despite the explosion in the growth of the Chinese populations in the Pacific and Gulf states between 1910 and 1926, the size of the Chinese immigrant community of central Mexico remained largely stable during these years (see table 3.2).[75]

The shift in Chinese geographical distribution patterns between the years 1910 and 1926, from concentration in northern Mexico to a more balanced pattern of settlement throughout the northern, Pacific, and Gulf states, reflects the declining importance of the Chinese immigrant smuggling trade after 1916. During the height of the illegal immigrant smuggling racket during the first decade and a half of the twentieth century, thousands of Chinese arrived at Mexican Pacific ports yearly with the intention of eventually entering the United States illegally through northern Mexico. During this early era of Chinese movement to Mexico, the Chinese focused their settlement in northern Mexico because of the important role played by border states such as Sonora and Chihuahua as entryway into U.S. territory as part of the immigrant smuggling trade, as well as because of the many economic opportunities offered by these industrializing and modernizing states. Whereas before 1916 Chinese immigrants chose to settle in particular regions such as northern Mexico based upon the twin factors of convenient accessibility to the United States and occupational/commercial opportunities, after 1916, with the demise of immigrant trafficking, geographical proximity to the United States became a less important factor for Chinese immigrants in deciding where in Mexico to settle. With the option of furtive entry into the United States less of a possibility after 1916, Chinese newcomers after this date appear to have selected their locations of settlement based primarily upon the factor of employment/commercial opportunities. No longer circumscribed by concern for geographical proximity to the United States, Chinese immigrants between 1910 and 1926 ventured throughout Mexico in search of economic opportunities. They successfully sought out and

Table 3.2. Geographic distribution of Chinese foreign nationals by region and state, 1926.

Central states		Northern states		Gulf states		Pacific states and territories	
Aguascalientes	31	Chihuahua	1,037	Campeche	108	Baja California	5,889
Distrito Federal	1,062	Coahuila	707	Quintana Roo	2	Chiapas	1,261
Durango	197	Nuevo León	216	Tabasco	67	Colima	43
Guanajuato	37	Sonora	3,758	Tamaulipas	2,916	Guerrero	7
Hidalgo	98			Veracruz	1,908	Jalisco	192
México	78			Yucatán	1,726	Michoacán	8
Morelos	9					Oaxaca	254
Puebla	22					Nayarit	164
Querétaro	1					Sinaloa	2,019
San Luis Potosí	288					Tepic	0
Zacatecas	113						
Total	1,936	Total	5,718	Total	6,727	Total	9,837

Source: Mexico, Secretaría de Gobernación, *El Servicio de Migración en México* (Mexico: Talleres Gráficos de la Nación, 1930), 36–38.

took advantage of such opportunities in the Pacific, Gulf, and central regions of Mexico and formed new thriving communities in such places as Chiapas, Sinaloa, Tamaulipas, Veracruz, and the Yucatán. Moreover, entrepreneurial Chinese immigrants during these years also successfully maintained and built upon the commercial infrastructures first laid and established during the early era of Chinese movement to Mexico in those areas of northern Mexico that were once strategic destinations along the transnational commercial orbit. In one such territory, Baja California, the Chinese constructed a commercial and residential capital that continues to exist to this day.

Conclusion

This chapter highlights the transnational nature of Chinese movement to Mexico during the late nineteenth and early twentieth centuries. In circumvention of, and adaption to, the Chinese exclusion laws, thousands of Chinese immigrants journeyed to Mexico in search of jobs and the chance to get smuggled into the United States. In collaboration with Mexican business and governmental interests, transnational Chinese businessmen devised impersonal systems of recruiting emigrants as contract laborers and undocumented coolies for haciendas, ranchos, and mines. These same entrepreneurial Chinese were also allegedly the leaders of a vast, transnational smuggling ring encompassing China, Mexico, Cuba, and the United States. The global economic network established by the Chinese Six Companies to facilitate the big business of transnational contract labor recruitment and human smuggling formed the basis for the Chinese transnational commercial orbit of the late nineteenth and early twentieth centuries. This orbit bound together the Chinese diasporic communities of the United States, Mexico, Cuba, and South America as an economic and geographic unit.

For Chinese immigrants, the journey to Mexico began aboard steamships that took them on circuitous journeys along the transnational Chinese commercial orbit of Asia and the Americas. Beginning in Hong Kong, Chinese immigrants were transported to Mexico via steamship lines that often took them through Japan, Cuba, and the United States. Although some Chinese landed directly at Mexican ports such as Mazatlán, Manzanillo, and Guaymas, others stopped first in San Francisco and traveled by train in transit to Mexican border towns in Sonora and Chihuahua. The most privileged of Chinese immigrants traveled to Mexico under the financial auspices of wealthy kin who had made their fortunes as merchants in the petit bourgeois sector of the Mexican economy; most Chinese were less fortunate and journeyed to Mexico, legally or illegally, as contracted laborers who had their passages paid in exchange for bitter labor.

Although many traveled to Big Lusong in search of economic opportunity and with plans of putting down roots, thousands of Chinese thought of Mexico as only a temporary layover en route to the United States. In resistance to the Chinese exclusion laws, thousands of Chinese used Mexico as a surreptitious gateway to Gold Mountain. Organized by entrepreneurial Cantonese immigrants of the San Francisco Chinese Six Companies in cahoots with transnational agents in China, Mexico, Cuba, and throughout the United States, the illegal traffic of Chinese immigrant laborers flourished well into the early twentieth century, until its demise following the interruption of transpacific steamship travel during World War I.

As we will see in the next several chapters, Chinese not only journeyed to Mexico along transnational paths and as part of transnational migration mechanisms; once arriving, they also lived transnational lives. Chinese immigrant men often maintained transnational marriages and families with Chinese women left behind in their home villages; they sometimes intermarried with Mexican women, who were sent, together with their cross-cultural progeny, to live in China; Chinese immigrants thrived as borderland merchants because of unique strategies of transnational commercial investment and wholesaling; and, they developed social, political, and legal networks through the establishment of transnational community organizations such as the Guo Min Dang and the Chee Kung Tong.

4
Gender, Interracial Marriage, and Transnational Families

Born in the Tew Lin village of the Taishan region of Guangdong on February 6, 1906, Ramon Wong Fong Song immigrated to Mexicali, Mexico, in 1924 and became a dry-goods merchant and restaurant owner.[1] In 1932, Wong made his first return visit to China and married Chin Yuk Lin. Following a two-year matrimonial visit, Wong returned to Mexico, leaving his wife behind in his native village and rejoining his brother and business partner, Samuel Wong Muy. Ramon and Samuel's parents, Wong Tow Chong and Fong Shee, as well as their six sisters and two other brothers, resided in the family village of Tew Lin.

Like Ramon and Samuel, the vast majority of Chinese immigrants to Mexico were male. Despite this gender imbalance, the Chinese community of Mexico was far from a "bachelor society." As exemplified by the life story of Ramon, significant numbers of Chinese male immigrants in Mexico maintained transnational marriages with Chinese women residing overseas in their home villages, and a few of the most privileged brought Chinese wives to live with them in Mexico. In addition to the maintenance of transnational and local marriages with Chinese women, Chinese men also intermarried with native Mexican women at relatively high rates. In contrast with the Chinese diasporic community of the United States, such high rates of racial intermarriage were a distinguishing feature of the Chinese of Mexico.

This chapter explores the topic of Chinese immigrant cultural adaptation by examining gender, marriage, and family patterns of the Chinese community of Mexico during the early twentieth century. In particular, it emphasizes the transnational nature of Chinese immigrant family life and looks at the transnational families that Chinese immigrant men formed with both Chinese and Mexican women. This chapter also analyzes the vehement opposition that Chinese-Mexican families faced in northern Mexico and examines popular cultural representations of Chinese-Mexican intermarriage through the lens of comedy sketches, cartoons, poetry, and corridos from postrevolutionary Mexico.

Table 4.1.   Comparison of male and female Chinese immigrant populations, 1895, 1900, 1910, 1921, 1926, 1930.

Year	Number of males	Number of females
1895	996	27
1900	2,647	13
1910	13,118	85
1921	14,227	245
1926	22,446	1,772
1930	16,254	2,711

Sources: Mexico, Ministerio de Fomento, *Censo general de la República Mexicana verificado el 20 de octubre de 1895, resúmen del censo de la república* (Mexico, D.F.: Dirección General de Estadística); Mexico, Secretaria de la Economía Nacional, *Quinto censo de población 1930, resúmen general* (Mexico, D.F.: Dirección General de Estadística); Mexico, Secretaría de Gobernación, *El Servicio de Migración en México* (Mexico: Talleres Gráficos de la Nación, 1930), 36–38.

Gender Patterns

Like the Wong brothers, most Chinese who immigrated to Mexico were male. Between 1911 and 1928, some 22,319 Chinese male emigrants and nationalized Mexican citizens were registered as entering Mexican ports from China, as compared with only 307 women during these same years.[2]

Mexican national census and governmental records for the years 1895, 1900, 1910, 1921, 1926, and 1930 further highlight the gender imbalance between male and female Chinese immigrants during these years (see table 4.1). The 1895 national census recorded only 27 Chinese female nationals out of a total Chinese immigrant population of 1,023 persons.[3] By 1910, although the Chinese overseas community in Mexico had grown to a size of 13,118, only 85 female Chinese nationals were registered as part of the census that year.[4] In 1926, at the height of Chinese settlement in Mexico, only 1,772 women were registered as Chinese foreign residents of Mexico, as compared with 22,446 men.[5] An examination of the 1930 national census manuscripts for the municipalities of Chihuahua City, Chihuahua, and Hermosillo, Sonora, underscores this similar trend favoring male immigration.[6] The review of a comprehensive sampling of 417 persons residing in Chinese households in Chihuahua City in 1930 revealed the presence of only two Chinese-born adult women. In the

1930 census manuscripts for the Sonora state capital of Hermosillo, only twelve Chinese-born adult women are recorded out of a comprehensive sampling of 408 persons living in Chinese households.

A comparison of the number of registered Chinese female immigrant entrances into Mexico between 1911 and 1928 with the rate of growth of the Chinese female population in Mexico during these same years reveals ostensible statistical discrepancies that appear to call into question the accuracy of Mexican government records. Whereas only 307 Chinese women were recorded as entering Mexico from 1911 to 1928, the Chinese female population in Mexico reportedly grew by 2,626 persons between 1910 and 1930.[7] Specifically, the number of Chinese women residing in Mexico increased dramatically during the second decade of the twentieth century. In 1921, the Chinese female population consisted of only 245, and by 1930 this number increased more than tenfold, to 2,711. In contrast, only 168 Chinese women are recorded as entering Mexican ports from China between 1921 and 1928. What accounts for these ostensible discrepancies between the numbers of registered female entrances and the disproportionate increase in the size of the Chinese female population in Mexico during these same years?

Although gross error in Mexican government statistical data gathering and census methodology is one possible explanation, a more plausible explanation relates to Chinese-Mexican intermarriage patterns and the concomitant birth of female offspring as a result of these unions. An examination of the 1930 census manuscripts for the municipalities of Chihuahua City and Hermosillo reveals a relatively high rate of intermarriage between Chinese male immigrants and Mexican women, as well as a smaller number of extramarital free unions between the two social groups. In Chihuahua City, based upon a comprehensive sampling of 304 Chinese males of varied age groups, twenty-eight Chinese men were registered as married to Mexican women as part of both Catholic and civil marital unions. Moreover, eleven extramarital free unions were recorded. Hermosillo census manuscripts record fourteen marriages and nine free unions between Chinese immigrant males and native Mexican females, based upon a sampling of 326 males of diverse ages.

Examination of the Chihuahua and Hermosillo census manuscripts further reveals that Mexican women were generally considered Chinese nationals for purposes of census statistical record keeping if their husbands were Chinese nationals.[8] On the other hand, Mexican women married to Chinese immigrants who had become nationalized Mexican citizens generally retained their status as Mexican nationals as recorded in the census materials. Female Mexicans involved in extramarital free unions with Chinese immigrants were also considered Mexican nationals for purposes of the census. Seventeen Mexican women from the Chihuahua sample and ten from the Hermosillo grouping were listed as Chinese nationals because of their marriage to Chinese immigrants who had not become nationalized Mexican citizens. This categorization of Mexican wives as Chinese nationals based upon the citizenship status of their husbands as Chinese nationals explains, in part, the disproportionate increase in the size of the Chinese female community when compared with the relatively small number of entrances of Chinese women immigrants into the country. Many of the women listed as Chinese nationals as part of Mexican national census publications, therefore, were not Chinese by birth but by marriage.[9]

Although this categorization of female Mexicans as Chinese nationals accounts for a significant amount of the increase in the size of the Chinese female population during the early twentieth century, a large proportion of the increase can be attributed to the birth of female children as a consequence of marital and extramarital unions between Chinese immigrant males and Mexican women, as well as between Chinese men and Chinese female nationals. An examination of the Chihuahua City and Hermosillo municipal manuscripts reveals that children born in Mexico as the result of marital unions between Chinese men and Mexican wives were usually counted in the census as Chinese nationals if their father was a Chinese national.[10] Children born as a result of free unions between Chinese male immigrants and Mexican women were usually recorded as Mexican nationals in the Chihuahua City census manuscripts and as Chinese nationals in the Hermosillo records.

Children born in Mexico to Chinese parents were included as Chinese nationals for census purposes where their father was a Chinese national. The Chihuahua manuscripts categorize forty females born in Mexico as Chinese nationals—thirty born to Chinese male nationals and their Mexican-born wives; four born to Chinese fathers as a consequence of extramarital unions with Mexican women; and six born to husbands and wives of Chinese descent and nationality. The Hermosillo census records list twenty-nine females born in Mexico as Chinese nationals—seventeen born to Chinese fathers and their Mexican wives; nine born to Chinese nationals and their Chinese wives; two born to Chinese fathers and their Mexican free-union partners; and, one born as a consequence of extramarital relations between a Chinese couple. In sum, a large amount of the increase in the size of the Chinese female population during the twentieth century can therefore be attributed to the birth of female children as a consequence of marital and extramarital unions between Chinese immigrant males and Mexican and Chinese women, and the subsequent categorization of many of their female offspring as Chinese nationals for purposes of the national census.

Marriage and Family Patterns

Like Ramon Wong, Ricardo Cuan immigrated to Mexico as a bachelor, leaving behind parents and siblings, and remained single for a number of years after his initial arrival in Mexico. As discussed in chapter 2, Ricardo Cuan immigrated to Guaymas, Mexico, from his native Kiukon village of the Nanhai District in Guangdong at the age of twelve.[11] Cuan made the journey to Mexico with his brother-in-law Manuel Ung, who owned a grocery store in Guaymas, and eventually became an established merchant in the city of Ensenada, Baja California. In an interview with an Immigration and Naturalization Service inspector in April of 1939, Cuan stated that his widowed mother, Chean Si, and two living brothers, Cuan Chim and Cuan Chaw, resided in Hong Kong. Presumably, Ricardo's parents and siblings Cuan Chim and Cuan Chaw remained in China while he went overseas to Mexico. In 1940, after about thirty years of residing in Mexico as a bachelor, Cuan was married by proxy to a woman he had never seen as part of a marriage arranged by his mother. The Chihuahua City and Hermosillo municipal manuscripts indicate that, like Ricardo Cuan and Ramon Wong, a large percentage of Chinese male immigrants arrived in Mexico as bachelors. The Chihuahua sampling revealed 153 single males over the age of 17 out of a total male population of 304, and the Hermosillo municipal records cite 142 single males out of a total male population of 326. Based upon Immigration and Naturalization Service interviews of Chinese immigrants such as Ramon Wong and Ricardo Cuan, it appears that many single emigrant males traveled to Mexico to find employment as a means of supporting parents, siblings, and other family members who stayed behind in China.[12] Moreover, through the sending of remittances, Chinese immigrant bachelors maintained transnational socioeconomic ties with their family members in China.

   In addition to serving as examples of the many bachelor males who migrated to Mexico during the late nineteenth and early twentieth centuries, the case studies of Ramon Wong and Ricardo Cuan provide insight into the trend of transnational marriages that was common among Chinese males. Both Wong and Cuan immigrated to Mexico at young, premarriageable ages and, after a time of establishing themselves financially as business owners, eventually entered into marriages with women residing in China. Whereas Wong returned to his native Taishan to marry Chin Yuk Lin at the age of twenty-six following an eight-year sojourn in Mexico, Cuan was married by proxy to a woman he had never met, after about thirty years of residing in Mexico. Moreover, both Wong and Cuan maintained transnational marriages, supporting their wives who remained in China through their income earned as Mexican merchants. An examination of the Chihuahua City and Hermosillo municipal census manuscripts confirms that this pattern of transnational marriage was quite common among Chinese male immigrants in Mexico. The Chihuahua sampling cites the presence of fifty married Chinese males whose wives were not registered in the census and therefore presumably resided in China. The Hermosillo manuscripts revealed the presence of ninety-six married immigrant adult males whose wives were not listed in the census and who may be presumed to have been living overseas in China.[13] This pattern of transnational marriage was also common among the diasporic Chinese living in the United States.[14]

Although the extant census manuscripts and Immigration and Naturalization Service interviews suggest that most Chinese male immigrants in Mexico who were married to Chinese women maintained transnational marriages, the available data also reveal that a few brought Chinese wives to live with them in Mexico. The Chihuahua census manuscripts record the presence of two Chinese-born wives, and the Hermosillo sampling reveals eight Chinese brides of Chinese immigrant males, in addition to one Chinese-born widow.

Besides the maintenance of transnational and local marriages with Chinese women, Chinese men also intermarried with native Mexican women at relatively high rates. The frequency of such intermarriage distinguishes the case of the Chinese in Mexico from that of their diasporic counterparts in the United States, who rarely intermarried with the mainstream white population, because of strictly enforced state legislative prohibitions. Based upon the comprehensive sampling of eighty married Chinese males residing in Chihuahua City in 1930, twenty-eight were married to Mexican women.[15] In Hermosillo, 14 of 119 Chinese immigrant marriages were to local Hispanic women.[16]

Figure 4.1. Rodolfo Ley.
Source: NA Laguna, Lee Chip or
Rodolfo Ley, Chinese Exclusion
Act Case File no. 4067/728.

The case studies of Rodolfo Ley (see fig. 4.1) and Pablo Chee provide examples of this not-infrequent phenomenon of intermarriage between Chinese male immigrants and Mexican women.[17] Rodolfo Ley left his native Nom Boo Haw Village in the Hoy Yin city of Guangdong in 1911 at the age of eighteen. Entering at the port of Manzanillo, Ley resided for a time in Tampico, where he became a dry goods/grocery merchant and met and married his Mexican wife, Maria Aguilar de Ley. While living in Tampico, the Leys had one son, Rodolfo Ley Jr., also known as Lee Kong. In 1923, the family moved to Mexicali, Mexico, where Rodolfo senior supported his wife and child as a business partner in the Quong Yuen Co. In April of 1931, Rodolfo, Maria, and Lee Kong traveled to China, where they remained for about a year. Rodolfo and Maria returned to Mexicali in 1932, leaving ten-year-old Lee Kong in China for school. Like Rodolfo Ley, Pablo Chee also immigrated to Mexico from Guangdong in the early twentieth century. Chee emigrated from the Kow Kong village in Nanhai, Guangdong, in November of 1901 and settled in Tapachula, Chiapas. Chee married Adelina Palomegus on February 6, 1909, in Tapachula, and the couple had a son, Manuel Jesús Chee, on January 10, 1910. Together with Adelina and Manuel, Pablo traveled to China in 1914, and in 1915; however, Pablo returned to Mexico, leaving his Mexican wife and child back in China to live in his home village. Manuel subsequently attended a British school in Guangdong, China. Following his return to Mexico, Chee increased his fortune as a successful businessperson engaged in a wide variety of commercial endeavors, serving as grocery and general merchandise merchant, and investing in several thousand acres of ranches, a hotel, and a saloon. He eventually also gained the right of legal domicile in the United States under the Section 6 merchant exemption. In 1924, Chee applied for permission from the U.S. Immigration and Naturalization Service to bring his wife and child from China to live in the United States.

These case studies of Rodolfo Ley and Pablo Chee demonstrate that Chinese male immigrants in Mexico in certain instances chose to intermarry with Mexican women rather than return to China to marry. As successful merchants, Ley and Chee could have easily arranged marriages with Chinese women from their home districts, as did Ricardo Cuan and Ramon Wong, yet instead they chose to marry Mexican nationals. It is not entirely clear from the historical record why Ley and Chee opted to buck Chinese tradition by finding themselves Mexican brides. One possible, but cynical, explanation is that intermarriage afforded them certain economic advantages. Marriage to Mexican nationals may have provided them with unique inroads to local Mexican economic networks and thereby served as a financial advantage.

Although it is difficult to explain why wealthy merchants like Ley and Chee chose to depart from traditional expectations and marry Mexican women, it is easier to understand why humble Chinese immigrants made this decision. Unlike successful immigrant businessmen, working-class Chinese could not afford to arrange for an overseas marriage and bring a wife to live with them in Mexico. With few financial resources, moreover, it was unlikely that they could return to China to marry. Rather than remain single, with little or no chance of finding a Chinese wife, it is likely that many of them viewed marriage to a Mexican woman as an attractive option.

As previously mentioned, these patterns of racial intermarriage were unique to the Mexican example. In the United States, Chinese men were strictly prohibited from intermarrying with white women because of strict antimiscegenation laws, which remained in effect until the late 1960s. In California, for example, intermarriage between Chinese and those defined by law as white was outlawed until 1968. Since persons of Mexican descent were legally categorized as "white," Chinese-Mexican intermarriage in the United States was legally prohibited until this time.

From the examples of Rodolfo Ley and Pablo Chee we learn also that Mexican wives of successful Chinese merchants occupied a status similar to that of native Chinese wives. Maria Aguilar de Ley and Adelina Palomegus de Chee both traveled with their husbands on extensive return trips back to China, which would not have been likely had they occupied a secondary concubine type of marital status. Moreover, Adelina remained in the home village of her husband for at least nine years together with her Mexican-born son Manuel, a practice that mirrored the transnational marriage patterns of Chinese immigrant males and their native Chinese wives.

In sum, the case studies of Rodolfo Ley and Pablo Chee, together with the data gathered from the Chihuahua City and Hermosillo 1930 census manuscripts, demonstrate that intermarriage between Chinese men and female Mexican nationals was not uncommon, and suggest that the Mexican wives of successful Chinese merchants enjoyed a status comparable to that of native Chinese brides.

In addition to civil and ecclesiastical marital unions, small numbers of Chinese male immigrants also engaged in extramarital free unions with Mexican women. The Chihuahua City census manuscripts list eleven free unions between Chinese men and Mexican female nationals; the Hermosillo records cite nine such extramarital relationships. The Hermosillo sampling also revealed the existence of one free-union relationship between male and female immigrants of Chinese descent.

Chinese male immigrants in Mexico sired many offspring as a consequence of their marital and extramarital unions with Chinese and Mexican women. The Chihuahua census manuscripts registered a total of 123 offspring of Chinese males and Chinese and Mexican women. Of this total, 90 children were the products of unions between Chinese men and their Mexican wives; 12 were the children of Chinese married couples; and, 18 were conceived as the result of extramarital free unions between Chinese males and Mexican women. The Hermosillo sampling records the presence of 83 children born in Mexico of ethnic Chinese fathers. Of this number, 48 were born of Chinese immigrant fathers and Mexican wives; 20 were products of marital unions between Chinese married couples; and 8 children were conceived within the context of extramarital free unions between Chinese males and Mexican women.

In addition to offspring produced as a consequence of marital and extramarital relationships with women in Mexico, some Chinese immigrant men also maintained transnational relationships with children conceived and residing in China as part of transnational marriages with native Chinese women. The examples of Federico Cham and Enrique

Chong are illustrative of this phenomenon.[18] Federico Cham married his wife, Chung Shee, on May 10, 1903, in his home village of Wuey Yuen in the Gow Ging District of China. Their eldest son, Quan Quai Fong, was born March 7, 1905, and their second son, Quan Sou Fong, was born two years later on December 7, 1907. In 1910, at the age of twenty-five, Federico Cham immigrated to Mazatlán, Mexico, leaving his wife, Quan Quai, Quan Sou, and daughter behind in Wuey Yuen village.[19] After residing in Mexico for ten years, Federico Cham gained legal entry and residence in the United States as a Section 6 Mazatlán merchant and became manager of a grocery store in Calexico, California.[20] A contemporary of Cham, Enrique Chong was born in the Ha Chun village of the Sun Ning District in 1886. Chong was married to Ho Shee on February 3, 1905, and the couple had two sons, Chong Sick Nom and Chong Charm Chun, born in 1906 and 1909 respectively. In January of 1922, Enrique Chong entered the United States at the port of New York as a Section 6 merchant and, prior to becoming a resident of the United States, appeared to have lived in Mexicali since at least 1919. In an interview with the U.S. Immigration Service in October of 1923, Enrique Chong stated that his wife, Ho Shee, and sons Chong Sick and Chong Charm were residing in his home village of Ha Chun. Presumably, Ho Shee, Chong Sick, and Chong Charm remained in China upon Enrique's initial immigration to Mexico.

From these vignettes of Federico Cham and Enrique Chong, we learn that male Chinese immigrants to Mexico sometimes left behind both wives and young children in their home villages. Pushed from their home villages by difficult socioeconomic conditions, married male emigrants like Cham and Chong moved to Mexico in search of greater economic opportunities, to provide for the livelihood of their families who remained in China. Moreover, we see from the example of Federico Cham that Chinese male immigrants sometimes maintained overseas transnational familial relationships with wives and children over the course of many years. When interviewed by Immigration Service officer A. C. Weisgerber in February of 1922 as part of an application for a merchant's return certificate, Federico Cham stated he had lived apart from his wife and children for twelve years. In a subsequent interview also associated with a return visit to China in 1934, Cham stated that, although his younger son, Quan Sou Fong, was then living in Los Angeles, California, his eldest son, Quan Quai Fong, and second wife, Kwock Shee, still resided in Guangdong, China. Based upon these examples of Federico Cham and Enrique Chong, it is likely that many of the 146 married Chinese males whose wives were not registered in the Chihuahua and Hermosillo 1930 census manuscripts maintained transnational familial relationships with both wives and children who remained in their home villages.

Based upon the previous discussion of marriage and family patterns among Chinese male immigrants in Mexico, it is clear that the Chinese overseas community in Mexico was far from a traditional bachelor society. Although the overwhelming majority of Chinese immigrants were male, based upon the case studies of Rodolfo Ley and Pablo Chee, and the Chihuahua City and Hermosillo manuscript records, we learn that intermarriage between Chinese men and female Mexican nationals was a relatively frequent phenomenon. Such patterns of intermarriage, moreover, distinguish the Chinese diaspora in Mexico from that of the United States, where racial intermarriage was almost nonexistent during this time period. As evidenced by the vignettes of Ramon Wong, Ricardo Cuan, Federico Cham, and Enrique Chong, and as implied by the Chihuahua and Hermosillo municipal records, many Chinese immigrant males maintained transnational familial relationships with wives and children remaining in their home villages. From the case studies of Ramon Wong and Ricardo Cuan, we may deduce that many who ventured to Mexico as bachelors likely returned to China to marry or became married by proxy while remaining in Mexico. From the life stories of Federico Cham and Enrique Chong, we learn that some Chinese males immigrated to Mexico during the early years of their marriage, leaving wives and young children behind in their home villages. Moreover, the Chihuahua and Hermosillo manuscripts reveal that a few Chinese emigrants brought Chinese wives to Mexico. Finally, the municipal census manuscripts of these two state capitals also demonstrate that the Chinese immigrant community of Mexico was not a traditional bachelor society, based upon the many records of Mexican-born offspring produced as a consequence of marital and extramarital unions between Chinese male immigrants and Chinese and Mexican women.

Popular Mexican Perspectives

Comedy, Cartoons, Poetry, and *Corridos*

Chinese-Mexican intermarriages were strongly condemned by mainstream Mexican society, and one finds frequent reference to them throughout popular Mexican culture of the early twentieth century.[21]

Spoken-word comedy recordings, cartoons, poetry, and *corridos* of these years comment upon a wide range of themes and topics pertaining to Chinese-Mexican unions, including courtship, marriage, cross-cultural children, abandonment, and even family relocation to China. As will be discussed in detail later in this chapter, much of this commentary was couched within broader nationalistic ideology of the Mexican Revolution.

Mocking Chinese Courtship Strategies

According to popular perception, wealthy Chinese immigrant merchants lured naive Mexican women into marriage by promising them lives of material comfort and prosperity. This courtship strategy is playfully depicted in a spoken dialogue recording titled, "El chino," which was commercially released by the Brunswick Record Corporation in 1937.[22] This comedic dialogue, set in Texas, parodies a conversation between a prosperous Chinese businessperson named Ching Choman and a young Mexican woman by the name of Maria. In the conversation, Ching aggressively courts the favor of Maria, who is already engaged to be married. As part of his courtship strategy, Ching tells Maria that he is very rich and promises to buy her whatever she wants in exchange for a marriage commitment. In addition, Ching tells Maria that her Mexican boyfriend is no good and useless, and he criticizes the boyfriend and other Tejanos for being lazy and depending upon their wives to support them. Despite Ching's persistent pleas in broken and heavily accented Spanish, Maria ultimately rejects him, insisting that she is an honorable woman.

> *Ching (C):* Maria, tomorrow I am going to give praise [go to church] and I want to take a nice virgin.
>
> *Maria (M):* Great, but this virgin already has a boyfriend. Besides who are you? I don't know you. I don't even know your name.
>
> *C:* My name is Ching Choman.
>
> *M:* Ching what? Well, what do you know, this guy just cussed at me. ["Ching" sounds like the first word of a very offensive Spanish phrase, "chinga tu madre," which translates as "screw your mother."]
>
> *C:* Don't get angry, Maria. I want to tell you that your boyfriend is no good, no good.
>
> *M:* What do you mean, no good?

C: A Texan never works. The poor woman always works to support him. . . . A pretty girl like you always wants nice dresses, many pairs of shoes. And this Chinese guy is very rich and will make a good husband. The one you have is useless.

M: So what.

C: Maria, I promise you eternal love. You will be the queen of my house, and I will buy you whatever you desire. As long as you give me . . . the heart of a divine and charming woman.

M: Hey, hey, you're going too far. If you keep it up, I'll give you a slap on the cheek.

C: Give me whatever you want as long as you give me something.

M: Listen, you, I am an honorable young lady.[23]

Condemning Interracial Marriage

Even though popular Mexican culture sometimes found humor in the courtship antics of Chinese male immigrants, Mexican women who married Chinese suitors were shunned and scolded as "dirty," "lazy," "unpatriotic," and "shameless." Chinese-Mexican marital unions were condemned as marriages of convenience in which lazy Mexican women avoided work, thanks to financial support from their Chinese husbands. Such cross-cultural relationships, moreover, were said to threaten the ruin of Mexican womanhood and to defile the Mexican nation. A number of cartoon sketches, poems, and corridos exemplify these popular critical attitudes.

Figure 4.2 unsympathetically portrays a Mexican woman suffering the consequences of an interracial marriage of convenience.[24] The cartoon's caption reads, "Oh wretched woman! . . . You thought you would enjoy a cheap life by giving yourself to a Chinese man, and instead you are a slave and the fruit of your mistake is a freak of nature."

According to the cartoonist, the woman entered into an interracial marriage hoping to secure for herself an easy life, free from financial worry. Instead, she has become a slave to her Chinese husband, and the reluctant mother of a subhuman, alienlike offspring that she now seeks to abandon.

An anonymous poem from around 1910 titled, "El destierro de los chinos" (Exile of the Chinese) expressed similar condemnation of Mexican women who chose to marry or become romantically involved with Chinese immigrant men.[25] The poem reads in part:

¡Ah infeliz!. . . . Creíste disfrutar de una vida barata al entregarte a un chino y eres
una esclava y el fruto de tu error es un escupitajo de la naturaleza . . . .

Figure 4.2. Imprisoned Mexican wife and unwanted cross-cultural offspring.
Source: José Angel Espinoza, *El ejemplo de Sonora* (Mexico, D.F.: n.p., 1932), 77, 36.

They haven't made a discovery
Paying with Chinese money,
They've only come to ruin
The female kind . . .

But we must make an effort
To tolerate imprudence.
The ones who are to blame
Are the wicked women.

They know no shame.
They begin to cry
About how comfortably they have lived
And their eventual decline.

Those wretched females,
Know no shame.
What's in it for them
Is pure convenience.

I tell you the truth,
Without fear of public outrage,
That she who lives with a Chinese man
Is a woman of pure convenience.

They don't like to work,
This shameless woman
She wants the Chinaman to support her
And keep her well dressed

And they like to boast
Without any brains
What they need
Is a little bit of shame

We hold the government responsible
Even though you may think me unwise
They should exile
Three types of people [Chinese, Mexican women who marry them,
     and Arabs].

The first should be the women
Who make unions with Chinese men
They know no shame
Because they are staining the nation

And we should give them their due
Right quick
Burn them with hot oil
With firewood and tar.

In harsh and inflammatory language, this poem excoriates Chinese immigrant men for bringing about the downfall of Mexican women, who are said to be bought off with "Chinese money." Mexican women who reciprocate the affections of Chinese men are chastised as wicked, shameless, and pitiful, and deserving of being burned with hot oil. Similar to the cartoon in figure 4.2, this poem asserts that Chinese-Mexican interracial unions are simply arrangements of convenience by which lazy Mexican women avoid work by relying on their Chinese lovers for financial support. Inserting a twist of revolutionary nationalism, the anonymous author of this poem also condemns such women as unpatriotic individuals who "stain" the Mexican nation.

Similar themes are expressed in a song titled "Los chinos" (The Chinese). Released by Columbia Records in 1913, just three years after the onset of the Mexican Revolution, the song echoes the sinophobic sentiment of the cartoon and poem. Composed by Eduardo Tavo in the traditional ballad style of a Mexican corrido, and performed by artist Gomez-Acosta, this song scolds Mexican women who date or marry Chinese men, calling them dirty and shameless women who marry for the love of money. It makes specific reference to the anti-Chinese agitation in Sinaloa during this period.

There goes the angry mob
So pay close attention
Only God knows what will happen
Here comes the big news
I don't know what will happen
But there will be no more silk outfits [in reference to the clothing of
   the Chinese]

I am saying this in reference to many young women
Young women of Mazatlán.
Go look for your way out [by marrying a Chinese man]
Because soon there will be none left

It started with a few Chinese
That had their stores closed down
And all of the women who did business with them
Cried all night

Many say that I am lying
Because I am telling the truth
They will fall in love with a Mexican
Only on rare occasions

Many Mexican women love the Chinese
Because they have no shame
And they aren't ashamed to make a Chinese bun in their hair.
They both make the braid together[26]

Then they go to the mirror
With their Chinese at their side
And one asks the other
Who did a better job fixing their hair

All Mexican women that love a Chinese man
Should be ashamed
And without hesitation
Should be shunned by all the people of Mexico

I say this because many women of Mexico
Dirty women
For the love of money
They make of themselves less than a woman of China.

I am leaving now, I am saying farewell
I am not from this area
But when they find you kissing a Chinese man
You will remember me

And you can say that I disappeared
And you can forget about me
Just pray to God that I don't return
To sing this corrido again

If a woman who hears these verses
Is married to a Chinese
She should not feel so proud
Because what I say is the truth
You will surely say
That I am a rude man
But still worse
Are the women of Mazatlán

This corrido situates sinophobic anti-miscegenation sentiment within the specific historical events of the Mexican Revolution. In addition to its explicit condemnation of intermarriage between Chinese men and Mexican women, this song recalls the violence perpetrated against the Chinese community of Mazatlán during the revolutionary years. In 1911–1913, revolutionary activists of Sinaloa organized public protests against the Chinese and sought to compel the Chinese to flee the city of Mazatlán under threat of mob violence.[27] In this corrido, Tavo paints an ominous picture of the anti-Chinese agitation: "There goes the angry mob . . . only God knows what will happen. Here comes the big news. I don't know what will happen. . . . [S]oon there will be none left" [referring to the Chinese community of Mazatlán]. The song mentions the forced closure of Chinese shops that occurred in Sinaloa during this period: "It started here with a few Chinese that had their stores closed down, and all of the women who did business with them cried all night."

It is against this historical backdrop of revolutionary mob violence perpetrated against the Chinese that Tavo presents his harsh critique of Chinese-Mexican intermarriage. Similar to the plaint of the previous poem and cartoon, he complains that Mexican women who pursue cross-cultural relationships with Chinese men do so "for the love of money" and as a dishonorable means of finding a way out of economic hardship. In addition, he derides such women as "shameful" and "dirty," and asserts that they "should be shunned by all of the people of Mexico." As a unique criticism not addressed in the previous two sources, moreover, the author chides the Mexican wives of Chinese husbands for their adoption of Chinese cultural norms. Specifically, he pokes fun at their selection of Asian hairstyle: "And they aren't ashamed to make a Chinese bun in their hair. They both make the braid together. Then they go to the mirror with their Chinese at their side and one asks the other who did a better job fixing their hair."

Defending Mexican Manhood

On a deeper level, this corrido and the previous sources suggest that Mexican men felt their manhood threatened by Chinese males who wielded greater economic—and presumably sexual—power. Thus, in the comedy sketch "El Chino," Ching tells Maria that her Mexican boyfriend is "no good," because "a Texan never works. The poor woman always works to support him." Revealing similar gendered insecurities, the anonymous, presumably male author of the poem "El destierro de los chinos" also alludes to Chinese economic power: "She who lives with a Chinese man is a woman of pure convenience. They don't like to work. . . . She wants a Chinaman to support her and keep her well dressed." In an effort to offset the Chinese male advantage, the corrido attempts to feminize Chinese men through critical reference to the long queue that Chinese immigrant males wore, which the song sarcastically compares to the woman's own hairstyle: "They both braid the hair together."

Defense of the sexual and economic honor of the Mexican male population of northern Mexico became a central goal of the anti-Chinese movement. It was a driving force in the attacks against Chinese merchants that took place in Sinaloa between 1911 and 1913 as part of the organized anti-Chinese campaigns. The perception of a Chinese sexual and economic threat was exacerbated by severe reductions in the Mexican male population of Sonora in the early twentieth century. Reacting to the Sonoran "man shortage" and to the perceived Chinese male advantage, a small group of Mexican shopkeepers and entrepreneurs formed the Commercial Association of Businessmen in Magdalena, Sonora, in 1916. This group stated as its explicit goal the elimination of the Asian merchant through all available legal means. The organized anti-Chinese campaigns culminated in the eventual expulsion of virtually the entire Chinese population from the state of Sonora in 1931.[28]

Criticizing Abuse, Polygamy, and Spousal Repatriation to China

While asserting that Mexican women were lured into interracial relationships by promises of wealth and an easy life, popular Mexican culture simultaneously characterized Chinese-Mexican intermarriages as relationships of abuse and slavery. The contrast between women's expectations of a luxurious life and the harsh reality of abusive marriages is reflected in the caption of the cartoon in figure 4.2: "Oh wretched woman! . . . You thought you would enjoy a cheap life by giving yourself to a Chinese man, but instead you are a *slave* . . ." (emphasis mine).

Other cartoons articulate this imagery of slavery and neglect even more clearly. In figure 4.3, two Mexican wives or concubines are depicted as the slaves of their polygamous Chinese husband, who is whipping them and using them as animals to plow his field in China. The harshness of

MUJER MEXICANA:—Si la locura o la ignorancia te hace esposa o manceba de un chino y éste te quiere llevar a su patria, antes que resolverte a seguirlo apura una dósis de veneno o clávate un puñal en el corazón......

Figure 4.3. Relocated Mexican concubines in China. *Source:* José Angel Espinoza, *El ejemplo de Sonora* (Mexico, D.F.: n.p., 1932), 77.

their experience is underscored by their attire and facial expressions: the two women are barefoot, clothed in tattered rags, and groaning from exhaustion and overwork. The abusive treatment of these Mexican women, moreover, is set in stark contrast to the serene Orientalist backdrop featuring snow-capped mountains and pagodas. Through their toil in the fields, it appears that the two Mexican concubines are slaving to support the opulent lifestyle of their Asian master, who makes his home in one of the extravagant pagodas nestled in the mountain valley.

The accompanying caption further highlights these themes: "Mexican Woman—If insanity or ignorance has led you to become the wife or concubine of a Chinese man and he wants to take you to his homeland, before you decide to follow him, take a dose of poison or drive a dagger into your heart. . . ." According to the cartoonist, therefore, the physical abuse and neglect in an interracial marriage with a Chinese man is so intolerable that suicide by poison or stabbing would be preferable.

In addition to this primary theme of slavery, this cartoon also highlights secondary themes of concubinage and polygamy. The cartoonist explicitly raises this issue through his caption, which refers to a *manceba* (concubine or mistress). However exaggerated, this caption provides limited qualitative evidence that some Mexican women served as concubines to Chinese immigrant men. This notion is supported by the quantitative data drawn from Sonora and Chihuahua census records that show the occurrence of free unions between Chinese men and Mexican women. Although the census manuscripts do not elaborate upon the nature of the free unions, it may be that some of the Chinese men who engaged in these unions with Mexican women remained married to Chinese women left behind in China. The cartoon allows room for such an interpretation: Although the setting is rural southern China, there is a conspicuous absence of any Chinese women in the picture. It may be implied that these two Mexican women are wives or concubines of secondary status who are laboring to support not only their Chinese husband but also the household of his preferred Chinese wife. This secondary concubine status of Mexican women is also conveyed by the lyrics of "Los chinos," which suggest that the Mexican wives hold a status below that of their Chinese counterparts: "I say this because many women of Mexico, dirty women, for the love of money *they make themselves less than a woman of China*" (emphasis added).

Finally, this cartoon also raises the interesting historical issue of spousal relocation to China. As happened in the case of Pablo Chee, some Mexican wives did return to China to live in the home villages of their Chinese husbands and raise their cross-cultural offspring.[29] Large numbers of Chinese-Mexican families also immigrated to China as part of the mass expulsions of the Chinese from northern Mexico.[30] It is estimated that at least two thousand individuals from five hundred Chinese-Mexican families had settled in China by the early 1930s. Attracted to its Iberian and Catholic culture, Chinese-Mexican families formed an ethnic enclave and community in Portuguese Macau.

Although Pablo Chee's narrative is neutral as to the experience of Adelina Palomegus in Guangdong, figure 4.3 vividly depicts the supposedly harsh life of Mexican women who chose to follow their Asian spouses to China. The caption issues a stern warning to those who might be considering such a move: ". . . before you decide to follow him, take a dose of poison or drive a dagger into your heart." Unfortunately, according to the historical record, this depressing depiction of life in China for Mexican women was sometimes a reality. Under the weight of intense familial, economic, and cultural pressures, many Chinese-Mexican families divorced, and hundreds of Mexican single mothers were left alone to raise their cross-cultural offspring in Macau. As a consequence, many Mexican women hoped to repatriate to Mexico. When confronted about the potential difficulties associated with a return to Mexico, some women stated, "Even if we have to scrape bittersweet potatoes in the sierra, we want Mexico."[31]

In the late 1930s, during the presidency of Lázaro Cardenas, many Mexican women in China petitioned the government of Mexico for permission to return to their homeland because of their unhappiness in China. Such permission was granted, and between 1937 and 1938 more than four hundred Mexican women, together with numerous children, returned to Mexico. Smaller numbers of Chinese-Mexican families were also allowed to repatriate in the years following World War II. In 1960, another small remnant returned to Mexico as a consequence of advocacy efforts spearheaded by Chinese-Mexicans who had come of age in Macau and had been deported to China together with their parents in the 1930s.

A different but equally negative outcome is suggested by the cartoon in figure 4.4. In this cartoon, the Chinese male character, dressed in merchant's garb, is shown with his back turned and hand waving in a gesture of dismissal. He is uttering an incomprehensible statement in Chinese, perhaps announcing his imminent departure. Through this combination of body language, speech, and nonverbal communication, it appears that the Chinese man is abandoning his Mexican wife and children after a short marriage of five years. This cartoon, therefore, may be viewed as representing a strong social critique against Chinese immigrant men who were thought to abandon both their Mexican wives and cross-cultural progeny after brief stints of marriage.

Like figure 4.2, this cartoon depicts marriages between Chinese men and Mexican women as relationships of abuse and neglect. It is a before-and-after depiction of a Mexican woman and her Chinese husband on their wedding night and five years into their marriage. In the first image we see a lustful, Mongoloid-looking Chinese male literally salivating over his beautiful, buxom Mexican bride. She is depicted as naive and eager, stylishly adorned in an elegant bedroom with an expensive standing mirror and an exotic Asian privacy partition. Five years later, the erstwhile Mexican maiden appears emaciated and disheveled, clothed in tattered rags and a servant's apron, bereft of the fine accoutrements bestowed upon her as gifts on her wedding night. The message of the cartoon is clear: lured into marriage by false promises of material prosperity, this Mexican

Figure 4.4. Mexican bride and Chinese husband on their wedding night and five years later. *Source:* José Angel Espinoza, *El ejemplo de Sonora* (Mexico, D.F.: n.p., 1932), 36.

woman has become the forsaken servant of a disinterested and abusive Chinese immigrant husband who married her for base sexual pleasure. Abandonment is her ultimate fate.

In addition, this cartoon offers a strong commentary on the issue of multiracial children. It depicts the progeny of the Chinese-Mexican union as gangly, degenerate Mongoloids. Though of both Chinese and Mexican ancestry, the cartoon children do not share any phenotypical character-istics with their Mexican mother and instead are drawn as miniature reflections of their Asian father. One implication of this portrayal is that the cartoonist (and the broader Mexican population) did not consider the offspring of Chinese-Mexican interracial unions to be legitimately Mexican. This popular perspective finds partial official legitimation in the Mexican municipal census manuscripts of 1930. In these records, Mexican census takers categorized the offspring of Chinese male nation-als and Mexican women as ethnically Chinese. If the Chinese fathers were nationalized Mexican citizens, the children were designated Mexican nationals for purposes of the census. But despite this legal classification, they were not treated as Mexican by the society.[32]

Racial Formation and the Mexican Revolution

Such critical portrayals of Chinese-Mexican children as racially degenerate were based upon the view that the Chinese represented a threat to Mexican mestizaje and the development of a unified national racial identity.[33] In the years following the revolution, mestizaje became the dominant paradigm of national and racial formation, and the mestizo was established as the unifying symbol of Mexican national identity.[34] Although there existed competing conceptions of mestizaje, and especially differing views about the proper means of incorporating the indigenous population into the Mexican mainstream, all versions of mestizaje excluded the Chinese. Even José Vasconcelos, the most well-known proponent of the theory of mestizaje, argued for the exclusion of the Chinese from membership in the Mexican racial community. Justifying Chinese exclusion, Vasconcelos wrote: "If we reject the Chinese, it is because man, as he progresses, multiplies less, and feels the horror of numbers, for the same reason that he has begun to value quality."[35] From the standpoint of the "ideal mestizaje," the Chinese represented a "step backward in the anthropological search for the prototypical [Mexican] man," and a threat to the "purity of Aztec blood."[36] Based upon the perceived Chinese threat to Mexican national ethnic identity formation, Chinese-Mexican interracial marriages were deemed particularly offensive because they resulted in the production of mixed offspring who departed from the ideal mestizaje of Spanish and indigenous. These critical attitudes are reflected in the cartoons that depict Chinese-Mexican children as misshapen, subhuman, degenerate Mongoloids.

Chinese-Mexican interracial marriages were deemed especially offensive to regional models of "blanco-criollo" racial formation in northern Mexico. Postrevolutionary racial theorists divided Mexico geographically into a "Creole north," an "indigenous south," and a "central region" characterized as mestizo. In Sonora, the birthplace of the organized anti-Chinese campaigns and the center of Mexican sinophobia, a male blanco-criollo identity predominated. The prototypical Sonoran was depicted in Mexican popular culture as a "white" male of Spanish ancestry with a racial identity distinct from that of the indigenous and mestizo majority populations of central and southern Mexico. Important mestizaje theorists such as Manuel Gámio, moreover, lauded the "blanco-criollo" racial characteristics of northern Mexico as a model for the future development of Mexican mestizaje. From the standpoint of the patriarchal blanco-criollo elite of Sonora, therefore, Chinese-Mexican intermarriages threatened to bring about the racial degeneration of the Sonoran people. The Sonoran elite condemned the offspring of Chinese-Mexican unions as "a new racial type still more degenerated than [Mexico's] naturally abject indigenous castes." They harshly depicted Chinese-Mexicans as "the product of filthy unions" who embodied the worst "vices and degeneration" of both Chinese immigrants and the Mexican lower classes.[37]

These elite regional attitudes toward Chinese-Mexican unions are reflected in the cartoon in figure 4.4. Consistent with the blanco-criollo racial identity of northern Mexico, the young woman in the cartoon is portrayed as fair-skinned, phenotypically white, and culturally westernized. In contrast, her Chinese husband is drawn as an unattractive, stereotypical Asian male with exaggerated Mongoloid features. Their children, of Chinese-Mexican ancestry, do not resemble their blanco-criollo mother but instead show the undesirable racial characteristics of their Asian father. The message of the cartoon is clear and consistent with localized Sonoran ideals of racial formation: Chinese-Mexican interracial unions threatened a racial degeneration of northern Mexico because they produced an inferior, nonwhite Asian racial type.

Popular critiques of Chinese-Mexican intermarriage were also bound up in larger discourses of economic nationalism. Revolutionary activists associated Chinese merchants with U.S. and European capitalist interests that they blamed for the downturn of the national economy and the commercial exploitation of the Mexican populace. Within this framework of economic nationalism, Chinese immigrants were portrayed as foreign exploiters of the Mexican people who, through intermarriage and numerical proliferation, promoted the ruin of the Mexican nation and Mexican womanhood. This perspective is clearly articulated in the poem, spoken-word dialogue, and corrido examined earlier in this essay. Tying the Chinese economic threat to the dangers of Chinese-Mexican intermarriage, the anonymous author of the poem "El destierro de los chinos" warns:

If the government lets them,
They will swamp our nation . . .
It is urgent to take steps
So that Arabs and Chinese

Don't overrun our country. . . .
Gentlemen, in your own homes,
Which of your household products come
From these two races?
They haven't made a discovery
Paying with Chinese money.
They've only come to ruin
The female kind.
That is the best thing they have done,
The dog-faced Chinese.
And that's why we ask
For the exile of the Chinese.
It is necessary that somebody takes notice
With care and attention
So that those wretched Chinese
Don't breed in our nation. . . .
The women that make a union with the Chinese . . .
Know no shame
Because they are staining the nation. . . .
Pray to God, man from China,
With all your heart
That they don't come and lynch you
If the revolution comes.

In the language and opinion of the author, the Chinese threatened to swamp or sink the Mexican nation through economic exploitation, racial intermarriage, and numerical reproduction. Though owing their livelihoods to the sale of their products to Mexican consumers, Chinese merchants were viewed as not contributing to national development— "They haven't made a discovery paying with Chinese money." Instead, implies the poet, Chinese merchants used their ill-gotten profits to entice Mexican women into marriage. Such unions engendered the "ruin of the female kind," and Mexican women who participated in them were said to "stain" the Mexican nation. As a final violent expression of revolutionary nationalism, moreover, the author warned Chinese immigrant males who engaged in cross-cultural marriages of potential death by lynching.

In contrast to the acerbic tone of "El destierro de los chinos," the spoken-word recording "El chino" demonstrates this connection between revolutionary nationalism and opposition to Chinese-Mexican intermarriage in a comedic and lighthearted way. In an interesting twist, the author of this comedy sketch accomplishes this through dialogue spoken by Ching, the Chinese antagonist of the skit. In halting Spanish, Ching proclaims to the Mexican maiden Maria:

> Mexico is good for foreigners. The Americans have oil wells. The English own large mines, large tracts of land. The Germans have hardware stores. The Spanish are owners of bars, markets, and bakeries. The Chinese own many restaurants and laundries. In conclusion, all the foreigners are making money. So what are the Mexicans doing? Nothing, because don't you see they are revolutionaries? Some wear green shirts, some red shirts and others gold shirts. Some yell out, "Long live Zedillo!" Others yell, "Death to Calles!" and still others, "Long live Cardenas!" All of them with their carbines doing "bang bang" here and "bang bang" there, that's all.

Consistent with the nationalistic perspective expressed in "El destierro de los chinos," Ching affirms that Chinese merchants, like their European and American counterparts, have profited greatly from their commercial relations with the Mexican people. Trivializing the aims of the Mexican Revolution, Ching jests that native Mexicans have been excluded from this financial bonanza because of their violent and misguided preoccupation with armed struggle.

This comedy sketch further emphasizes the economic theme when it portrays Ching as seeking to lure Maria into marriage through his wealth earned as a foreign businessman:

> *Ching (C):* A pretty girl like you always wants nice dresses, many pairs of shoes. And this man Chinese guy is very rich. . . . I will buy you whatever you desire . . .
>
> *Maria (M):* And how did you earn a living?
>
> *C:* I was the owner of the Clan de Tonali, cabaret and resort.
>
> *M:* The famous resort they advertise on the radio?
>
> *C:* That same one, the same one. . . .

The author of "El chino" therefore threads together the twin themes of economic nationalism and Chinese-Mexican interracial marriage. Like the anonymous composer of "El destierro de los chinos," he depicts the Chinese as foreign capitalists who have become rich at the expense of the Mexican populace. With their wealth earned as leeches on the Mexican economy, moreover, they seduce "honorable" Mexican women into cross-cultural relationships through extravagant promises of financial security and material wealth. This comedic dialogue and poem clearly demonstrate that popular critiques of Chinese-Mexican unions were often couched within broader discussions of revolutionary economic nationalism. As previously discussed in the analysis of the corrido "Los chinos," moreover, such popular criticism unfortunately also sometimes expressed itself in sinophobic violence.

Law 31 and Legal Prohibitions against Chinese-Mexican Intermarriage

Sinophobic popular sentiment and opposition to Chinese-Mexican interracial marriage found official government sanction in antimiscegenation laws passed by the Sonoran state legislature on December 13, 1923. "Law 31" prohibited marriage between Mexican women and Chinese males under penalty of a 100–500-peso fine to be enforced by local municipal authorities. The text reads:[38]

Law Number 31

"ALEJO BAY, Constitutional Governor of the Free and Sovereign State of Sonora, to its inhabitants, let it be known:

"That the H. State Congress, has sent to me the following Law No. 31 WHICH PROHIBITS THE MARRIAGE OF MEXICAN WOMEN TO CHINESE PERSONS.

FIRST ARTICLE—Prohibits the marriage of Mexican women with persons of the Chinese race, even if they obtain a Mexican naturalization card.

SECOND ARTICLE—Marital life or illicit union between Chinese men and Mexican women will be punished with a fine of 100 to 500 pesos, subject to justification of the act, according to the means established by common law and will be applied by the municipal authorities in the place where the infraction is committed.

As antimiscegenation legislation, Law 31 embodied and articulated the popular perspectives expressed in the spoken-word comedic recording, cartoons, poetry, and corrido previously examined. Known as one of the "nationalistic laws" of the organized anti-Chinese campaigns, it sanctioned the racist and revolutionary attitudes of the Mexican populace by officially punishing Chinese-Mexican intermarriages. In a virulent expression of revolutionary nationalism, article 1 of the law barred intermarriage even with Chinese men who had become naturalized Mexican citizens. Article 2 extended the law's reach beyond the official institution of civil and ecclesiastical marriage to enforce strictures upon Chinese immigrant men and Mexican women engaged in extramarital free unions.

Although an ostensible victory for revolutionary opponents of Chinese-Mexican interracial marriage, Law 31 was not widely or consistently enforced by Sonoran state and local officials. According to José Angel Espinoza, a prominent leader of the organized anti-Chinese campaigns, official application of these laws was limited because of the systematic bribery of magistrates, judges, and government officials by Chinese community organizations known as "tongs." In addition, Chinese community groups hired high-class Mexican lawyers (derisively labeled "chineros") who successfully defended the right of Chinese men to marry freely with Mexican women.[39] Commenting upon the success of Chinese immigrants in resisting the application of the antimiscegenation laws, Espinoza lamented, "The rich Chinese tongs gathered money, paid attorneys, bribed magistrates and judges, and laughed, with the cunning and cynical laughter of a stubborn and calculating coolie."[40]

Although in most instances Chinese immigrants managed to evade enforcement of Law 31, the case of Francisco Hing represents an interesting legal anomaly and counterexample.[41] In violation of Law 31, Hing, a Chinese immigrant, married a Mexican woman in the state of Sonora. Although he was a naturalized Mexican citizen, his marriage was deemed invalid by local Sonoran officials in accordance with article 1 of the antimiscegenation statute. Taking his claim all the way to the highest court of the land, Hing challenged the constitutionality of Law 31 in an effort to secure official legal recognition of his marriage. In September of 1930, however, the Mexican Supreme Court rejected Hing's legal claim and affirmed the constitutionality of Sonora's antimiscegenation laws by an overwhelming majority.

Conclusion

Although most Chinese immigrants were male, the Chinese overseas community in Mexico was far from a traditional bachelor society. Some left wives and children behind in their home villages. Others who entered Mexico as bachelors eventually returned to China to marry, only to return to Mexico in order to support their new brides and children who remained in China. These Chinese male breadwinners maintained close transnational ties with their wives, children, and other family members in Guangdong.

For those who did not opt for a traditional Chinese nuptial, inter-marriage with Mexican women was an attractive option and a relatively common occurrence. Cross-cultural marriages were common among both wealthy Chinese merchants such as Pablo Chee and Rodolfo Ley and humble immigrants who could not afford to arrange for an overseas marriage or return to China to marry. As a consequence of their marital and extramarital unions with Mexican women, Chinese male immigrants sired many offspring in Mexico. This phenomenon of racial intermarriage is unique when compared to the experience of the Chinese diasporic community of the United States during this same time period. In the United States, Chinese immigrants were barred from marrying whites as a consequence of strict antimiscegenation laws, and therefore intermarriage was a rare occurrence.

Indicative of the widespread nature of Chinese-Mexican intermarriage in Mexico, one finds frequent reference to such cross-cultural unions throughout popular Mexican culture. Spoken-word comedy recordings, cartoons, poetry, and corridos of the time cast strong social commentary upon such themes as courtship, concubinage, polygamy, spousal abuse, abandonment, and family relocation to China. Interracial marriage with prosperous Chinese merchants was scornfully depicted as a shameless shortcut by which slothful Mexican women avoided the need to work and secured lives of material comfort. Mexican women who reciprocated the affections of Chinese immigrants were shunned and condemned as "dirty," "wretched," "lazy," and "unpatriotic." Popular Mexican culture, moreover, portrayed Chinese cross-cultural marriages as relationships of abuse, slavery, and neglect, and furthermore rejected the offspring of such unions as subhuman, degenerative, and unworthy of full inclusion within the Mexican national community. On a deeper, less obvious level, these popular-culture sources also reveal that Mexican manhood was threatened by Chinese males who wielded economic and sexual power that was attractive to Mexican women. Such popular criticism of Chinese-Mexican interracial marriage, moreover, was often couched within larger discourses of revolutionary economic nationalism. Opponents of

Asian-Latino interethnic unions identified Chinese merchants with the western foreign economic menace and complained that Chinese cross-cultural marriages promoted the ruin of the Mexican nation and the female race. Critical portrayals of Chinese-Mexican children as racially degenerate, moreover, were based upon the view that the Chinese represented a threat to Mexican mestizaje and the development of a unified national racial identity.

5
Employment and Community
Coolies, Merchants, and the Tong Wars

Santiago Wong Chao arrived in Mazatlán, Mexico, in 1907 at the age of nineteen. During his first twelve years of residence in Mexico, Wong worked as an employee in both Mexican and Chinese-owned stores, as a laborer on a Chinese-owned ranch, and as a waiter in a hotel café.[1] In 1919, after more than a decade spent in various unskilled labor positions, Wong acquired interest in the Quong Lung Hing grocery store in Cananea, Sonora. Even after becoming a merchant in 1919, however, Wong subsequently reverted to employment as a laborer on Chinese Mexicali cotton ranches between 1924 and 1926, following the sale of his interest in the Sonora grocery business and his failure to secure other meaningful employment. Like many other Chinese immigrants, Wong maintained a transnational marriage relationship with his wife and proxy bride Lim Sem, who resided in Taishan, Guangdong.

As evidenced by this life story of Santiago Wong Chao, Chinese male immigrants found employment in various types of occupations during their tenure in Mexico. Contrary to the existing historiography that emphasizes the role of the Chinese as petit bourgeois members of the Mexican commercial sector, and which denies the substantive presence of Chinese immigrants in laboring and working-class positions, the Chinese found employment throughout a broad spectrum of employment categories.[2] Although large numbers of Chinese did work as agricultural contract laborers and urban unskilled employees, as did Wong Chao, many did eventually transition into employment as merchants involved in the grocery and dry-goods trade. The first part of chapter 5 is devoted to examining in greater detail this broad vocational diversity of the Chinese community of Mexico as well as the distinct demographic profiles of the Chinese working and bourgeois classes.

The second part of this chapter analyzes the transnational business practices that allowed merchants like Santiago Wong Chao to prosper as key financial players along the transnational commercial orbit. Their businesses were often capitalized by family members residing in the

United States and China, and they usually purchased goods for their shops from Chinese and American wholesalers across the border in "el otro lado." Utilizing a loophole in U.S. immigration policy, Chinese merchants managed to cut inventory costs by regularly crossing over the northern border to purchase goods directly from American wholesalers. These transnational business practices were key factors that allowed Chinese merchants to outsell their Mexican competitors, and they also represent two important economic activities of the transnational commercial orbit.

Despite disparities in socioeconomic level, Chinese immigrants in Mexico banded together through the formation of transnational community organizations. The Chinese used these transnational organizations as important vehicles for defending their legal, economic, and political interests in the face of racial discrimination by the mainstream Mexican populace. As evidenced by the "tong wars," these transnational community organizations also sometimes ran into conflict among themselves. The final portion of this chapter looks at some of the transnational community organizations formed by the Chinese of Mexico and describes the tong wars fought by two of these organizations—the Guo Min Dang and Chee Kung Tong—over the control of the opium trade.

Employment Diversity of the Chinese of Mexico

The Chinese community of Mexico was vocationally diverse and comprised of two distinct socioeconomic tiers. Agricultural laborers and urban unskilled employees formed the poor, illiterate, and socially unconnected underclass of the Chinese community. Merchants and skilled artisans such as tailors represented the privileged, wealthier, and oftentimes more assimilated social class of the Chinese immigrant community.[3]

The statistics drawn from the 1930 Mexican national census demonstrate the occupational diversity of the Chinese community of Mexico (see table 5.1). A comprehensive sampling of Chinese immigrant households from the state capitals of Hermosillo and Chihuahua City drawn from 1930 municipal census manuscripts further confirms this pattern of Chinese occupational diversity and highlights the presence of Chinese immigrants in a wide variety of both commercial and laboring activities (see table 5.2). The occupational categories are adapted from those utilized by the 1930 Mexican national census summary.

As reflected in the national census and municipal manuscript statistics, Chinese immigrants established themselves in a variety of occupations.

Table 5.1. Occupational distribution of Chinese immigrants in Mexico, 1930.

Total Chinese population		18,965		
Occupational category	**Percentage**	**Total numbers**	**Men**	**Women**
Agriculture, livestock, fishing	21.84	4,142	4,133	9
Mining	0.39	74	74	0
Various industries (tailors, shoemakers, carpenters, bakers, etc.)	6.65	1,262	1,248	14
Communications and transportation (telegraph, telephone employees, maritime employees, etc.)	0.22	42	42	0
Commerce	36.61	6,961	6,909	52
Public administration	0.11	21	21	0
Free professions	0.21	40	36	4
Domestic sphere (maids, servants, housewives)	9.64	1,829	692	1,137
Other occupations (commercial employees, clerks, mechanics)	4.81	912	898	14
Unproductive occupations, without occupation, occupation unknown (students, minors)	19.42	3,682	2,201	1,481

Source: Mexico, Secretaría de la Economía Nacional, *Quinto censo de población 1930, resúmen general* (Mexico, D.F.: Dirección General de Estadística).

Table 5.2. Chinese immigrant occupational distribution, Chihuahua City, Chihuahua; Hermosillo, Sonora, 1930.

Total sampling Chihuahua City and Hermosillo = 767

Occupational category	Total/Chihuahua and Hermosillo	Percent of total
Agriculture	108	14.08
Mining	1	0.13
Various industries	46	6
Commerce	229	29
Professions	2	0.26
Domestic sphere		
Housewives, daughters, etc.	84	10.95
Paid domestics, servants	6	0.78
Commercial employees, clerks, mechanics	65	8.47
Minors, students	202	26.34
Unskilled, low-skilled employees (cooks, barbers, etc.)	24	3.14

Sources: Statistics compiled from Mexico, Dirección General de Estadística, *Censo de población del municipio de Chihuahua, Chihuahua, 1930* (Salt Lake City: Filmado por la Sociedad Genealógica de Utah, 1987); *Censo de población del municipio de Hermosillo, Sonora* (Salt Lake City: Filmado por la Sociedad Genealógica de Utah, 1988), Mormon Family History Center of West Covina.

Although a large percentage of the national total—36.71 percent—were involved in commerce, significant numbers of Chinese were not merchants. Small numbers of Chinese were professionals and public administrators, and a few found employment within the mining, communications, and transportation industries. One-third of the Chinese community (33.3 percent) were employed as farmers, agricultural laborers, fishermen, laundrymen, bakers, tailors, and artisans of various types, commercial employees, and sales clerks. Roughly one-fifth (19.42 percent) were students, minors, and without occupation. Finally, close to 10 percent were involved in employment related to the domestic sphere. Of this number, although many were servants and/or maids of Mexican families, the vast majority were likely the stay-at-home wives and daughters of Chinese males who worked at home without monetary remuneration.[4]

Based upon examination of a comprehensive sampling of Chinese households from the Chihuahua City and Hermosillo municipal census manuscripts, Chinese farmers and agricultural laborers ranged in age from teenagers to senior citizens in their sixties and seventies (see table 5.3).[5] Most, however, were between twenty-six and sixty years old, and the majority of those from this age category were in their forties. As for marital status, the great majority of Chinese farmers and rural agricultural workers were single, a substantial number had wives in China, and a few maintained free-union relationships with Mexican women. The majority, moreover, were also illiterate, and most remained Chinese citizens. Finally, although some agricultural employees possessed ostensible kinship connections with others in their household or hacienda, the great majority did not appear to be bonded by familial ties with others in Mexico.

Alejandro Chan, Manuel Yong, Low Quan, and Luis Chong provide representative examples of the occupational profiles of Chinese agricultural laborers. Typical of the common occupational profile, Alejandro Chan was a farm laborer who worked in Guaymas, Santa Rosalia, and Mexicali during his residence in Mexico.[6] Chan was single, had no relatives in Mexico or the United States, and worked as a farm worker from the time of his initial arrival in Mexico in 1910 at the age of twenty-two until the time of his illegal entry into the United States in 1918. In that year he was apprehended by U.S. immigration authorities for illegal entrance into the United States near the port of Calexico, together with two other Chinese immigrants—Manuel Yong and Low Quan. Like Chan, and fitting the age profile of Chinese agricultural laborers, Yong and Quan were aged thirty and twenty-five, respectively. Yong worked in Mexico as an agricultural worker; Quan was formerly employed as a farmer. Further matching the occupational profile, moreover, Quan, like Chan, was single, but Yong was married, presumably maintaining a transnational marriage relationship. Like Chan, Yong, and Quan, Luis Chong was a farm laborer in Mexico who was arrested by immigration officials for surreptitious entry into the United States at Calexico, California. Chong arrived in Mexico in 1912 at the seaport of Manzanillo and worked as a farm worker in Tampico and Mexicali for a period of about four years before attempting to enter the United States. Similar to Chan and consistent with the occupational profile, Chong possessed no immediate kinship connections with persons residing in either Mexico or the United States. Slightly

Table 5.3. Demographic profiles of Chinese farmers, rural laborers, and mayordomos of Hermosillo and Chihuahua City, 1930.	
Numbers	96
Ages	
14–25	6
26–35	11
36–40	17
41–50	37
51–60	20
61–75	5
Marital status	
Single	55
Married to Chinese wife	29
Married to Mexican spouse	6
Free union	5
Literacy	
Literate	40
Illiterate	56
Citizenship	
Chinese national	92
Mexican citizen	4

Note: Marital statistics do not include one widow.

Source: Statistics compiled from Mexico, Dirección General de Estadística, *Censo de población del municipio de Chihuahua, Chihuahua, 1930* (Salt Lake City: Filmado por la Sociedad Genealógica de Utah, 1987); *Censo de población del municipio de Hermosillo, Sonora* (Salt Lake City: Filmado por la Sociedad Genealógica de Utah, 1988), Mormon Family History Center, West Covina.

Table 5.4. Demographic profiles of low-skilled/unskilled Chinese urban employees of Hermosillo and Chihuahua City, 1930.	
Numbers	27
Ages	
15–25	1
25–40	9
40–50	12
50–60	4
60–70	1
Marital status	
Single	14
Married to Chinese wife	7
Married to Mexican spouse	1
Free union with Mexican woman	5
Literacy	
Literate	16
Illiterate	11
Citizenship	
Chinese national	25
Mexican citizen	2

Source: Statistics compiled from Mexico, Dirección General de Estadística, *Censo de población del municipio de Chihuahua, Chihuahua, 1930* (Salt Lake City: Filmado por la Sociedad Genealógica de Utah, 1987); *Censo de población del municipio de Hermosillo, Sonora* (Salt Lake City: Filmado por la Sociedad Genealógica de Utah, 1988), Mormon Family History Center, West Covina.

younger than the average Chinese agricultural laborer, at the time of his apprehension by border officials Chong was nineteen years old.

Unskilled and low-skilled Chinese urban employees closely matched the profile of their farming *paesani* (see table 5.4).[7] Similar to their compatriots employed in agricultural positions, unskilled and low-skilled Chinese immigrants who worked in jobs such as cooks, barbers, gardeners, and waiters ranged in age from teenagers to persons in their sixties. The largest number of low-skilled employees fell within the age bracket 26–50, and a sizable number ranged from 51 to 70 years old. Moreover, most were single, a few maintained transnational marriages with Chinese wives, and a substantial number maintained marriage and/or free-union relationships with Mexican women. Unlike their fellow immigrant farmworkers, the majority of unskilled Chinese immigrant employees were literate. Similar to their farming counterparts, however, most did not become Mexican citizens and did not possess ostensible familial connections with others residing in Mexico.

The example of Santiago Wong Chao demonstrates the common profile of both low-skilled immigrant employees and agricultural laborers and suggests that agricultural and unskilled employees may often have derived from the same immigrant sociological cross-section.[8] As previously mentioned, Wong arrived in Mazatlán, Mexico, in 1907 at the age of nineteen. Like many in the agricultural and low-skilled employment categories, he spent the decade of his twenties working as a rural farm laborer and unskilled urban employee. Following a brief stint as a merchant, Wong reverted to employment as a laborer on Chinese Mexicali cotton ranches. Similar to many agricultural and urban unskilled employees, Wong also maintained a transnational marriage relationship with a woman in China. Like most members of the agricultural and low-skilled employment categories, moreover, Wong retained his Chinese citizenship despite his more than twenty-year residence in Mexico.

Chinese immigrants employed in various industries as tailors, bakers, butchers, shoemakers, launderers, artisans, and candy makers, like their compatriots employed in agricultural and urban unskilled labor positions, clustered in the 26–50 age category. Skilled industrial employees and tradesmen were almost equally divided between bachelors and married men. A significant number maintained transnational marriages, and some carried on free-union relationships with Mexican women. Like low-skilled laborers, the great majority of skilled workers were literate and retained their Chinese citizenship status. Finally, although the majority of artisans and tradesmen possessed no ostensible familial connections with others in Mexico, close to one-third of those sampled did appear to have kinship ties with others in their immediate household (see table 5.5).

José Chong exemplifies this skilled-tradesman profile.[9] Similar to most of his compatriots of the "industries" category, Chong worked as a tailor while in his late twenties and early thirties. Consistent with the tradesman profile, moreover, Chong was both single and a citizen of China. Although it is not clear from the historical record whether he worked together with immigrant kinsmen during his two-year tenure as a journeyman tailor, it appears that Chong was hired by the Yew Kew Tailor Company of Mexicali based upon familial connections. Moreover, Chong did possess immediate familial connections in Mexico, in the form of his older brother José Chong Cuy, who acted as guardian and source of financial support during his early years of residence in Mexico.

Hermosillo and Chihuahua Chinese merchants ranged in age from teenagers to elderly immigrants in their sixties and seventies (see table 5.6).[10] Like their skilled-tradesmen counterparts, they concentrated in the age category of 26–50 years old, although significant numbers of Chinese merchants were in their fifties, and a smaller number fell into the 15–25 age bracket. Paralleling members of the other occupational categories, the majority of Chinese merchants were single, although a large number were married to Mexican women and/or had Chinese wives residing overseas in the patria. Unlike immigrant farmers, urban laborers, and skilled artisans, however, some merchants brought Chinese wives to live with them in Mexico. Although the number of Chinese women residing in Mexico as the spouses of immigrant merchants was small, the phenomenon is noteworthy because it did not occur with members of other occupational categories. In addition, whereas trivial numbers of agricultural laborers, low-skilled employees, and artisans became Mexican citizens, small but significant numbers of merchants established Mexican national citizenship. Similar to immigrant artisans, the vast majority of Chinese merchants were also literate. Finally, merchants much more frequently possessed apparent familial connections with others in their household than did members of the occupational categories. Roughly one-half of all immigrant merchants sampled possessed such kinship ties.

Ensenada businessman Ricardo Cuan illustrates the common immigrant merchant profile.[11] Cuan owned a 6 percent interest in the Rafael Chan and Company partnership, which was formed around the establishment of a general mercantile store that sold dry goods, hardware,

Table 5.5. Demographic profiles of Chinese "industrias" of Hermosillo and Chihuahua City, 1930.

Numbers	56
Ages	
15–25	5
25–40	27
40–50	17
50–60	4
60–70	3
Marital status	
Single	25
Married to Chinese wife	17
Married to Mexican spouse	7
Free union with Mexican woman	6
Literacy	
Literate	37
Illiterate	19
Citizenship	
Chinese national	54
Mexican citizen	2

Note: Marital statistics do not include one widow.

Source: Statistics compiled from Mexico, Dirección General de Estadística, *Censo de población del municipio de Chihuahua, Chihuahua, 1930* (Salt Lake City: Filmado por la Sociedad Genealógica de Utah, 1987); *Censo de población del municipio de Hermosillo, Sonora* (Salt Lake City: Filmado por la Sociedad Genealógica de Utah, 1988), Mormon Family History Center, West Covina.

Table 5.6. Demographic profiles of Chinese merchants of Hermosillo and Chihuahua City, 1930.

Numbers	214
Ages	
15–25	24
26–35	47
36–40	54
41–50	60
51–60	24
61–64	1
65–70	3
71–75	1
Marital status	
Single	109
Married to Chinese wife	64
Married to Mexican spouse	24
Free union with Mexican woman	12
Literacy	
Literate	182
Illiterate	32
Citizenship	
Chinese national	196
Mexican citizen	18

Note: Marital statistics do not include widows.

Source: Statistics compiled from Mexico, Dirección General de Estadística, *Censo de población del municipio de Chihuahua, Chihuahua, 1930* (Salt Lake City: Filmado por la Sociedad Genealógica de Utah, 1987); *Censo de población del municipio de Hermosillo, Sonora* (Salt Lake City: Filmado por la Sociedad Genealógica de Utah, 1988), Mormon Family History Center, West Covina.

and groceries. Cuan served as manager, bookkeeper, and buyer for the six-man firm, and his 6 percent share in the company consisted of a 7,500-peso investment. As remuneration for his services and investment, Cuan received a salary of 500 pesos per month, housing accommodations in the store building, and potential dividends. He began his commercial career while only a teenager in the city of Merida, Yucatán, where he operated a perfume shop together with his nephew Pablo Cuan for eight years. In 1927, at the age of twenty-seven, Cuan traveled to the Baja California city of Ensenada, where he entered into the Rafael Chan Company partnership. Like many immigrant merchants, Cuan was married to an overseas Chinese bride. (Chan was reportedly married by proxy to a woman in China as part of an arranged marriage in 1940. Apparently, however, because Cuan was unable to return to China to carry out the arrangements, the marriage was not carried out.) Moreover, following the pattern of significant numbers of Chinese merchants, Cuan became a citizen of Mexico in 1928. Finally, as was common among members of his occupational category, Cuan immigrated to Mexico as part of familial connections of the transnational commercial orbit and possessed various kinship ties with others in Mexico. As discussed in chapters 2 and 3, Cuan traveled to Mexico in 1910 or 1911, together with his brother-in-law Manuel Ung, who was an established merchant in the city of Guaymas, Sonora. As previously mentioned, Cuan operated a perfume business in the Yucatán, together with his nephew Pablo Cuan.

Occupying employment positions closely tied to their merchant compatriot counterparts, commercial employees and clerks comprised the final vocational category for analysis.[12] "Dependientes" and "empleados particulares" most frequently ranged in age from twenty-six to sixty years old (see table 5.7). Although most were bachelors, a substantial number of those sampled maintained transnational marriages, and very few had Mexican wives or free-union partners. Like merchants, the vast majority of employees and clerks were literate, with more than two-thirds of those sampled recorded as being able to write and/or read. In addition, commercial employees retained their Chinese citizenship almost without exception. Finally, similar to merchants, close to half of all clerks and employees sampled possessed ostensible kinship ties to others in their household.

As exemplified by the vignettes of Ricardo Cuan and José Chong, members of the privileged merchant and skilled artisan class likely immigrated to Mexico as part of a system of serial chain migration based

Table 5.7.   Demographic profiles of "dependientes," "empleados particulares," and mechanics of Hermosillo and Chihuahua City, 1930.

Numbers	55	Literacy	
Ages		Literate	41
10–14	2	Illiterate	14
15–25	10	**Citizenship**	
26–40	23	Chinese national	54
41–50	13	Mexican citizen	1
51–60	7		

Marital status

Single	33
Married to Chinese wife	17
Married to Mexican spouse	2
Free union with Mexican woman	1

Note: Marital statistics do not include two minors whose marital status was not designated.

Source: Statistics compiled from Mexico, Dirección General de Estadística, *Censo de población del municipio de Chihuahua, Chihuahua, 1930* (Salt Lake City: Filmado por la Sociedad Genealógica de Utah, 1987); *Censo de población del municipio de Hermosillo, Sonora* (Salt Lake City: Filmado por la Sociedad Genealógica de Utah, 1988), Mormon Family History Center, West Covina.

upon ties of kinship. As discussed in detail in chapter 3, chain migration may be defined "as that movement in which prospective migrants learn of opportunities, are provided with transportation, and have initial accommodation and employment arranged by means of primary social relationships with previous migrants."[13] "Serial migration," moreover, is a form of chain migration, whereby passage financing, housing accommodations, and employment opportunities are arranged by the established immigrant friends and family of potential emigrants. Privileged members of the merchant class traveled the transnational commercial orbit from China to Big Lusong as part of the systems of kinship serial migration.

Exemplary of this pattern of serial migration, Ricardo Cuan immigrated to Mexico with the assistance of his brother-in-law Manuel Ung, who was an established grocery merchant in Guaymas, Sonora. Upon his initial arrival in Guaymas as an adolescent, moreover, it appears that Cuan remained financially dependent upon his brother-in-law, as Cuan did not work during his early years in Mexico, but rather spent his first three years attending a local Mexican school. In addition, further consistent with the serial migration model, his first employment as a perfume merchant in the Yucatán was also arranged through familial connections, as evidenced by the fact that his first business partnership was formed together with his nephew Pablo Cuan.

José Chong's experience of immigration to Mexico and initial settlement also exemplifies this pattern of serial migration. Like Ricardo Cuan and consistent with the model of serial chain migration, José Chong traveled to Mexico under the supervision of close kin. Whereas Cuan journeyed to Mexico together with his brother-in-law, however, José Chong traveled to Mexico presumably under the guardianship of his elder brother José Chong Cuy. Further paralleling the experience of Cuan, Chong attended a local Mexican school during his early years of residence and subsequently remained financially dependent upon familial support for his economic livelihood. As a serial chain migrant, moreover, Chong was placed in his first employment as a tailor ostensibly through kinship connections. In addition, evidencing the close social ties of artisan and merchant members of the immigrant upper class, and further demonstrating the nepotistic nature of Chinese business partnerships, José Chong left his tailor position at the Yew Kee Company after two years of employment to become a salesman and partner of Las Quince Letras grocery store together with his older brother José Chong Cuy.

In addition to these examples of Ricardo Cuan and José Chong, the high incidence of kinship connections among merchants and skilled craftsmen as reflected in the Hermosillo and Chihuahua City census manuscripts further suggests that many members of the privileged immigrant upper class traveled to Mexico as part of a system of kinship-based serial migration. The common appearance of ostensible familial connections among members of merchant and artisan households in the census records strongly implies that many of the merchant and skilled artisan class likely migrated to Mexico in a pattern similar to the experiences of Cuan and Chong—with the assistance of family members who had earlier made the journey to Big Lusong and achieved a measure of financial success within the Mexican commercial sector.

As chain migrants, moreover, members of the privileged immigrant class also established ethnic employment niches or "chain occupations."[14] According to the chain occupation concept, ethnic employment niches are created when established members of the immigrant community direct their newly arrived family and friends to job opportunities within specific areas of employment in which they have previously worked during their tenure in the host country. As evidenced by the examples of Ricardo

Cuan and José Chong, and as suggested by the census data, many established Chinese merchants and skilled artisans not only assisted their kin in immigrating to Mexico but also helped them to acquire employment within commerce and industry. As a consequence, the Chinese created chain occupations as grocers, dry-goods merchants, tailors, shoemakers, bakers, launderers, butchers, and candy makers. Moreover, through this process of chain migration and the creation of chain occupations developed a privileged class of immigrant merchants and skilled artisans and craftsmen.

Although the core membership of the Chinese immigrant upper class likely developed through such mechanisms of serial chain migration, the historical record indicates that some probably gained entrance to the privileged merchant ranks through merit and in the absence of significant familial connections. The case study of Santiago Wong Chao supports this claim. As previously discussed, following his arrival in Mexico at the age of nineteen in 1907, Wong Chao worked in various low-skilled urban and agricultural positions for twelve years before becoming a merchant in Cananea, Sonora. Unlike Ricardo Cuan and José Chong, Wong Chao arrived in Mexico seemingly without strategic kinship connections. This lack of familial connections is evidenced by his participation in menial labor activities after entering Mexico, as opposed to immediately entering the commercial sector as did Ricardo Cuan. Moreover, his absence of kinship connections is further suggested by the names of his employers during his first decade of work in Mexico. Wong's first employer was a Guaymas grocery merchant named Wah Chong; his subsequent employers were a Mexican grocer by the name of Salazar, a Chinese café owner named Jim Wong, and a Chinese ice cream parlor owner by the name of Carlos Cinco. That Wong Chao did not share the same surname as most of his employers seems to suggest that he did not share close kinship ties with any of them. Although Santiago shared the same surname as the Chinese café owner Jim Wong, it is not likely that they were closely related, because he worked for Jim Wong for six years in the menial position of waiter, without marked socioeconomic mobility, and subsequently went to work in the ice cream parlor owned by Carlos Cinco. If Santiago had shared close familial ties with Jim Wong, he would likely have been elevated from waiter to partner in the business over the duration of the six years. Although Wong Chao labored in various unskilled and low-paid agricultural and urban employee positions for twelve years after his arrival in Mexico, he eventually became a merchant, at different times purchasing interests in the Quong Lung Hing firm of Cananea and the Yeon Ton y Compañía grocery store partnership in Tijuana. In sum, it appears that Santiago Wong Chao entered the ranks of Mexico's successful Chinese merchants through merit and the sweat of his brow. Without strategic familial connections to facilitate his entrance into the immigrant commercial sector, he worked for over a decade in various inglorious menial labor positions to save capital and establish the necessary commercial connections to allow for investment in his first mercantile partnership. By virtue of merit, Wong Chao established himself as a successful Tijuana merchant and earned the reputation of being "well received" and of having "good connections."[15]

In addition to often possessing filial social connections, members of the privileged merchant and skilled trades category also appear to have been more assimilated than their immigrant counterparts of the laboring underclass. This higher level of cultural assimilation is evidenced by the substantial numbers of merchants and skilled tradesmen who engaged in nonplatonic relationships with local Mexican women, and also by the significant numbers of Chinese businessmen who became Mexican citizens. Although the majority of both merchants and artisans remained single during their tenure of residence in Mexico, large numbers married or carried on free-union relationships with Mexican women. Representative of this phenomenon are merchants Rodolfo Ley and Pablo Chee.[16] Rodolfo Ley began his career as a dry goods and grocery merchant immediately after entering Mexico in 1911. Before becoming sole proprietor of the El Progreso Dry Goods Store of Mexicali in 1933, Ley served as partner in another Mexicali firm, the Quong Yuen Company. While affiliated with the Quong Yuen partnership, moreover, Ley supplemented his income through investments in five cotton ranches. Prior to settlement in Mexicali, Ley resided in Tampico, where he met and married his Mexican wife, Maria Aguilar, and where he and his wife became the parents of their first child, Rodolfo Ley Jr. As the sole owner of El Progreso, and without close kin residing with him in Mexico, Rodolfo Ley Sr. operated his dry goods business together with his wife and three hired clerks. Of these three employees, two were Mexican and one was Chinese.

Like Ley, Pablo Chee was also a merchant in the borderlands of Mexicali and Calexico, California. Although initially residing in Mexico for twenty-one years, Chee eventually resettled in the United States as a Section 6 merchant but maintained extensive business interests on both sides of the border.[17] In Mexicali, Chee owned a general merchandise and grocery establishment, a popular hotel, and saloon. In addition, Chee was a silent partner in a Calexico grocery company, conducted a profitable cotton-selling business in Calexico, and at one time owned a 65 percent interest in a 1,240-acre cotton ranch located in the vicinity of Sesbania, Mexico. Chee originally emigrated from the Nanhai District of Foshan City in Guangdong to Tapachula, Chiapas, in 1901. In Tapachula, he met and married his Mexican wife, Adelina Palomegus. Manuel J. Chee was born to Pablo and Adelina in 1911, and in 1915, Manuel and his mother were sent to live in Hong Kong, where Manuel was placed in an English school. Following the relocation of his wife and son and a brief visit to China, Pablo Chee resettled in Mexicali where he resumed his merchant activities and resided for seven years before being admitted to the United States as a Section 6 merchant in January of 1922.

In addition to patterns of intermarriage between Chinese male immigrants and local Mexican women, the phenomenon of "delayed family migration" is further indicative of the increased level of acculturation among members of the commercial class.[18] A type of chain migration, delayed family migration occurs when established lone male immigrants who had originally immigrated based upon serial chain relationships bring their spouses and children to live with them in the host country. In the case of Italian delayed family migration of the early twentieth century (the case study from which this concept of delayed family migration derived), lone Italian males brought their wives and children over to live with them in the United States after failing to procure the wealth and savings that would have allowed them to return to southern Italy with markedly increased social status. In contradistinction to the Italian case, it appears that Chinese merchants brought their wives and children over to northern Mexico, not based upon a failure to become financially successful, but rather, precisely because of their financial success. If, as in the Italian case, delayed family migration among Chinese male immigrants was the result of the failure to accumulate sufficient savings to allow for increased social mobility, then we would expect to have seen this phenomenon develop among members of the humbler socioeconomic tier comprised of agricultural and unskilled urban laborers. No examples of such delayed family migration among members of the laboring class are evident in the Hermosillo and Chihuahua City samplings, however. On the contrary, the only examples of this familial migration are found among the most economically prominent of all Chinese immigrants—merchants. For this reason, it appears that the option of bringing a Chinese wife overseas to Mexico was likely a *privilege* enjoyed only by the most economically successful immigrant merchants. Confirming this hypothesis, the Hermosillo and Chihuahua City census manuscripts reveal a small but significant number of examples of merchant families comprised of merchant husbands, Chinese-born wives, and their offspring. Had the Chinese not been expelled from the state of Sonora in 1931, and had the anti-Chinese movement not progressed so vociferously as a consequence of the Great Depression, it is likely that this incipient trend of familial chain migration would have continued to become more common among other merchants, and that it may have even spread among artisans and members of the lower socioeconomic stratum. Instead, as a consequence of the inhospitable environment created by the anti-Chinese campaigns, migration to Mexico came to a halt, many returned to China, and the natural development of the Chinese community in Mexico, which would have included increased delayed family migration, was stunted after 1931. The Kong and Chan families, residents of Chihuahua City and Hermosillo respectively, represent examples of the incipient phenomenon of family chain migration prior to 1931 (see tables 5.8 and 5.9).[19]

In both examples, the family patriarchs appear to be established merchants who had brought their Chinese wives to live in Mexico as part of a system of delayed family migration. With a Mexican-born child of sixteen years old, Guillermo Kong had likely lived in Mexico for more than twenty years at the time of the 1930 census. Although it is possible that Guillermo Kong initially immigrated to Mexico together with his wife, Josefina Wong de Kong, based upon the qualitative data collected from Immigration and Naturalization Service interviews related to other Chinese merchants, it is more probable that he first made the journey to Mexico as a bachelor or lone married male. Based upon his age (42) at the time of the 1930 census, it is likely that he first traveled to Mexico as a young man in his early twenties during the first decade of the twentieth century. After several years of establishing himself as a Mexican merchant, Kong probably sent for his wife (to whom he had been married prior to immigrating to Mexico or subsequently as part of a proxy marriage) to reside with him in Chihuahua. Soon after, they likely gave birth to their first child, Arturo, and began to build their family in Mexico.

As in the case of Kong, the census data related to Agustín Chan strongly suggest that his wife, Ley Wong Day de Chan, immigrated to Mexico as part of a system of delayed family migration. Although Agustín Chan was forty-eight, and his wife Ley Wong thirty-six years old in 1930,

Table 5.8.   The Kong family, Chihuahua City, Chihuahua, 1930.

Name	Position in household	Age	Occupation	Birthplace
Guillermo Kong	Husband/father	42	Merchant	China
Josefina Wong de Kong	Wife/mother	32	Housewife	China
Arturo Kong Wong	Son	16	Student	Chihuahua
Luisa Kong Wong	Daughter	14	Student	Chihuahua
Roberto Kong Wong	Son	12	Student	Chihuahua
Raul Kong Wong	Son	10	Student	Chihuahua
Guillermo Kong Wong	Son	8	Student	Chihuahua
Rosa Elena Kong Wong	Daughter	5	Minor	Chihuahua
Estela Kong Wong	Daughter	2	Minor	Chihuahua
Emma Kong Wong	Daughter	2 mos.	Minor	Chihuahua

Source: Mexico, Dirección General de Estadística, *Censo de población del municipio de Chihuahua, Chihuahua, 1930* (Salt Lake City: Filmado por la Sociedad Genealógica de Utah, 1987), Mormon Family History Center, West Covina.

Table 5.9.   The Chan family, Hermosillo, Sonora, 1930.

Name	Position in household	Age	Occupation	Birthplace
Agustín Chan	Father/husband	48	Merchant	China
Ley Wong Day de Chan	Wife/mother	36	Housewife	China
Jorge Chan	Son	6	Student	Sonora
Agustín Chan, Jr.	Son	5	Minor	Sonora
Guadalupe L. Chan	Daughter	8	Student	Sonora

Source: Censo de población del municipio de Hermosillo, Sonora (Salt Lake City: Filmado por la Sociedad Genealógica de Utah, 1988), Mormon Family History Center, West Covina.

their oldest child, Guadalupe L. Chan, was only eight years old at the time the census was taken. These data place Agustín at forty years old and his wife at twenty-eight years old at the time of the birth of their first child. Based upon qualitative data collected from the Immigration and Naturalization Service merchant interviews, it was not uncommon for men to be married while in their late teens or early twenties. In addition, lone male migrants sometimes immigrated to Mexico in their late teens and early twenties without making return visits to their home villages for more than a decade. The fact that Agustín became a father at such a late age seems to imply that he immigrated to Mexico and was separated from his wife for a very lengthy period of time before being reunited and given the opportunity to produce offspring. Agustín Chan likely immigrated to Mexico in his twenties or early thirties as either a bachelor or a recently married lone male emigrant. After a lengthy period of establishing himself as a merchant in Mexico, he likely sent for his wife (to whom he had been married before leaving for Mexico or subsequent to immigrating as part of a proxy marriage). Shortly after the arrival of his transnational spouse, Agustín and Ley Wong probably had their first child, Guadalupe L. Chan, and began building their lives together in Sonora.

Higher levels of cultural assimilation among members of the privileged socioeconomic tier are further evidenced by the significant numbers of merchants who became naturalized Mexican citizens. Chinese merchants took on Mexican citizenship for several possible reasons: (1) their Mexican spouses requested that they do so, in order that their wives and children not lose their status as Mexican citizens; (2) Mexican citizenship status probably afforded special governmental protection in the face of sinophobic attacks, which they would not have possessed as resident aliens; (3) naturalization may have entitled Chinese immigrants to certain economic advantages, such as the right to own property; and (4) Mexican citizenship status (at least in the early years) might have provided a legal loophole with regard to the exclusionary immigration laws of the United States that forbade the entrance of Chinese nationals, but which allowed for the mostly unencumbered flow of Mexican nationals.

Ricardo Cuan provides an example of an assimilated Chinese merchant who not only became a naturalized Mexican citizen but also became active in local civic, military, and commercial affairs.[20] In addition to being a Mexican citizen, Cuan was a registered civilian member of the Mexican military according to Mexican law. As a Class A registered member of the civilian defense of the city of Ensenada, moreover, Cuan participated in biweekly military drills. In addition to his military involve-ment and perhaps as part of an effort to increase local business con-tacts and opportunities, Cuan was also active in local Mexican business organizations. He was a member of the Rotary club and also served as councilor of the Ensenada Chamber of Commerce. As part of his Rotary club activities, moreover, Cuan developed a close relationship with the American consul of Ensenada. He met weekly with both the American consul and vice consul of Ensenada, and as part of Cuan's application for renewal of border-crossing privileges in 1940, American consul Gerald A. Mokma even personally visited the Immigration and Naturalization Service offices of San Ysidro on behalf of Cuan to verify Cuan's merchant status. In addition to exemplifying the high level of cultural assimila-tion of Chinese merchants, Ricardo Cuan's active involvement in local Mexican military, civic, and commercial affairs also challenges the twin stereotypes of Chinese immigrant social isolation and rootlessness. Cuan's example demonstrates that Chinese merchants were not simply isolated and disaffected immigrants seeking to earn a quick fortune and repatri-ate, but rather savvy commercial entrepreneurs who put down social roots in Mexico, contributed to local civic development, and cultivated mainstream political and commercial relationships to promote their professional interests.

It is worth noting that Ricardo Cuan, Agustín Chan, Rodolfo Ley, Pablo Chee, and other members of the Chinese merchant class experi-enced much higher levels of acculturation to mainstream Mexican society than their diasporic counterparts in the United States during this same time period. These differing levels of acculturation can be attributed, in part, to the racial exclusivity of U.S. marriage and citizenship laws as compared to those of Mexico. In the United States, antimiscegenation laws remained in effect in most states until the Supreme Court decision of *Loving v. Virginia* in 1967. These state legislative restrictions barred Chinese immigrants from assimilating into U.S. mainstream society through intermarriage to Euro-Americans. Chinese immigrants were also hindered from acculturating to U.S. society based upon federal legislation that banned them from becoming naturalized citizens. The Naturaliza-tion Act of 1870 excluded Chinese and other nonwhites from naturalized citizenship until the passage of the MacCarran-Walter Act in 1952. As discriminatory as Mexican society may have been to Chinese immigrants, Mexican law did allow them the rights of intermarriage in most states as well as the right to become naturalized citizens.

Whereas merchant and skilled artisan members of the privileged immigrant socioeconomic tier often experienced high levels of assimilation and traversed the transnational commercial orbit to Mexico as part of networks of familial chain migration, agricultural laborers and urban low-skilled employees likely immigrated to Mexico as part of a system of "impersonally organized migration."[21] Whereas chain migration occurs within the context of primary social relationships based upon kinship and friendship, impersonally organized migration involves the "impersonal recruitment and assistance" of potential emigrants by persons with whom migrants share no close social connections. Many Chinese immigrant laborers were impersonally recruited to work in Mexico as part of the coordinated efforts of Chinese businessmen, Mexican industrialists and government officials, and transnational coolie smugglers. Following the failure to attract sufficient numbers of native laborers and European emigrants to areas of booming industrial expansion in the Mexican northern frontier and lower coastal regions, Mexican industrialists successfully lobbied for the systematic recruitment of Chinese immigrant laborers as part of official government diplomatic negotiations between Mexico and China, and established commercial agreements with Chinese merchants of San Francisco to allow for the systematic recruitment and transportation of Chinese immigrant laborers. As part of the system of impersonal recruitment that developed from these negotiations, Chinese laborers were recruited under contract at Chinese ports such as Hong Kong and Shanghai and, upon arrival in Mexico, distributed throughout cities and haciendas in various menial labor positions. In addition to familial chain migration, contract labor recruitment was another important migration mechanism that helped to facilitate the movement of Chinese immigrants to Mexico. Such labor recruitment also represented a central economic activity of the Chinese transnational commercial orbit.

Chinese laborers traveled to Mexico as part of this system of impersonally organized migration because of their lack of access to familial chain migration networks. Whereas members of the privileged class of merchants and artisans such as José Chong and Ricardo Cuan relied upon established immigrant kin to cover their immigration expenses and provide them with initial housing accommodations and employment opportunities, members of the laboring class in many cases possessed no such kinship connections with others residing in Mexico. As a consequence, emigrant laborers likely had no other choice but to immigrate based upon systems of impersonal recruitment. As reflected by the examples of Alejandro Chan, Manuel Yong, Low Quan, Luis Chong, and Santiago Wong Chao previously discussed in this chapter, most Chinese agricultural and urban unskilled laborers lacked close familial ties with others in Mexico. Moreover, the Hermosillo and Chihuahua City census manuscripts reveal a low incidence of ostensible kinship connections among rural agricultural and urban unskilled laborers. This lack of familial connections among most Chinese laborers strongly suggests that many members of the lower socioeconomic tier likely traveled to Mexico as part of the system of impersonal recruitment organized by Chinese merchants and Mexican industrial interests.

As a consequence of their lack of familial ties to other established residents of the Chinese overseas community, moreover, Chinese immigrants who traveled to Mexico as impersonally recruited laborers were also likely excluded from more desirable employment opportunities in commercial and skilled trade chain occupations. Many members of the immigrant laboring class were probably unable to secure employment as merchants and skilled artisans because these ethnic employment niches appear to have been often organized around networks of kinship.

In addition, Chinese laborers were also likely precluded from membership within the merchant and skilled trade ranks because of the lack of business capital and preexisting trade skills. Since the majority of immigrant agricultural laborers and urban low-skilled employees sampled were illiterate, it seems reasonable to assume that most Chinese from the laboring class hailed from poor peasant backgrounds. As a consequence, upon arrival from China they likely lacked either the capital necessary to invest in a commercial partnership or the preexisting skills necessary to begin employment as an artisan. Because of the absence of close filial ties, moreover, they could not borrow from family members the financial resources necessary to become merchants, nor could they easily obtain artisan apprenticeships, which were likely reserved for chain migrant relations.

In addition to the lack of kinship connections with others in Mexico, members of the Chinese immigrant underclass differed from their compatriots of the merchant and skilled trade category based upon their lower level of assimilation. Whereas substantial numbers of merchants and artisans engaged in marital and free-union relationships with Mexican women, few agricultural laborers were involved in nonplatonic relationships with local women. In this aspect of marital relations, urban unskilled laborers more closely resembled merchants and artisans than their rural laboring counterparts, as substantial numbers were married to or engaged in free-union relationships with Mexican women. Similar to their rural compatriots, however, and further indicative of their lower level of cultural assimilation, few urban workers became Mexican citizens. Finally, in contrast with the data available for merchants, and as further reflective of lower acculturation levels, no evidence of delayed family migration among the immigrant underclass is present in the Hermosillo and Chihuahua City census manuscripts.

Borderlands Merchant Types

U.S. Immigration Service officials of the early twentieth century defined a merchant as "a person buying and selling goods at a fixed place of business and who, for at least one year prior to his application [to the Immigration Service for special merchant legal privileges such as permission to cross into U.S. territory from Mexico for business purposes] has not engaged in any manual labor, except such as is necessary in the conduct of his business as a merchant."[22] Notwithstanding this broad, overarching merchant definition, a review of Immigration Service Chinese Exclusion Act case files for Chinese borderland merchants residing in the Mexican cities of Mexicali, Tijuana, and Ensenada, and the American cities of Calexico and Nogales, reveals the existence of four Chinese merchant *types* during the early to mid-twentieth century: the immigrant merchant *magnate*, the *medium-sized* merchant, the *small merchant*, and the *sole proprietor*.[23] Merchants from each of these categories were key players in the development and ultimate success of the Chinese transnational commercial orbit of the U.S.–Mexico borderlands. A close examination of their demographic profiles and common business practices provides an important glimpse into the day-to-day operations of the transnational economic orbit.

The Chinese borderlands merchant magnate played a foundational role in the orbit because of the large size of his business investments and the far transnational reach of his commercial endeavors.[24] He possessed personal commercial investments ranging from $20,000 to $75,000 and maintained a diversity and multiplicity of investments in hotels, restaurants, cotton ranches, grocery stores, and general merchandise firms. In addition, he was likely the primary investor in a large merchant firm that possessed upward of $100,000 in capital stock and which was simultaneously financially interested in several lucrative business ventures. In addition, because of the extensive resources wielded by the magnate and his company, the firm likely also owned both the buildings and the land upon which their businesses were situated. Finally, both the high-class merchant and his firm were likely involved in transnational commerce, purchasing from sellers and selling to buyers on both sides of the international line.

Calexico borderlands merchant Pablo Chee serves as the model for this magnate type.[25] In 1923, Chee's personal wealth was conservatively appraised at $125,000, and in 1923 alone he conducted approximately $80,000 in business transactions in the United States and $100,000 in Mexico. He possessed financial interests of $75,000 gold in Mexico and maintained cash deposits of $1,500 in two Calexico banks, and the merchandise value from all his Mexican business interests amounted to approximately $40,000. Chee transacted much of his transnational business from an office located in the Dool Building of Calexico, and he enjoyed an outstanding reputation in the larger Anglo business community of Calexico. When asked by Immigration Service officials to comment on the financial wealth of Pablo Chee, one Anglo businessman commented, "[If] he would give us an order for $10,000.00 worth of stuff, it would go there on his own say, without any money," and, "he has unlimited credit as far as our firm is concerned, and we have made him sales as high as $5,000.00 on open account." As previously discussed in this chapter, moreover, Pablo Chee was financially interested in a wide variety of commercial enterprises. Chee made his fortune as a vendor of cotton, cotton ranch owner, liquor retailer, hotel and restaurant proprietor, owner of a grocery and general merchandise store, and silent partner in a Calexico-based grocery company.

Although Chee had no partners in his cotton-selling business, his Mexican hotel, saloon, and grocery store were owned and run as part of a larger commercial partnership known as Pablo Chee and Company. As the principal investor, Pablo Chee was one of five transnational partners with financial interests ranging from $1,000 to $75,000 (see table 5.10).

The ostensible kinship connections shared by the partners, and the large amounts and transnational nature of the investments of the company members, stand out as the more salient characteristics of the partnership list. Consistent with the profiles of Chinese merchants of Hermosillo and Chihuahua City, as previously discussed in this chapter, four of the partners of the Pablo Chee firm appear to be connected by ostensible ties of kinship based upon the commonality of family names—Pablo Chee, Chee

Table 5.10.   Partnership list of Pablo Chee and Company, Mexicali, Mexico (1924).

Name	Amount of interest	Date acquired	Occupation	Residence
Pablo Chee	$75,000	May 1920	Manager	Calexico
Chee Chung Huey	$20,000	May 1920	Asst. Manager	Mexicali
Quan Yuet	$1,000	January 1923	Mgr./Grocery Dept.	Mexicali
Chung Wee Cho	$25,000	May 1923	Silent Partner	San Francisco, California
Chung Puey	$25,000	May 1923	Silent Partner	Oakland, California

Source: Laguna Niguel, National Archives, Pablo Chee, Chinese Exclusion Act Case File no. 2295/7.

Chung Huey, Chung Wee Cho, and Chung Puey (see fig. 5.1). Immigration Service interviews, moreover, confirm the immediate family relationship shared by brothers Pablo Chee and Chee Chung Huey; Chung Wee Cho and Chung Puey, in turn, would appear to be more distant relatives of Pablo and Chee Chung, based upon their surname of Chung. In addition, the size of the investments of these kindred partners—$75,000, $20,000, $25,000, and $25,000, respectively, stands out as unusually large in comparison with the typical investment of $500 to $1,000 usually contributed by average merchants. Finally, the transnational nature of the investments of Chung Wee Cho and Chung Puey—both resided in the San Francisco Bay area—is worthy of note. The two were possibly cousins of Pablo Chee and Chee Chung who were invited to invest their savings in the commercial enterprises of their immigrant relatives who had established themselves as successful merchants at the opposite end of the state. This example of transnational familial partnership provides a clear illustration of the kinship ties that unified Chinese immigrants of the transnational commercial orbit in both Mexico and the United States.

Representative of a well-established, high-class Chinese firm, the Pablo Chee partnership owned both the building and the land upon which their hotel, saloon, and stores were situated. This property was valued

Figure 5.1. Chung Puey.
Source: Laguna Niguel,
California, National Archives,
Pablo Chee, Chinese Exclusion
Act Case File no. 2295/7.

at approximately $145,000 and was covered under an insurance policy of $85,000. In addition, as a high-class commercial operation, the firm supplied its hotel and bar from a variety of transnational vendors, purchasing whiskey and alcohol from Canada and Mexico and other items from Calexico, Los Angeles, and San Francisco.

Whereas the Chinese merchant magnate possessed extensive commercial investments of upward of $20,000, the medium-sized merchant maintained a much smaller business ownership of approximately $3,000.[26] In addition, although the magnate merchant possessed a multiplicity and diversity of investments, the medium-sized businessman likely focused his investment in only one or two commercial enterprises, because of his limited financial resources. The members of his firm were likely tied together by bonds of kinship, contributed humbler investments of capital ranging from $100 to $1,000, and may have resided in other parts of Mexico or even in China. Active firm members received monthly salaries ranging from $60 to $100 plus room and board, and they sometimes benefited from regular dividends; silent partners, on the other hand, probably did not receive salaries and may have received nothing beyond the appreciation of the business value. The medium-sized merchant firm, moreover, likely traded in groceries, dry goods, and hardware and may have carried on both wholesale and retail commerce. The value of merchandise on hand probably varied from firm to firm, ranging anywhere from smaller stock values of $3,000 aimed at retail consumers to extensive stocks of goods worth upward of $80,000 intended for sale to both wholesale and retail purchasers. Similar to the merchant magnate firms, these firms also likely purchased their own supplies from transnational wholesale vendors located in the United States. Their goods were sometimes delivered across the international line, moreover, by Mexican merchant trucking cooperatives or through the use of personal transportation vehicles. Finally, as smaller commercial enterprises, the firms of medium-sized merchants may have sometimes owned the buildings in which their businesses were situated; more often, however, they likely owned neither the land nor the physical premises of their commercial establishments and were forced to rent from Mexican landlords at a monthly rate of about $60.

Exemplifying the mid-size Chinese immigrant merchant, Ricardo Cuan possessed a 15,000-peso (approximately $3,000) 6 percent interest in the Ensenada mercantile firm of Rafael Chan and Company.[27] Unlike merchant magnate Pablo Chee, who maintained a multiplicity of commercial investments, Cuan involved himself in no other personal commercial investments outside of his participation in the Ensenada business. As consideration for his services as manager, bookkeeper, and buyer for the partnership, Cuan received a monthly salary of 500 pesos (about $100), potential dividends, and his own room located in the store building.[28] As the sole buyer for the company, Cuan traveled across the U.S. line every fifteen days to purchase supplies for the business from several wholesale firms in San Diego, such as the Klauber Wangenheim, Wellman-Peck, and Western Metal Supply companies. His monthly U.S. purchases totaled approximately $8,000, and his orders were transported to Ensenada by the cooperative trucking association of Tijuana and Ensenada. This example of transnational wholesaling provides a unique illustration of the day-to-day operations of the transnational commercial orbit. As part of this orbit, Chinese merchants like Cuan frequently crossed the international line to purchase supplies for their Mexican shops. This practice of transnational wholesaling represented another important activity of the Chinese transnational commercial orbit of the U.S.–Mexico borderlands.

Like Pablo Chee, Cuan enjoyed an excellent business reputation, as reflected by the many personal endorsements he received from established members of the commercial communities of both Mexico and

Table 5.11.   Partnership list of Rafael Chan and Company, Ensenada, Mexico, 1943.

Name	Initial investment	Position/Status	Residence
Rafael Chan	3,000 pesos	President/Active	Hong Kong
Juan Chim	2,000 pesos	Silent Partner	Hong Kong
Ricardo Cuan	500 pesos	Manager/Active	Ensenada
Roberto Chan	1,000 pesos	Active Partner	Ensenada
Rafael Leon	500 pesos	Active Partner	Ensenada
You (Yau) Chong	1,500 pesos	Silent Partner	Puebla, Mex.
Yee Chong		Silent Partner	Puebla, Mex.

Source: Laguna Niguel, National Archives, Cuan Sun (Ricardo Cuan), Chinese Exclusion Act Case File no. 14036/88.

the United States. According to Immigration and Naturalization Service documentation, Cuan "[gave] the impression of being a high type of Chinese merchant," and one manager of a Tijuana wholesale grocery firm stated of Cuan: "I regard him very highly; the commercial experience I have had with him has been very good; he has been honest and exact in every transaction we have had."[29]

Rafael Chan and Company, of which Cuan served as manager, conducted a general mercantile trade in both wholesale and retail commodities, specializing in groceries, meats, clothing, hardware, perfume, and the like. It maintained stock on hand valued at around 400,000 pesos (approximately $80,000) and did an impressive $10,000 in gross monthly wholesale and retail sales.[30] Similar to the firm of magnate Pablo Chee, Rafael Chan and Company consisted of various transnational investors (see table 5.11).

As with Pablo Chee and Company, many members of Ricardo Cuan's business enterprise appear to be bonded by ostensible ties of kinship based upon the commonality of family names. Rafael Chan and Roberto Chan, and You Chong and Yee Chong appear to be kinsmen. Although the other three members of the partnership do not share similar surnames with others in the list, it is likely that some or all of them are also tied together by kinship to other members of the group through maternal or marriage lines. In addition, similar to the partnership of Pablo Chee and Company, the Rafael Chan firm was comprised of certain transnational partners. Although residing in Mexico during the early years of the company's existence following its formation in 1927, Pablo Chee and Juan Chim returned to China in 1935, the former continuing to serve as president of the partnership for a time despite his transnational residence, and the latter presumably continuing his investment as a silent partner. In contrast with the merchant magnate firm of Pablo Chee and Company, and indicative of their humbler commercial status, members of the Rafael Chan and company all contributed small initial investments of under $1,000. Although Ricardo Cuan's personal interest in the company was valued at 15,000 pesos (about $3,000) in 1943, making him "a high type of Chinese merchant," his small initial investment of only 500 pesos betrays his humble small-merchant roots.[31]

Finally, in further contrast to the firm of Pablo Chee, and reflective of its status as a mid-level business enterprise, Rafael Chan and Company did not own the land upon which their store was situated, and was not invested in or connected with any other businesses outside of their single general merchandising venture. Although Ricardo Cuan's firm did own a new store building valued at $7,000, unlike its more established business counterparts, it did not own the property upon which the establishment was located. In addition, whereas the high-level Chee partnership was simultaneously interested in a diversity of businesses, including a hotel, saloon, and grocery store, the Chan company limited its commercial investments to its single general merchandising venture.

Of all four merchant types, small merchants were the backbone of the Chinese transnational commercial orbit, because they were the most numerous.[32] Whereas the magnate and the medium-sized merchant maintained initial investments ranging from $3,000 to $75,000, the small merchant entered the merchant ranks with usual investments of about $500 to $1,000. Similar to the medium-sized merchant, Chinese small merchants generally limited their personal investment to one or two businesses based upon their limited resources. In addition to their primary investment in the firm in which they served as active members, they might possess other small interests in commercial enterprises such as the store of a relative, a restaurant, or a cotton ranch. Humble immigrant entrepreneurs, moreover, often pooled their resources with other small to medium-sized investors in partnerships of three to forty-five persons. Firm members often shared ties of kinship, and active partners received monthly salaries ranging from approximately $30 to $75, together sometimes with room and board.

Small merchant partnerships ran grocery stores, dry goods stores, and restaurants. They maintained stock on hand valued at $4,300 to $35,000 and boasted gross annual sales of $24,000 to $160,000, and yearly profits of $1,800 to $3,000. Like their magnate and medium-sized counterparts, small entrepreneurs purchased their supplies from various transnational suppliers in Mexico and the United States. Finally, most small Chinese merchants, similar to their medium-scale merchant compatriots, rented their commercial properties, both land and building.

Federico Cham clearly illustrates this small merchant profile.[33] Typical of Chinese small merchants, Cham possessed a $1,000 investment in the Calexico grocery and general merchandise firm of Yat Sang Company. In addition, further consistent with the small-entrepreneur profile, Cham maintained no commercial investments outside of his involvement with the Yat Sang Company, of which he was manager. His firm conducted a wholesale and resale trade in American and Mexican groceries and general merchandise, purchasing its products from U.S. suppliers such as the Standard Oil Company. The Yat Sang Company, moreover, conducted transnational commercial sales on both sides of the international line. In addition to its earnings generated from sales in its U.S. stores, the Yat Sang Company sold large quantities of its merchandise to Chinese immigrant merchants residing in Mexico, at one time averaging $5,000 in sales per month in Mexicali. These wholesaling activities provide another glimpse into the daily operations and transnational scope of the Chinese commercial orbit. Building upon a humble early capitalization of about $10,000, the firm maintained stock on hand ranging from $4,000 to $10,000 and achieved annual sales of up to $110,000.

The Yat Sang Company was comprised of transnational partners located in China and throughout the United States (see table 5.12).

Like the firms of magnate Pablo Chee and mid-sized merchant Ricardo Cuan, the Yat Sang Company was conspicuously marked by familial ties among its members. Eight of the firm's twelve partners shared the same surname as other members of the firm, with four of the active partners—Quan Kim Tong (Federico Cham; see fig. 5.2), Quan Bow (José Quan), Quan Yut Hong, and Pon Fook Kim—possessing familial names in common with four of the silent investors who resided in disparate locations throughout California and China. Immigration and Naturalization Service interviews, moreover, reveal that silent partners Quan Sow and Quan Lun Hong were both butchers of the Chin Sam Market located on Ninth Street in Oakland, California, and that Chan Chang Qui and

Table 5.12.   Partnership list of the Yat Sang Company, Calexico.

Name	Interest	Date acquired	Position/ Status	Residence
Quan Kim Tong (Federico Cham)	$1,000	Dec. 1920	Manager	Calexico
Leung Yum (Francisco Leung)	$1,000	June 1921	Salesman	Calexico
Quan Bow (José Quan)	$1,000	June 1921	Salesman	Calexico
Pon Fook Kim	$1,000	April 1923	Salesman	Calexico
Lau Wing	$1,000	April 1921	Salesman	Calexico
Quan Yut Hong	$1,000	April 1923	Salesman	Calexico
Quan Lun Hong	$1,000	Dec. 1920	Silent	Oakland
Quan Sow Hong	$1,000	Dec. 1920	Silent	Oakland
Quang Chung	$1,000	Dec. 1920	Silent	Los Angeles
Quan Ho Kean	$1,000	Dec. 1920	Silent	Los Angeles
Pon Fook Chew	$1,000	Dec. 1920	Silent	Guangdong, China
Chan Chang Qui	$1,000	Dec. 1920	Silent	Los Angeles

Source: Laguna Niguel, National Archives, Federico Cham, Chinese Exclusion Act File no. 25100/38.

Quan Chung were both merchants of the United Meat Market in Los Angeles. It is likely that most, if not all, of the silent investors of the Yat Sang Company were kinsmen of active members who resided in Calexico. These silent partners, (with the exception of Pon Fook Chew who was an active member of the firm before his return to China), moreover, were probably invited by their relatives residing in Calexico to join as investors in the Yat Sang Company. In return for their initial investments of $1,000, these silent members sometimes received dividends based upon the annual profit of the business. Active members, in addition to such dividends, were paid $75 a month and provided with room and board.

The sole proprietor represents the final borderlands merchant type.[34] The capitalization of independent Chinese entrepreneurs rivaled that of their small to medium-sized merchant counterparts who invested as

Figure 5.2. Federico Cham.
Source: Laguna Niguel,
California, National Archives,
Federico Cham, Chinese
Exclusion Act Case File no.
25100/38.

part of collective business partnerships. Sole proprietors controlled business assets and/or made initial business investments ranging from about
$4,000 to upward of $10,000. They owned shops that specialized in the
sale of groceries, dry goods, feed, grain, clothing, yard ware, and notions;
purchased their supplies from transnational suppliers in San Francisco,
El Paso, Los Angeles, Calexico, and Mexico; and maintained stock on
hand valued at $4,000 to $8,000. Sole proprietors conducted monthly
sales of about $2,000 and averaged annual profits ranging from about
$2,000 to $4,800. In addition, although independent entrepreneurs had
no official business partners, their Mexican and Chinese wives sometimes worked together with them to run their stores. Despite the lack of
business partners, Chinese sole proprietors also sometimes employed
Mexican and Chinese employees in positions such as salesmen, clerks,
and delivery personnel. Finally, independent entrepreneurs also leased
their store facilities from Anglo and Mexican landlords at rents of $20 to
$100 a month. Some resided on their store premises together with their
families, while others chose to make their home in a residence separate
from their commercial establishment.

Rodolfo Ley was the sole proprietor of El Progreso clothing and dry
goods store of Mexicali.[35] Formerly a partner in a four-member Mexicali

grocery firm known as Sang Yuen y Compañía, Ley established his sole proprietorship on July 15, 1933. Ley ran his clothing and dry goods business together with his wife, Maria Refugio Aguilar de Ley, and in addition employed one Chinese and two Mexican individuals who served as store clerks.[36] El Progreso featured an eclectic selection of shoes, yard goods, notions, and clothing for men, women, and children; it was described by one Immigration and Naturalization Service agent as: "[being] composed of one medium sized room where the business of the store is conducted and in which a large amount of the merchandise on hand is kept. To the rear of the room above-mentioned is a smaller room used for a stockroom. Underneath both rooms is a basement also used as a stockroom and where most of the merchandise is kept. All three rooms are well stocked with merchandise, clothing, footwear, yard goods and notions."[37] Adjoining the clothing shop on either side were a dry goods business and a barber shop.

Although some of Rodolfo Ley's store inventory was of Mexican manufacture, most of his stock was produced in the United States. Ley crossed regularly into the United States to buy goods for his business establishment, making average monthly purchases of about $500 from suppliers such as the Butler Brothers of San Francisco, Nasef Ellis of Los Angeles, Sam Ellis of Calexico, and the Farah Manufacturing Company of El Paso, Texas. The value of his stock of merchandise was appraised at approximately 40,000 pesos, or $8,000.[38]

El Progreso's total assets in 1939 amounted to 51,000 pesos, or approximately $10,000. This total amount included the above 40,000 pesos ($8,000) worth of merchandise, 1,500 pesos ($300) in store fixtures, 7,000 pesos ($1,400) of cash on hand and in the bank, 1,000 pesos ($200) in accounts receivable, and one Ford automobile valued at 1,500 pesos ($300). To cover his investment in goods and fixtures, Ley carried a fire insurance policy of 30,000 pesos ($6,000). His daily sales averaged 500 pesos ($100), and in 1938 his net annual profits amounted to approximately 10,000 pesos, or $2,000.

El Progreso conducted business Monday through Friday, from 7:00 a.m. to 6:00 p.m., Saturday, from 7:00 a.m. to 9:00 p.m., and was closed for business on Sunday. As remuneration for their store services, Ley's Chinese employee was paid a monthly salary of sixty pesos, plus room and board, and his Mexican clerks were given weekly salaries of thirty-five pesos. The Leys drew no regular salary from the store's profits but rather only withdrew living expenses from business revenues.

As was common business practice among small and medium-sized merchants, Rodolfo Ley and his wife leased their store facilities from a Mexican company by the name of Compañía Inviciones, for a monthly rent of 100 pesos. Unlike many lone immigrant male merchants, however, the married couple chose to live in a residence separate from their dry goods and clothing establishment. Cross-cultural marriages and successful business partnerships like that of Rodolfo and Maria once again distinguish the Chinese of Mexico from their diasporic counterparts of the United States, who rarely intermarried because of strict antimiscegenation laws.

The Transnational Commercial Orbit and Chinese Mercantile Success: Transnational Capital Investment and Wholesaling

Chinese borderlands merchants such as Pablo Chee, Ricardo Cuan, Federico Cham, and Rodolfo Ley were highly successful. As will be discussed in great detail in the following chapter, Chinese mercantile success engendered deep resentment on the part of the Mexican middle classes of northern Mexico and led to the organized anti-Chinese campaigns of the early twentieth century. The economic prosperity of the Chinese merchant class was facilitated by two common business practices or "class resources"—transnational capital investment based upon ties of kinship and transnational wholesaling. According to Light and Bonacich, Korean immigrants of Los Angeles experienced success as entrepreneurs because of their exploitation of various "class" and "ethnic" resources.[39] They assert that class resources are those resources enjoyed only by the privileged middle- and upper-class contingencies of an immigrant community, such as high levels of prior education, large amounts of personal capital, and prior commercial skills. Ethnic resources, on the other hand, are those resources such as nepotistic hiring patterns, rotating credit associations, the utilization of unpaid family labor, and sojourner attitudes that are shared by an entire immigrant population regardless of socioeconomic background. This analytical framework proposed by Light and Bonacich to explain contemporary Korean entrepreneurial success in Los Angeles is also a useful model for understanding the economic success of Chinese immigrant entrepreneurs in northern Mexico during the late nineteenth and early twentieth centuries. These business practices, moreover, represented two important activities of the Chinese transnational commercial orbit.

Strategic kinship connections provided immigrants of the merchant class with access to the class resource of transnational capital. Chinese borderlands merchants formed unique transnational business partnerships based upon the financial contributions of family members residing in China, Mexico, and the United States. The Yat Sang Company of Federico Cham exemplifies the business practice of transnational capital investment. Although the daily affairs of the firm were supervised and conducted by six partners residing in Calexico, California, the remaining silent partners lived in disparate locations in Los Angeles, Oakland, and Guangdong, China. Each of the partners, both silent and active, contributed $1,000 toward the early capitalization of the business, which amounted to an impressive capital base of $12,000 in 1923. As previously discussed, moreover, the twelve partners of the firm were all connected by bonds of kinship. As shown by this example, Chinese borderland merchants were able to begin new commercial enterprises by drawing from a multiplicity of transnational familial sources. Although the financial resources of any individual Chinese immigrant might be insufficient to start a business, this strategy enabled Chinese entrepreneurs to become partners in well-capitalized commercial ventures.

The Mexicali-based firm of Pablo Chee and Company further demonstrates this strategy of pooled commercial investment, which was common among merchants of the Chinese transnational economic orbit. Although Pablo Chee managed the Mexicali firm and was its principal investor, he himself was a U.S. resident of Calexico, California. The assistant manager of the firm, Chee Chung Huey, and the grocery department manager, Quan Yuet, resided in Mexicali, Mexico. The two silent partners, Chung Wee Cho and Chung Puey, lived in San Francisco and Oakland, California. This partnership list clearly demonstrates the transnational nature of Chinese business ventures in Mexico and is also a clear example of the larger Chinese transnational commercial orbit of the late nineteenth and early twentieth centuries. Although the firm was based in Mexico, Pablo Chee, the main partner and primary investor, lived in Calexico, California. Based upon a special border-crossing permit issued by the U.S. Immigration and Naturalization Service, Chee crossed regularly into Mexico to manage his business affairs. Moreover, although the firm's two other managers resided in Mexicali, Mexico, the two silent investors lived hundreds of miles away, in the Bay Area of San Francisco. As with the Yat Sang Company, moreover, most of the firm's members appear to be connected by ostensible ties of kinship based upon the commonality of family names. Marked by ties of kinship and a multinational capital base, the Pablo Chee Company clearly evidences the operation of a Chinese transnational commercial orbit of the early twentieth century that encompassed northern and eastern California and the borderlands of Baja California, Mexico.

Another aspect of the transnational commercial orbit that helped Chinese merchants to prosper involved the provision of wholesale supplies and goods for sale in Mexican shops. Chinese grocery and dry goods merchants in Mexico purchased much of their store inventory from Chinese and Anglo wholesalers of the United States. Exemplifying this phenomenon, Lee Kwong Lun served as an economic middleman between Chinese store owners in Sonora, Mexico, and California wholesalers. Taking orders from Chinese retailers, Lee Kwong wrote letters to San Francisco wholesalers who delivered goods to Mexico by train for sale in Chinese shops. As another example, the Pablo Chee Company also purchased supplies for its hotel and bar from various transnational vendors. The firm bought alcohol from Canada and Mexico and other items from Calexico, Los Angeles, and San Francisco. The Yat Sang Company averaged $5,000 per month in sales in Mexicali.

Chinese merchants purchased supplies for their Mexican businesses not only through commercial middlemen like Lee Kwong, but also by crossing regularly into the United States and ordering directly from wholesale suppliers. Special border-crossing permits issued by the Immigration and Naturalization Service granted certain Chinese borderlands merchants the legal right to enter the United States to purchase supplies for their Mexican stores. Chinese immigrants not entitled to legal residence in the United States were granted such commercial permits if they could prove that they were "bona fide" merchants, "well anchored" in Mexico, and that they desired to cross over the international border for legitimate business purposes.[40] As part of the application process for the border-crossing privilege, Immigration and Naturalization Service agents visited and inspected the purported business establishments of Chinese merchants in Mexico. In addition, they conducted lengthy interviews in which Chinese merchants were queried extensively as to their immigrant and family history in China and Mexico. These interviews were often conducted in Chinese or Spanish using an interpreter, and translated into English for purposes of the transcript record. Below is an excerpt from one such interview given by Chinese Mexicali merchant Rodolfo Ley on October 24, 1939:

Q. (Examining Inspector W. J. Young): In what dialect will you testify duering [*sic*] this investigation?

A. (Rodolfo Ley): See Yip.

Q.: What are your names?

A.: Lee Chip is my Chinese name, Rodolfo Ley is my Mexican name.

Q.: When and Where [*sic*] were you born and of what country are you a citizen?

A.: I was born on K.S. 18 yr-1-19 (Feb. 17, 1892), in Hoy Yin Village, Hoy San District, Canton, China. I am a citizen of China. . . .

Q.: Are you the same Lee Chip who made a statement to an inspector of this Service at the U.S.I. and N.S. office, Calexico, Calif., on October 21, 1938, in connection with your application for extension of the Border Crossing Privilege?

A.: Yes . . .

Q.: What is your wife's name?

A.: Maria Aguilar de Ley . . .

Q.: When and where were you married to Maria Aguilar?

A.: I have been married to her for 20 years. I was married in Mexicali, Mexico, I don't remember the exact date.

Q.: Do you have any children by this marriage?

A.: I have one son, Rodolfo Ley, who is 16 years old . . .

Q.: What is your occupation?

A.: I am the sole owner of the El Progreso Dry Goods Store at 355 Reforma Avenue, Mexicali, B.C., Mexico . . .

Q.: What class of merchandise is sold by the "El Progreso"?

A.: We sell mens [*sic*], women's and children's ready to wear, clothes, foot-wear, yard goods and notions . . .

Q.: What are the assets of the "El Progreso" at present?

A.: Merchandise on hand, 40,000 pesos; fixtures, 1,500 pesos; cash on hand and in bank, 7,000 pesos; accounts receivable, 1,000 pesos; one Ford Sedan, 1,500 pesos; total assets, 51,000 pesos. (the present value of a peso is approximately 20 cents, U.S. money) . . .

Q.: What is the average amount of your monthly purchases in the United States? [emphasis added]

A.: About $500 per month. I have here the month of August, $1050.41; September, $532.63 and from October 1 to 24, 1939, $1048.27. (Presents invoices of purchases from Butler Bros., S.F., Calif.; The Farah Mfg. Co., El Paso, Tex, Nasef Ellis, L.A. Calif., and Sam Ellis, Calexico, Calif., and others, which substantiate this statement) . . . .

Like Rodolfo Ley, Ensenada businessman Ricardo Cuan also made regular trips to the United States to purchase supplies for his Mexican business.[41] As the sole buyer for a mercantile firm known as Rafael Chan and Company, Cuan traveled to San Diego, California, every fifteen days to acquire supplies for his business from several wholesale firms such as the Klauber Wangenheim, Wellman-Peck, and Western Metal Supply companies. As contrasted with Ley's smaller monthly purchases of approximately $500, Cuan made monthly purchases on behalf of the Rafael Chan firm of up to $8,000. Cuan's merchandise orders were transported to his business in Mexico by the cooperative trucking association of Tijuana and Ensenada, and, unlike Ley's sole proprietorship, which was limited to retail sales, Cuan's firm engaged in a general mercantile trade consisting of both wholesale and retail commodities. It is likely that the wholesale trade of Rafael Chan and Company targeted smaller-scale Chinese merchants and street peddlers who could not acquire border-crossing privileges and who therefore could not acquire American products directly from U.S. wholesalers and manufacturers. Through this import-wholesale scheme, established Chinese merchants such as Ricardo Cuan may have created a distinct transnational ethnic distribution system involving U.S. suppliers/manufacturers, Chinese importers/wholesalers, and Chinese retail merchants.

In an interview with the U.S. Immigration and Naturalization Service in application for border-crossing privileges on April 14, 1943, Cuan describes his firm's reliance upon goods purchased in the United States:

Q. (Wm. E. Addis, Examining Inspector): For what purpose do you desire that your border crossing card be renewed?

A. (Cuan, in Spanish): I wish this privilege to be extended so that I may continue making trips to San Diego, Calif. to purchase merchandise in connection with my business in Ensenada, B.C., Mexico.

Q.: Has there been any change in the nature of your business since you last made a statement in this office on Oct. 5, 1942?

A.: No, I still have a general merchandise store; both wholesale and retail, selling groceries, dry goods and hardware . . .

Q.: How often do you cross the line to the United States on these purchasing trips?

A.: Every 15 days . . .

Q.: Are all these purchases made in San Diego?

A.: Yes, the main purchases are made at Klauber Wangenheim Co., Wellman-Peck Co., and Western Metal Supply Co. Then I also shop around for bargains on potatoes and other produce where I can do the best.

As exemplified by this interview excerpt of Ricardo Cuan and the previous transcript of Rodolfo Ley, Chinese borderlands merchants regularly crossed into the United States and purchased clothing and various manufactured goods from American wholesale companies for sale in their own retail establishments. In addition, more sophisticated mercantile firms such as Rafael Chan and Company also engaged in the wholesale trade of merchandise acquired in the United States, passing on such goods at wholesale prices to willing—and likely Chinese—"comerciantes" of Mexico.

As demonstrated by these examples, therefore, another important activity of the Chinese transnational commercial orbit consisted of the provision of wholesale supplies and goods for sale in Mexican shops. Chinese merchants in Mexico filled their shops with American-manufactured items ordered directly from wholesale suppliers, and indirectly from middlemen like Lee Kwong and the Yat Sang Company, as part of an organized transnational wholesale supply network encompassing northern Mexico, eastern California, Los Angeles, and the San Francisco Bay Area. This business practice of transnational wholesaling helped the Chinese to prosper as borderlands merchants.

In addition to the class resources of transnational capital recruitment and transnational wholesaling, Chinese merchants also exploited various ethnic resources such as nepotistic hiring patterns, unpaid or low-wage partnership labor, and sojourner attitudes. Large numbers of Chinese commercial employees and clerks sampled from municipal census manuscripts possessed ostensible kinship ties with others in their household, suggesting that Chinese merchants often hired their employees on the basis of familial connections. Although they frequently hired clerks to assist them, active partners also appear to have provided much of the labor required for the day-to-day operations of their shops. Moreover, because most Chinese merchants were unmarried sojourners, or had wives and children still residing overseas in their home villages, they lived simply and frugally, residing in their business establishments and likely subsisting on their own mercantile supplies.

Nepotistic hiring patterns, unpaid or low-wage partnership labor, and sojourner attitudes allowed Chinese entrepreneurs to maximize commercial profits through the reduction of business overhead costs and living expenses. By working in their own shops and hiring family members and paesani as employees, Chinese merchants drastically reduced overhead expenses related to labor. In addition, by living in their shops and drawing their basic subsistence requirements from their own stock of goods, Chinese entrepreneurs saved large amounts of money that could in turn be reinvested into their businesses and/or sent to China as familial remittances.

In sum, Chinese immigrants of the merchant class thrived as entrepreneurs in northern Mexico because of the class resources and business practices of transnational capital recruitment and transnational wholesaling. In addition, their utilization of certain ethnic resources such as familial and partnership labor, and sojourner attitudes, allowed them to maximize commercial profits through the minimization of expenditures related to business overhead, room, and board.

Community in Big Lusong

Despite wide disparities in socioeconomic level, Chinese immigrants in Mexico banded together through the formation of transnational associations based upon region of origin, surname, and political ideology.[42] The Chinese of Mexicali and Baja California developed various regional associations for immigrants hailing from places such as Nanbing, Zhongshan, Hoy Yin, and Hoy Pin, many of which survive to this day. In addition, they created two types of surname associations—those comprised of members who shared a single family name and those whose membership consisted of individuals of several last names. Examples of these surname organizations include the Asociación Lim Sei Ho Tong, which bonded together those with the family name of Lim, the Asociación Ma Kiem Tu Tong for those of the last name Ma, and the Asociación Long Kong, comprised of members with the surnames of Liu, Kuan, Chiong, and Chio.[43] Chinese immigrants of Baja California and other parts of Mexico also formed transnational organizations based upon political ideology, such as the Guo Min Dang and the Chee Kung Tong, which were overseas branches of mainland Chinese political parties.[44] The Guo Min Dang and the Chee Kung Tong linked the Chinese of Mexico not only to the political happenings of their homeland but also to other Chinese diasporic communities that formed their own overseas branches of these political organizations.

The Guo Min Dang represented the largest political party of the Chinese parliament during the second decade of the twentieth century and labored for the twin goals of freedom from western imperialism and the establishment of republican democracy. Through the creation of a Mexican overseas branch of the Guo Min Dang, or Nationalist Party, immigrant Chinese remained connected to the political happenings of their native China. In addition, the Chinese government partnered with the Guo Min Dang and appointed members of this organization as its official spokespersons to the Mexican government.[45]

The Union Fraternal China and the Lung Sing Tong were two other major Chinese immigrant organizations that were closely affiliated with the Guo Min Dang. The Union Fraternal China was first organized in the early twentieth century as a mutual aid society for overseas Chinese in Mexico, and by the 1920s its leadership was dominated by members of the Guo Min Dang.[46] The Lung Sing Tong was allegedly founded by members of the Mexican Guo Min Dang to counteract the financial power of their Chee Kung Tong rivals through organized participation in the trafficking of opium and the management of casinos.

Founded centuries before as an organization dedicated to the overthrow of the foreign Manchurian dynastic rulers of China, in contradistinction to the revolutionary Guo Min Dang party, the conservative Chee Kung Tong supported the traditional Chinese monarchical system.[47] Chinese immigrants pledged their allegiance to the traditional dynastic model through their membership in the Mexican overseas branch of the Chee Kung Tong, or Masonic Society. Beyond these political dimensions, the Chee Kung Tong also played a central role in both Chinese labor recruitment and small-scale commercial trade. As previously discussed in chapter 3, Ramon Corral partnered with transnational merchants of the Chee Kung Tong society of San Francisco to develop a system for recruiting Chinese contract labors to northern Mexico. In addition, another important function of the Chee Kung Tong was to organize and unify Chinese businessmen of various stripes, including merchants, shopkeepers, small industrialists, and hotel owners.[48] Notwithstanding its ostensible origins as a political and commercial organization, both Chinese and Mexican observers of the early twentieth century depict the Chee Kung Tong as a source of various forms of vice, including opium and gambling.[49] According to an official statement of the Guo Min Dang of October 1922: "In the United States, China, Japan, Mexico, and in general in every country in which you have a member of the CHEE KUNG TONG, there will be opium, gambling, and immorality."[50]

Although members of the Mexican branch of the Chee Kung Tong identified themselves as Masons and appropriated Masonic insignias as part of their official letterhead, the Chee Kung Tong was not officially affiliated with the international Masonic order and was publicly denounced by the Mexican Grand Lodge of the Pacific.[51] In a letter dated October 22, 1924, Mexican Mason Ing. Juan L. Paliza rebuked Chee Kung Tong representatives Tomas Wang and Guadalupe Chin for their organization's unauthorized appropriation of the Masonic title:

> The Supreme Council of Mexico, which is the highest Masonic authority in our country, and with which I am actually directly related to, distributed, in the past year, a circular to all the Masonic Powers (Grand Lodges) of the Republic, informing them of a recent agreement by the International Masonic Congress of Lausanne, in which was given a list of false Masonic societies, and among them appeared and continues to appear the "Chee Kung Tong," which is an ancient and well organized association as you have said, but which is not masonic, according to the opinion of all the masons of the world, as duly represented in said Congress.[52]

The ideological, political, and financial conflicts of the Mexican branches of the Guo Min Dang and Chee Kung Tong parties engendered unfortunate violent outbursts between the years of 1922 and 1924 known as the "tong wars." According to José Angel Espinoza, prominent leader of the Mexican anti-Chinese campaigns, although the ostensible proximate cause of the tong wars was disagreement between the organizations related to political developments of mainland China, the tong wars were precipitated largely by a financial conflict of interest between the two groups related to control of the opium trade in Mexico.[53] The political tension between the two parties stemmed from the exclusion of the latter from political power within the Chinese government following the triumph and rise to power of Sun Yat Sen and his Nationalist Party. In response to their political disaffection, the Chee Kung Tong wielded its financial influence to initiate a wave of political change in the hopes of wresting political power from their Guo Min Dang rivals and taking the reins of governmental leadership. In addition, Espinoza claims that the Chee Kung Tong financed their political war against the Guo Min Dang largely through the trafficking of opium. Despite these historical political roots of conflict between the two groups, Espinoza asserts that the tong wars of Mexico between 1922 and 1924 were sparked largely by a less noble materialistic cause—the desire to control the opium trade.

According to Mexican historian José Luis Trueba Lara, the origin of the tong wars cannot be attributed to a nefarious desire on the part of the Guo Min Dang to wrest control of the drug trade away from the Chee Kung Tong. Instead, Trueba argues, the tong wars were the result of deep-seated political and economic divisions between the two groups in Mexico.[54] According to Trueba, the Guo Min Dang ousted the Chee Kung Tong from substantial political power by seizing control of the leadership of the Chinese Fraternal Union in 1911. This wresting of power was made possible, in part, because of political leverage that the Guo Min Dang gained in Mexico after its party gained control of the Chinese national government that same year. Following this rise to national prominence and authority in China, members of the Nationalist Party were named as China's official representatives to Mexico. This newfound political clout is what allowed the Guo Min Dang to seize control of the Chinese Fraternal Union.

Capitalizing upon its institutional authority, the Guo Min Dang worked actively over the next decade to effect the expulsion of its Chee Kung Tong rivals from Mexico. The Nationalist Party tried to accomplish this by slandering the Chee Kung Tong through the submission of letters to the Mexican government that claimed that the Chee Kung Tong was an association of drug traffickers and human smugglers. In the short term, these efforts were ultimately unsuccessful, serving only to deepen the divisions and tensions between the two transnational organizations. In 1922, in response to these deepening hostilities, the Chee Kung Tong ousted the Guo Min Dang from economic power in Sonora by seizing control of the Chinese Chamber of Commerce in Cananea.

In retaliation, members of the Guo Min Dang traveled to Cananea, Sonora, and initiated a multifaceted attack against their rivals. According to Trueba, they "[took] with them a considerable part of their war arsenal that they had at their disposal" and filed a formal complaint against the Chee Kung Tong society with local Mexican officials. On April 25, 1922, members of the Chee Kung Tong society responded by shooting and killing Manuel Juan and Federico Juan Qui, rival members of the Nationalist Party. This first wave of murders began the tong wars, and over the course of the next two months numerous Chinese were targeted and shot, including the president of the Chee Kung Tong. The following excerpt from a letter written by former Chee Kung Tong party head Hoi Ping ordering the assassination of Guo Min Dang rival "Diablo Hau" illustrates the deep-seated enmity and rivalry that fueled the tong wars:

> Today, wanting to make the acquisition, we must only accomplish the assassination secretly, because this way it will not implicate the rest of us, and with such luck, they will approve everywhere of this type of assassination: SECRETLY . . . In the meantime, we will wait on the matter regarding the Devil Hau; if you are able to do it, do it; if you must call it off, call it off; but the main and important thing is to seek the general wellbeing.[55]

In reaction to the many violent shootings and murders, Mexican citizens of Cananea, Imuris, Magdalena, and various cities throughout Sonora wrote letters of protest to Governor Francisco S. Elias requesting the expulsion of the Chinese who were responsible for the tong wars. One such telegram from residents of Magdalena stated:

> Town of Magdalena and surrounding neighborhoods unanimously ask this Government to make their own the protests of this town against the disorder caused by Chinese citizens in Sonora and at the same time we ask you to please go before the President of the Republic in denouncing the disorder and that the town of Magdalena is actively protesting asking that Article 33 of the Constitution in regards to troublesome foreigners be applied.[56]

In response to the fervent pleadings of Sonoran residents and the petition of Governor Elias, on June 24, 1922, President Alvaro Obregon issued an expulsion order against Chinese who had actively or passively participated in the recent killings. On August 8, 1922, nearly three hundred individuals were transported by train to Sinaloa and deported to China via the port of Mazatlán. Conspicuously, most of those deported were members of the Chee Kung Tong, and none were members of the rival Guo Min Dang. What were the reasons behind this "lopsided" justice? Unfortunately, the historical record does not speak directly to this issue. Circumstantial evidence does seem to indicate, however, that the Guo Min Dang was given a "pass" by the Mexican government, perhaps because of its official diplomatic relationship to the national leadership of China or because of a collusive deal that was brokered behind the scenes. For example, President Obregon received an "anonymous list" that assigned complete culpability for the tong wars to specific members of the Chee Kung Tong; drawing from the information contained on this list, the federal and state governments initiated a wave of arrests of Chee Kung Tong affiliates who were eventually deported. As further evidence of collusion between the Mexican federal government and the Guo Min Dang, Chee Kung Tong arrestees were denied due process and the opportunity to respond to the criminal charges filed against them, despite desperate pleadings made on their behalf by Juan Lin Fu, interim president of the Chee Kung Tong. Following unsuccessful appeals to Sonoran officials, on June 27, 1922, Lin Fu sent a telegram to President Obregon alleging that his compatriots had been arrested, jailed, and denied due process by the Sonoran state government:

> From the 12th of this month by order of the Governor bi-national members have been held in the jail of this city [Cananea] and from other parts of the state whose this society represented many but others do not belong to any society [. . .] without being notified of the motives for arrest or being allowed to defend themselves. We exhausted all possible means with no success in the Governor conceding to guarantees [. . .]. I plead with you respectfully Mr. Governor to order to allow the imprisoned countrymen to defend themselves [. . .] I implore before you Mr. President in the name of humanity for the justice for my countrymen.[57]

Unmoved by Lin Fu's letter, Obregon upheld his deportation order and replied the following day:

> In regards to your message yesterday.—I let you know that due to executive duties of my position, in light of unacceptable behavior that has threatened safety caused by a considerable number of Chinese that has resulted in a series of murders. [. . .]
>
> And in virtue that those responsible for such deplorable events do not appreciate the hospitality of Mexico, I therefore will apply to them Article 33 [sic], as quarrelsome foreigners to see if the frenzied fighting occurring among the own Chinese can be contained, because otherwise, more severe measures will take place and therefore decree for larger expulsions.

Despite the expulsions that were carried out on August 8, 1922, the tong wars continued over the course of the next two years, and "the frenzied fighting occurring among the own Chinese" was not contained. During two years of bloody skirmishing between the rival organizations, there occurred a total of thirty-nine assaults, which left twenty-five dead and nine wounded. The Chee Kung Tong Party bore the brunt of these casualties, with fourteen of their members killed as a consequence of the assassinations and bloody feuding.

In sum, Chinese immigrants of Mexico bridged disparities in socioeconomic levels and promoted the well-being of their community through the formation of organizations based upon regional origin, familial ancestry, and political ideology. Despite these efforts at community building, disagreement over the political course of events in their homeland bitterly divided Chinese immigrants, leading to the extreme factionalism of the Mexican branches of the Chee Kung Tong and Guo Min Dang political parties, and eventually engendering the bloody outbursts that came to be known as the "tong wars."

Conclusion

Contrary to the claims of the existing historiography, Chinese immigrants of Mexico during the early twentieth century were vocationally diverse and formed two distinct socioeconomic tiers. The impoverished underclass of the Chinese community was comprised of agricultural laborers and urban unskilled employees. In addition to their poverty, members of the Chinese working class were characterized by a lack of significant familial connections with others of the immigrant community. Because of their lack of close kinship ties to others in Mexico, Chinese laborers made their overseas journey across the transnational commercial orbit as part of a system of impersonally organized labor recruitment. As part of this system, emigrant laborers were systematically recruited under contract at Chinese ports by representatives of the Chee Kung Tong of San Francisco, transported to Mexico by steamship, and distributed throughout cities and rural estates in various menial labor positions. As a further consequence of their lack of familial connections, moreover, such migrants were likely excluded from the more lucrative and desirable commercial and industrial chain occupations that appear often to have been organized around networks of kinship. Finally, members of the Chinese immigrant underclass exhibited a low level of cultural assimilation into the society of their host country, as evidenced by low rates of racial intermarriage and citizenship naturalization.

Merchants and skilled artisans comprised the privileged, wealthier, and more assimilated social class of the Chinese overseas community. Their greater privilege, wealth, and access to lucrative employment opportunities were often shaped by their kinship ties to other more established immigrants residing in Mexico. As exemplified by the case studies of Ricardo Cuan and José Chong, many members of the privileged merchant and artisan class traversed the transnational commercial orbit and arrived in Mexico as part of a system of kinship-based serial chain migration. As part of this pattern of familial chain migration, established immigrant kinsmen sponsored the overseas voyages of their family members, provided them with initial housing accommodations, and placed them in exclusive "chain occupations" within the fields of commerce and industry. Lastly, as reflected by high rates of racial intermarriage and citizenship naturalization, as well as by the incipient trend of delayed family migration, immigrant merchants and artisans appear to have been more acculturated than their working-class counterparts. This high level of acculturation is also in direct contradistinction to the experience of Chinese immigrants in the United States during this same time period. The acculturation efforts of the Chinese diasporic community of the United States were hindered in large part because of racist societal norms and laws that barred the Chinese immigrants from intermarriage and naturalization.

Notwithstanding the common characteristics shared by merchant members of the Chinese upper class, the examination of U.S. Immigration Service records reveals the existence of four distinct Chinese merchant types: the immigrant merchant magnate, the medium-sized merchant, the small merchant, and the sole proprietor. Each of these merchant types played a key role in the development and ultimate success of the Chinese transnational commercial orbit. The Chinese borderlands merchant magnate played a foundational role in the transnational economic orbit because of the large size and diversity of his commercial investments. His commercial investments ranged upward of $70,000, and he was also actively involved in transnational sales to clients in both Mexico and the United States. In contrast to the high-class merchant magnate, the medium-sized merchant maintained a much more modest business ownership of approximately $3,000 and probably limited the scope of his investment to one or two commercial projects, because of his limited financial resources. The mid-level merchant was likely part of a kinship-based business partnership that traded in goods such as groceries, dry goods, and hardware, and which was comprised of transnational and/or local members who contributed humble investments of capital ranging from $100 to $1,000. As remuneration for his services as active member of his family firm, the mid-level merchant received a monthly salary of $60 to $100, plus room and board.

The third merchant type—the small businessman—was the most common among Chinese immigrants and as such was the backbone of the transnational commercial orbit. The small merchant shared many of the same characteristics of his mid-level counterpart, except for the size of his initial capital outlay. The small merchant entered the commercial ranks with a limited personal investment of $500 to $1,000, and like the medium-sized merchant limited his investment to one or two business enterprises. The final borderlands merchant type was the sole proprietor. Independent Chinese entrepreneurs managed stores and business enterprises that rivaled those of their small to medium-sized merchant counterparts who invested as part of larger commercial partnerships. Sole proprietors controlled financial assets and contributed capital investments of $4,000 to $10,000, maintained large inventories valued at $4,000 to $8,000, and realized annual net profits of close to $5,000.

The great success of Chinese borderlands merchants was tied to two specific transnational business practices—transnational capital investment based upon ties of kinship and transnational wholesaling. This first business practice enabled Chinese merchants of Mexico to form formidable and well-capitalized commercial firms by pooling small amounts of capital from family members residing in various local and transnational locations in Mexico, the United States, and China. Transnational wholesaling was another commercial practice that helped the Chinese to thrive as borderlands merchants. Chinese grocery and dry goods merchants in Mexico purchased much of their store inventory from Chinese and Anglo wholesalers of the United States. They purchased these goods either directly from U.S. wholesalers by making regular trips across the international line based upon a special border-crossing privilege or indirectly, through economic middlemen who crossed the border themselves to solicit their business. These two business practices were instrumental in facilitating Chinese commercial success, and they also represented two important activities of the Chinese transnational commercial orbit of the Americas.

Finally, despite differences in vocation and socioeconomic level, Chinese immigrants banded together through the development of community organizations based upon region of origin, kinship, and political affiliation. Mainland Chinese political developments of the early twentieth century, however, discouraged such efforts at community building and deeply divided Chinese immigrants. The toppling of the Qing dynasty and the resultant rise to political prominence of the Nationalist Party at the exclusion of the centuries-old Chee Kung Tong stirred the waters of political conflict among the overseas Chinese residing in Mexico, leading ultimately to the bloody tong wars of 1922–1924. As we will see in the next chapter, the violence of the tong wars and the commercial success of Chinese borderland merchants engendered the organized anti-Chinese campaigns of the early twentieth century and led to the ultimate expulsion of the Chinese from the state of Sonora in 1931.

6
Mexican Sinophobia and the
Anti-Chinese Campaigns

On the afternoon of June 22, 1913, Chinese store clerk Ramón Wong was murdered by a Mexican Constitutionalist revolutionary in the city of Nogales, Mexico, allegedly over a disagreement about the price of cigarettes.[1] Prior to the shooting death of Wong, the Mexican soldier had unsuccessfully attempted to purchase cigarettes at another Chinese store located near the U.S. consular headquarters of Nogales. After entering this first commercial establishment, the soldier handed fifteen cents of Mexican currency to the Chinese shopkeeper and requested cigarettes. Although expecting three packs of cigarettes in exchange for his money lying on the store counter, the soldier was much chagrined as the clerk gave him only two packs. In response, the soldier drew his gun and demanded three packs, leading to a verbal altercation between the two. Following their argument, the soldier left the store and traveled one block west down International Street, presumably in search of another store to buy cigarettes. The revolutionary soldier then entered the Chinese business establishment owned by Ramón Wong. Following an alleged disagreement over the price of cigarettes, Wong was shot in the back, the bullet entering "one and a half inches to the right of the spinal column," passing "downward and forward towards the left," and piercing his heart. He died instantly. Upon arrest, the soldier claimed that the shooting was accidental and that Wong was shot after the gun was unintentionally dropped on the ground. American consul of Nogales, Frederick Simpich, issued a report to the secretary of state two days after Wong's death concluding: "In my opinion, and in the opinion of everyone here who knows the attitude of lower class Mexicans toward Chinese, this is untrue. The range of the bullet was *downward,* and the Chinese was behind the counter when killed. It would have been a physical impossibility for a gun, falling and striking the floor and exploding from the contact, to have discharged a bullet in the direction traveled by the bullet which killed Ramón Wong."[2]

As exemplified by this unfortunate account of the death of Chinese merchant Ramón Wong, some members of the Mexican lower classes responded violently to the Chinese economic presence in Mexico. Members of the lower socioeconomic classes sometimes violently voiced their hostility against the Chinese through murders, lootings, and robberies, and also nonviolently through anti-Chinese rallies and protests. Although subaltern reaction and protest were generally sporadic and unplanned, lower-middle-class discontent toward the Chinese immigrant community expressed itself in the form of organized anti-Chinese campaigns. Propagandists of the anti-Chinese movement couched their complaints against the Chinese within a framework of economic nationalism, decried Chinese-Mexican racial intermarriage, portrayed the Chinese as a serious public health nuisance, and alleged that Chinese immigrants were a major source of vice and crime. Lower-middle-class leaders of the sinophobic campaigns spread their message and recruited support for their cause through the creation of anti-Chinese clubs, organizations, and periodicals, and through the promotion of boycotts and protests.

At the core of both lower-middle-class and working-class animosity toward the Chinese was a fervent economic nationalism. Members of both socioeconomic classes blamed the Chinese and other resident foreigners for the downturn of the Mexican economy during the early twentieth century. In addition, they resented the economic success achieved by the Chinese as part of the transnational commercial orbit. Many from the Mexican working class believed that the Chinese had become rich at the expense of humble Mexicans, blamed the Chinese for the depreciation of Mexican currency and rising food costs, and chided Chinese immigrants for their occupation of categories of employment traditionally reserved for Mexican women. Through the organized anti-Chinese campaigns, lower-middle-class Mexican merchants sought to break the Chinese commercial monopoly in northern Mexico and eliminate the Chinese merchant, with whom they could not compete.

This chapter examines the diverse responses of the Mexican population to the Chinese presence in Mexico. Although the major focus is the anti-Chinese campaigns and lower-middle-class and proletariat responses to the Chinese, this chapter also explores the perspectives and attitudes of two other important Mexican sociopolitical groups: the industrial and commercial elite of frontier and tropical Mexico and the Mexican federal government. A final aim of this chapter is to dispel the popular misconception that the Chinese were passive victims of Mexican discrimination. To this end, this chapter highlights some of the legal, extralegal, and diplomatic tactics by which the Chinese community of Mexico defended itself during the anti-Chinese campaigns.

Table 6.1.   Documented Chinese murders, 1911–1919.

Monterrey	1
Chihuahua	48
Piedras Negras	373
Mazatlán	9
Mexico City	129
Total	560

Source: "Note," Index Bureau 312.93/172–312.93/181, microfilm roll "Chinese Question in Mexico, 1910–1930," Record Group 59, General Records of the Department of State, Decimal File 312.93, 1910–1929, 1930–1939; 704.9312, 1910–1929, 1930–1939, University of Arizona Main Library.

Subaltern Perspectives and Responses

Unfortunately, the murder of Ramón Wong was not an isolated incident during the years of the Mexican Revolution. Between 1911 and 1919, at least 814 Chinese were killed in various states throughout Mexico by soldiers or unknown individuals (see table 6.1).[3] Based upon a review of U.S. consular reports, most of these murders appear to have been committed by disgruntled revolutionary soldiers.[4] Such anti-Chinese violence eclipsed that experienced by the Chinese diasporic communities of the United States and the rest of the Americas during the twentieth century.[5]

In addition to such killings, violent Mexican subaltern reaction against the Chinese immigrant population during the revolutionary years 1910–1920 also expressed itself in the form of robbery and looting. The looting of Chinese shops commonly occurred at the initiation of revolutionary soldiers and with the participation of civilian members of the Mexican lower socioeconomic classes.[6] According to one common scheme, revolutionary soldiers would force their way into a Chinese shop and scare away the Chinese proprietors through the wielding and firing of weapons. Following the flight of the Chinese businessmen from their stores, the soldiers, accompanied by civilian mobs, would then proceed to raid the commercial establishment of its stock of merchandise. This pattern of military-civilian looting occurred in several Sonoran towns, such as Cananea, Nacozari, and Arizpe, and sometimes included the involvement of both men and women.[7] In other instances, civilian mobs raided Chinese merchants without the assistance of renegade revolutionary soldiers.[8] In addition, according to one American consular agent, it was a "favorite past-time" of Mexican soldiers to rob Chinese merchants, strip them of all their clothing, and tie them up to a tree or post in a remote region to remain until a passerby came along to free them.[9] The looting of Chinese shops became so widespread and common during the years of the Mexican Revolution that detailed notarized merchandise inventories were sent to U.S. diplomatic representatives in Mexico, by and on behalf of some Chinese merchants. Chinese immigrants appealed to U.S. consular authorities for protection because they lacked official Chinese diplomatic representation in Mexico. In addition, because Chinese merchants often shared commercial connections with American businesses in Mexico, U.S. diplomatic officials felt a moral obligation to provide a limited level of political protection for the Chinese.

Precautionary measures such as the compilation of merchandise inventories were ostensibly carried out in anticipation of future military and civilian raids, and to facilitate the process of governmental compensation in the event of such looting.[10] Mexican looters robbed Chinese commercial establishments of both merchandise and cash, and individual merchant firms sustained losses ranging from several hundred to tens of thousands of dollars.[11] In addition, raiding civilian and military mobs sometimes stormed numerous Chinese businesses of a particular city. On July 19 and 29, 1915, for example, looters sacked forty-four Chinese commercial houses in Cananea, Sonora, robbing them of $527,752.90 worth of cash and goods, and, "[w]ith the exception of a few Chinese medicines, such articles as could not be moved or used by the Mexicans were deliberately destroyed." During the early years of the Mexican Revolution up to circa 1911, Chinese immigrants filed 608 property claims totaling $1,137,227.04 (U.S.) in economic losses.[12] Although claims were presented in various states throughout Mexico, most were filed by Chinese immigrants residing in the northern states and territories of Coahuila, Chihuahua, Sonora, and Baja California.

The Massacre of Torreón

The most horrendous incident of Mexican subaltern violence perpetrated against Chinese immigrants during the early revolutionary years took place in the city of Torreón, Coahuila, on May 14 and 15, 1911. On May 15, 303 Chinese and five Japanese immigrants were murdered by Maderista revolutionary soldiers under the command of military leaders Jesús Castro, Sixto Ugalde, Enrique Macías, and others.[13] In addition to the many lives taken as a consequence of the massacre, Chinese immigrants of Torreón and the city's neighboring vicinity suffered financial losses of $849,928.69 as a consequence of the looting and robbery that accompanied the murders.[14] The massacre of Torreón was the worst act of violence committed against any Chinese diasporic community of the Americas during the twentieth century.

At the turn of the twentieth century, Torreón was a burgeoning northern industrial boomtown that boasted a total population of approximately 35,000, as well as nine banks and "magnificent business houses."[15] The Chinese community of Torreón consisted of about six hundred to seven hundred persons in 1911, immediately prior to the events of May 14 and 15. In addition, the Chinese colony of Torreón was economically prosperous, with members invested in a wide array of commercial activities, including small-scale trade, real estate, the laundering industry, and vegetable gardening. The Chinese community even operated its own bank and hotel.

In September of 1910, and early in May 1911, several events occurred in Torreón and the surrounding vicinity that set the stage for, and eerily foreshadowed, the massacre of May 15. On September 16, 1910, anti-Chinese sentiment was aroused in Torreón by the presentation of an inflammatory speech that criticized the existence of the large Chinese community of the city. Incited by the sinophobic oration, local residents of Torreón carried out a protest demonstration that day, which involved the stoning of Chinese businesses and residences but did not include the perpetration of physical violence against Chinese immigrants themselves.[16]

Just one week before the massacre of Torreón, anti-Chinese hostility was further aroused during a civic parade organized by Maderista revolutionary supporters as part of Cinco de Mayo celebrations in the neighboring city of Gómez Palacio, Durango. In honor of Mexican liberation from French colonial rule, revolutionists sponsored a series of civic activities on May 5, which included circuses, serenades, and parades. During the parade march, revolutionary leaders and supporters presented speeches that were, presumably, nationalistic in emphasis. One such speech was given by Jesús C. Flores, a stonemason by trade and a leader of the Maderista faction. In his nationalist call to revolution, Flores condemned the wealthy resident foreigners of Mexico who profited based upon the exploitation of the Mexican working class. In addition, he specifically singled out Chinese immigrants as a major cause of such economic troubles. According to Delfino Ríos, an eyewitness of both the Flores speech and the massacre at Torreón, Flores chided the Chinese for having "taken over even the work of the women, depriving them of their livelihood," and advocated "that, therefore, it was necessary . . . even a patriotic duty, to finish with them."[17] Moreover, in his nationalist tirade, Flores criticized Chinese immigrants for not being good citizens, and for their practice of sending their savings as remittances to China instead of spending in the Mexican economy. Commenting upon the effects of Flores's speech upon its audience, and referring to Flores's call to do away with the Chinese of Mexico, Delfino Ríos stated: "These latter words made an impression and remained fixed in the minds of these unthinking, ignorant people and 'patriotism,' which was in a state of effervescence, was prepared to break out at the opportune moment." Following the celebrations of the Fifth of May, Maderista revolutionary forces of the cities of Gómez Palacio and Ciudad Lerdo prepared for an attack upon Torreón. As part of their preparation for the upcoming siege of Torreón, Maderista leaders gathered troops from among the subaltern class of these two towns and allegedly issued a call "to the mobs from which the troops had been drawn."

In anticipation of the imminent attack of revolutionary forces, on May 12, 1911, the Chinese Merchants' and Laborers' Society of Torreón published a circular that eerily foreshadowed the terrible events that were to take place only a few days later. The circular warned members of the Chinese colony of the impending attack and of the probability of mob violence. In addition, it suggested certain safety precautions to minimize risk to life and property.[18] The circular was distributed among the Chinese stores, in the central marketplace, and throughout the Chinese community. The circular warned:

> Brothers, attention! Attention! This is serious. Many unjust acts have happened during the revolution. Notice has been received that before ten o'clock today the revolutionists will unite their forces and attack the city. It is very probable that during the battle a mob will spring up and sack the stores. For this reason we advise all our people, when the crowds assemble, to close your doors and hide yourselves and under no circumstances open your places for business or go outside to see the fighting. And, if any of your stores are broken into, offer no resistance but allow them to take what they please, since otherwise you might endanger your lives. THIS IS IMPORTANT. After the trouble is over we will try to arrange a settlement.

Although the cautionary circular announced the arrival of Maderista forces on May 12, the revolutionary army did not attack Torreón until the morning of May 13.[19] Torreón was defended by the federal army of General Lojero, which consisted of about 670 men adorned in yellow khaki and known as the Yellow-Jackets. On the morning of May 13, the revolutionary army of four thousand men stormed the city from all sides for forty-two hours but were successfully warded off by the small number of federal troops. In addition, as part of their strategy of attack, Maderista soldiers fired upon federal forces from the Chinese vegetable gardens located east of Torreón, using the homes of Chinese residents as protection. Some Chinese employees and residents of the gardens, moreover, were robbed and forced to prepare food for members of the revolutionary army during the siege of Torreón. The homes of some Chinese residents of the gardens were also sacked by Maderista troops, and 112 lost their lives at the hands of the invading soldiers.

Despite his successful defense of Torreón during the first two days of skirmishing, General Lojero withdrew his federal troops from the city in the early morning hours of May 15.[20] It was reported that Lojero evacuated his Yellow-Jacket soldiers because of a shortage of ammunition. Some also asserted that Lojero had been given orders to retreat, and others stated that the withdrawal was influenced by the sympathies extended by local residents toward the invading Maderista revolutionary forces.

Following the retreat of the federal army, revolutionary troops stormed the city of Torreón.[21] Joined by civilian mobs from the cities of Lerdo, Gómez Palacio, San Pedro, Viesca, Matamóros, and Torreón, Maderista soldiers looted and pillaged both business establishments and private homes. Four thousand individuals participated in the looting of Torreón. According to one eyewitness:

Business places and private residences without number were swept entirely clean and it was a sight to witness the lower classes carrying away bureaus, chairs, sewing machines, phonographs, pianos, etc., which they rolled along like bales of cotton. The doors of these houses had been opened by the revolutionists who incited the masses to enter and take possession of the contents. Some of the houses after being robbed were set on fire, which was the fate suffered by the jail, the police headquarters building, the Inferior Court, and Court of Letters and the Municipal Treasury.[22]

Chinese homes and commercial establishments were also specifically targeted by marauding military and civilian mobs.[23] Members of the Chinese colony of Torreón were robbed of all their possessions, and their private residences and businesses were completely sacked and destroyed during the raids of May 15. In an investigational report of the Torreón massacre dated June 7, 1911, American consular agent G. C. Carothers described in detail the destruction carried out upon two Chinese commercial establishments of the city:

> Next we went to the Chinese Laundry where four had been killed, and the laundry practically demolished. Bombs had been thrown on the roof, the windows and doors either destroyed or stolen, the machinery broken to pieces and everything that could be carted away, stolen. . . . The Puerto de Shanghai building was next visited. All of the doors and windows of the building were destroyed. The Chinese Bank, which had been moved into this building a few months before, was demolished, safes blown open and contents taken, furniture destroyed, all papers and valuables stolen. Seventeen Chinamen were killed here. I am told that many on the second floor had been cut to pieces and the pieces thrown out through the windows.[24]

As evidenced by this consular report description, many Chinese residents of Torreón were also brutally murdered by revolutionary forces and civilian mobs during the events of May 13, 14, and 15.[25] Nearly one-half of the Chinese colony of Torreón died during these three days of military activity.[26] Allegedly, all Chinese that could be found were murdered. They were killed with swords and guns, in their homes and in the streets, in a variety of disturbing ways. According to one report:

> The town was searched for Chinese and all who could be found were murdered in the most brutal and horrifying manner. In one instance the head of a Chinaman was severed from his body and thrown from the window into the street. In another instance a soldier took a little boy by the heels and battered his brains out against a lamp post. . . . In another instance a Chinaman was pulled to pieces in the street by horses hitched to his arms and legs. . . . No language can adequately depict the revolting scenes which attended this carnival of human slaughter. . . . The mind recoils in horror from the contemplation of such an atrocity.[27]

In all, 303 Chinese lost their lives during the massacre of Torreón. Table 6.2 lists those Chinese murdered in different commercial establishments of the city.

Table 6.2. Chinese murdered in commercial establishments of Torreón.

Name of store	Number killed	Name of store	Number killed
La Kin Chan	0	La Esperanza	3
Sam Sing	1	Zaragoza	3
Lim Wong King	1	Gee Hop	18
Suc. de la Plaza	3	Joaquín Wong	2
Hop Yick	1	Juan Sing	2
Hing Sing	2	La Gitana	2
Wong Lee	4	Wong New	4
Hop Lee	7	Hung Lee	11
Ciudad Mexico, S.A.	2	Chee Sing	2
Joaquín Quinto	2	Chew King Sing	2
Wing Hong Long	2	Juan Mau	?
Honam	3	Total	77

Source: "Report of Investigation of Chinese Massacre That G. C. Carothers, American Consular Agent, Torreón, Coahuila, Mexico, Made June 7, 1911," enclosed in American Consul Charles M. Freeman to the Honorable Secretary of State, Durango, Mexico, 10 June 1911, microfilm roll "Chinese Question in Mexico, 1910–1930," Record Group 59, General Records of the Department of State, Decimal File 312.93, 1910–1929, 1930–1939; 704.9312, 1910–1929, 1930–1939, University of Arizona Main Library, 6.

Despite the profound loss of life that occurred on May 15, many lives were also saved that day by the intervention of Mexican and foreign resident Good Samaritans.[28] Such Good Samaritans protected the lives of Chinese residents of Torreón by hiding them in their private homes and by misleading Maderista soldiers as to their whereabouts. In a manner reminiscent of the biblical account of Rahab, one Mexican tailor saved the lives of eight by standing in the rain all night in front of a Chinese laundry and lying to revolutionary soldiers about the whereabouts of the Chinese who were present in the building. In another similar instance, a twenty-year-old tailor protected the lives of seventy by running atop the roof of a restaurant building where the Chinese were hidden, waving his arms, and misdirecting the angry mob that sought to take their lives.

In a final noteworthy example, one Hermina Almaráz saved the lives of eleven Chinese who were sheltered in her home by telling the Maderista troops who sought to enter "that they could only enter the house over her dead body." The soldiers had killed her father (who incidentally was a leader of the Maderista faction) while trying to break into the house, but after hearing these words of Hermina, they abandoned the home and the eleven Chinese who were therein concealed.

The massacre of Torreón ended some time in the mid-afternoon of May 15 upon the arrival of commanding officer Emilio Madero, who brought the looting mobs under control through the use of military force.[29] Following the massacre, and in response to the many injustices committed against its national subjects residing in Torreón, the Chinese government hired the Anglo-American law firm of Wilfley and Bassett to investigate the events of May 15 and to secure monetary indemnities from the Mexican government for its failure to protect the Chinese residents of Torreón as required by the 1899 Chinese-Mexican treaty. It is interesting to note that the Chinese government chose to hire an American, as opposed to a Mexican, law firm to represent its legal interests. Although it is not clear from the historical record exactly what factored into this decision, one reason could be that Wilfley and Bassett was an international law firm that specialized in defending foreign political and economic interests in Mexico. As a well-established international law firm, moreover, Wilfley and Bassett would have likely possessed not only the requisite legal expertise but also important political connections that could be utilized to summon diplomatic pressure from the U.S. government on behalf of the Chinese. Specialized legal expertise and strategic diplomatic ties were, therefore, probably important factors that influenced the hiring of the American law firm of Wilfley and Bassett.

Named partner Arthur Bassett, together with Chinese diplomatic representative Owyang King and Mexican presidential representative Licenciado Antonio Ramos Pedrueza, conducted an investigation of the Torreón events within several days after the massacre.[30] Based upon the results of the joint investigation, the law firm of Wilfley and Bassett drafted comprehensive legal memoranda that appealed to the Mexican government for large monetary indemnities based upon the breach of treaty stipulations and the authority of a wide breadth of international case law.[31] Two years later, in January of 1913, following further negotiation between the two nations, Mexico agreed to pay the Chinese government an indemnity of approximately $3,200,000 in compensation for the lives of its subjects lost in the massacre of Torreón.[32] Despite this diplomatic agreement, as of December 1913 the indemnity remained unpaid.[33]

Subaltern Organized Protest

As evidenced by the anti-Chinese protest speeches and demonstrations of September 1910 and May 5, 1911, which preceded the Torreón massacre, members of the Mexican lower socioeconomic classes also voiced their opposition to the Chinese immigrant community through the use of organized protest.[34] Subaltern men and women protested against a perceived Chinese socioeconomic threat through the organization of anti-Chinese rallies and the presentation of sinophobic, nationalistic speeches. Illustrative of the nationalistic character of anti-Chinese subaltern protest, one speech, originally scheduled to be presented as part of an anti-Chinese demonstration in Mazatlán, Sinaloa, in March of 1912, was themed, "He who protects the Chinese is a traitor to his country."[35] Exemplary of the protest rallies organized by members of the Mexican lower socioeconomic classes against Chinese immigrants, wives of Mexican mine laborers sponsored a large anti-Chinese demonstration on February 24, 1914, in Cananea, Sonora. This demonstration, moreover, followed the presentation of a letter of protest to officials of the American-owned Cananea Consolidated Copper Co. by Mexican labor leaders. Taking place on the main thoroughfare of the Ronquillo District of that city, the protest rally attracted a large crowd of four hundred to five hundred persons, consisting of both men and women. During the rally, female demonstrators presented a series of speeches, condemning all foreigners and demanding the forcible expulsion of the Chinese colony of Cananea. Following the speeches, the demonstration participants continued their protest through the looting of a nearby Chinese laundry. Upon arrival at the Chinese laundry, the crowd "pulled down the sign in front of the laundry, broke the door and windows, and stole the clothing found in the laundry and took what money was in the till, amounting to about ten pesos in small change."[36] Two of the Chinese present in the laundry were pulled into the thoroughfare by the demonstrators and beaten with stones.

Sources of Subaltern Discontent

Subaltern discontent toward Chinese immigrants stemmed from the perception that the Chinese, together with other foreign elements, were responsible for the downturn in the Mexican economy.[37] In their minds, members of the Mexican working classes lumped Chinese immigrants and American capitalists together and categorized them as the wealthy foreign class that had profited from the exploitation of the humble Mexican populace.[38] They blamed the Chinese and other foreigners for Mexican monetary depreciation and the concomitant rise in the cost of food and basic provisions.[39] In the face of depressed wages—during the years of the Mexican Revolution, laborers and soldiers received as little as one and a half pesos per day—devalued currency, and unaffordable costs of provisions, it appears that Mexican laborers and soldiers sometimes resorted to looting to provide for themselves and their families, and that they assigned responsibility for their economic situation to foreign elements such as the Chinese.[40] Further hostility toward Chinese merchants in the state of Sonora arose from the perception of governmental favoritism toward Chinese businessmen, and from resentment toward state officials for the recruitment of Chinese immigrants.[41] U.S. consular records indicate, moreover, that antipathy toward Chinese merchants may have also been stirred by the perceived hoarding of provisions on the part of Chinese merchants.[42] Finally, as described in the earlier narrative of the massacre of Torreón, members of the Mexican lower socioeconomic classes also criticized Chinese immigrants for taking over categories of employment traditionally occupied by Mexican women, and for draining the domestic economy through the sending of their savings earned in Mexico as overseas remittances.[43] Because Chinese male laborers filled such types of employment positions, they were criticized for robbing Mexican women of their economic livelihoods. Furthermore, in contrast with members of other resident foreign groups who contributed to the Mexican economy by spending large amounts of their incomes domestically, Chinese immigrants were criticized for subsisting on small amounts of money and for sending most of their earnings to China as remittances.

Lower-Middle-Class Perspectives and Responses: The Anti-Chinese Campaigns of 1916–1935

Whereas Mexican subaltern discontent toward Chinese immigrants expressed itself largely in the forms of unplanned violent outbreaks and sporadic organized protests and rallies, lower-middle-class reaction against the Chinese community took the form of organized anti-Chinese campaigns, which began in 1916 and which culminated in the expulsion of the

Chinese from the state of Sonora in 1931. The origins of the organized anti-Chinese movement in Mexico can be traced back to a meeting of Mexican small businessmen in the city of Magdalena, Sonora, on February 5, 1916.[44] Disgruntled by the economic success achieved by Chinese merchants as part of the transnational commercial orbit, participants evaluated the impact of the Chinese mercantile presence in Sonora and established a Mexican business organization called the Junta Comercial y de Hombres de Negocios (Council of Commerce and Businessmen). Francisco C. Lopez was named president of the organization's board of directors, and José Maria Arana was awarded the position of "first ranking member."

Junta members also developed a written manifesto that listed the goals of their organization and enumerated their complaints against the Chinese.[45] The organization dedicated itself to: (1) the promotion of the interests of the Mexican businessman through all possible means, and (2) the use of all measures allowed by law to bring about the extinction of the Asian merchant. In addition, according to the group's written manifesto, Chinese immigrants represented unfair competition for Mexican merchants because of their dishonest business practices and the low prices they offered for their merchandise. Junta members criticized Chinese merchants for committing fraud in their use of weights and measures, for tax evasion, and for selling their goods at prices with which Mexican businessmen could not compete. Moreover, they condemned the Chinese as a public health threat and asserted that Chinese immigrants denied Mexican youth employment opportunities and forced them to emigrate in search of work. Copies of the group's manifesto were to be mailed to all the towns of Sonora in the hope of establishing other juntas throughout the state. Unlike their subaltern counterparts who condemned the economic presence of all foreigners in Mexico, members of the Junta Comercial welcomed the participation of all Mexican and foreign businessmen in their organization, with the sole exception of Asians.

The junta's early manifesto of 1916 unabashedly reveals the primary motivation underlying the founding of the organized anti-Chinese movement—lower-middle-class Mexican businessmen sought to eliminate the Chinese merchant with whom they could not compete. As discussed in chapter 5, Chinese immigrants developed transnational business practices and a multinational economic orbit that allowed them to prosper—above and beyond that of their Mexican competitors. This economic success engendered deep resentment on behalf of aspiring Mexican merchants and led to the birth of the anti-Chinese campaigns. As will be later discussed in great detail, the movement's leaders would eventually develop a sophisticated propaganda campaign against the Chinese aimed at recruiting support among the larger Mexican population through an appeal to a wide array of noneconomic factors (portraying the Chinese as the source of vice within Mexican society, threats to public health, and seducers of Mexican women, to name a few). In addition, Mexican merchants sought to co-opt the Mexican working classes into their movement by highlighting the Chinese failure to employ native laborers in their shops and business establishments.[46] Despite the development of such consensus-building rhetoric, however, the 1916 manifesto betrays the true motivation of the movement's founders—Lopez, Arana, Davila, Grijalva, and others, formed the Junta Comercial y de Hombres de Negocios because of their inability to compete successfully with Chinese immigrant businessmen.

Anti-Chinese Campaign Propaganda

To promote their cause and garner support among the Mexican populace, lower-middle-class leaders of the anti-Chinese movement developed a comprehensive corpus of sinophobic rhetoric and propaganda. Capitalizing upon the nationalistic fervor sparked by the Mexican Revolution, they couched their complaints against the Chinese within a framework of patriotic nationalism. Leaders of the anti-Chinese campaigns described their efforts as a movement "Por la Patria y Por la Raza" (For the Fatherland and For the Race), involving a "cuestión moral de nacionalísmo" (moral question of nationalism).[47]

In addition, anti-Chinese propagandists appealed to revolutionary economic nationalism to gain support for their movement. Similar to their subaltern compatriots, they identified the Chinese as being part of the prosperous foreign economic class that had come to dominate the economy at the expense of Mexican nationals.[48] In a letter to José Maria Arana (see fig. 6.1), chief spokesperson of the early anti-Chinese movement, Luis L. León of the Partido Revolucionario Sonorense of Hermosillo (Sonoran Revolutionary Party of Hermosillo) expressed this perspective of economic nationalism that sought to link Chinese immigrants together with other foreign capitalists: "I believe that a true nationalism, aimed at destroying, not only the eminent Chinese monopoly, but also even the monopoly over the Fountains of wealth of the state by other foreigners, such as the North American companies, will . . . give us strong sympathy in all of the Republic."[49]

......y quienes no oyeren mis palabras, mañana llorarán la agonía de la Patria que fuimos incapaces de defender.

José María Arana.

Figure 6.1. Cartoonist's depiction of José Maria Arana, chief spokesperson of the Mexican anti-Chinese movement. Sign reads: "MEXICAN: OF EVERY PESO THAT YOU BUY FROM A CHINESE BUSINESS, FIFTY CENTS GOES TO SHANGHAI AND THE OTHER FIFTY CENTS SERVES TO SHACKLE YOU AND TO PROSTITUTE THE WOMEN OF YOUR RACE!!!" *Source:* José Angel Espinoza, *El ejemplo de Sonora* (Mexico, D.F.: n.p., 1932), 33.

As part of their rhetoric of economic nationalism, moreover, proponents of the anti-Chinese campaigns asserted that Chinese immigrants monopolized retail commerce at the expense of native Mexican merchants and that they hindered the development of national commerce.[50] In addition, they maintained that the Chinese represented unfair labor competition, filled jobs traditionally occupied by Mexican women, and charged overinflated prices for basic foodstuffs.[51] As depicted in figure 6.1, leaders of the sinophobic movement also criticized Chinese merchants for sending remittances back to family members in China instead of investing their economic profits in Mexico. Such remittances represent another important economic activity of the Chinese transnational commercial

El sudor y la mugre entran también en la receta china para la elaboración del pan.....

Figure 6.2. Cartoonist's depiction of unsanitary conditions of Chinese bakery. Caption reads: "Sweat and grime also enter into the Chinese recipe for the production of bread." *Source:* José Angel Espinoza, *El ejemplo de Sonora* (Mexico, D.F.: n.p., 1932), 69.

orbit and were an important means by which families of Guangdong maintained their financial livelihoods.

Building upon their rhetoric of nationalism, as discussed in great detail in chapter 4, "anti-chinistas" decried intermarriage between Chinese immigrants and Mexican women, stating that such marital unions engendered the ruin and degeneration of the Mexican race.[52] Propagandists characterized such interracial unions as relationships of abuse and slavery, and they portrayed the offspring of such unions as degenerative mongoloids.

As part of their propaganda campaign, leaders of the anti-Chinese movement also condemned Chinese immigrants as representing a major public health threat (see figs. 6.2 and 6.3).[53] They criticized Chinese immigrants for bringing over diseases from China such as syphilis, trachoma, and leprosy, and for passing on contaminated foods and goods to the

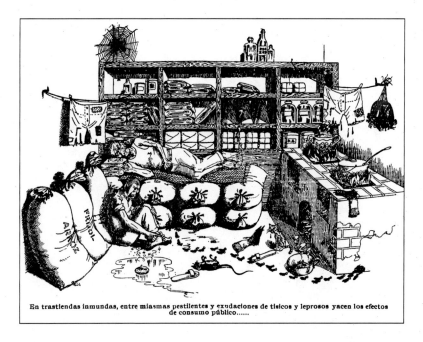

En trastiendas inmundas, entre miasmas pestilentes y exudaciones de tísicos y leprosos yacen los efectos de consumo público......

Figure 6.3. Pictorial representation of disease-ridden Chinese storeroom. Cartoon caption reads: "In filthy backrooms, amongst pestilent miasmas and tubercular and leprous discharges lay the goods for public consumption." *Source:* José Angel Espinoza, *El ejemplo de Sonora* (Mexico, D.F.: n.p., 1932), 67.

Mexican public. According to propagandists, Chinese merchants kept consumer goods such as rice and beans in filthy back storerooms that were infested with disease and doubled as living quarters. In addition, they depicted the kitchens of Chinese bakers and cooks as unsanitary and germ-ridden threats to public health. Immigrant waiters, laundrymen, and sales clerks, moreover, were also portrayed as furtive carriers of exotic diseases hidden beneath their daily apparel.

As a final element of sinophobic rhetoric, proponents of the anti-Chinese movement criticized the Chinese immigrant community for being a major source of vice and crime. They described Chinese immigrant organizations such as the Chee Kung Tong and the Lung Sing Tong as "mafias" and asserted that such groups promoted illegal immigration from China, gambling, and the Mexican opium trade. According to

Y, en México, el tráfico de la "nieve" y el opio se han generalizado con la presencia de los chinos que, discretos y listos, buscando "lopa pa'laval" en las rúas. . . . , y, en los cafés, entre cierta gente que saben distinguir, inician a los "principiantes".

Figure 6.4. Chinese immigrant posing as launderer and furtively peddling opium to Mexican addict. Caption reads: "And, in Mexico, the traffic of 'snow' and opium has spread with the presence of the Chinese, who, discreet and shrewd, seek 'clothes for washing' in the streets . . . and, in the cafés, amongst certain people that they [the Chinese] know how to distinguish, they initiate the 'inexperienced.'" *Source:* José Angel Espinoza, *El ejemplo de Sonora* (Mexico, D.F.: n.p., 1932), 228.

anti-chinistas, the Chinese furtively peddled opium or "nieve" (snow), in public streets and cafés, under the guise of laundrymen seeking "lopa pa'laval" (clothes for washing), and they smoked the drug in the secrecy of their homes, business establishments, and "templos de vicio" (temples of vice) (see fig. 6.4).[54] Propagandists also decried the violent tong wars, which they claimed were fought by warring Chinese mafia factions over control of the opium trade (see fig. 6.5).[55]

Cegando a veces vidas preciosas del país que les brinda hospitalidad inmerecida, las maffias chinas se disputan la preponderancia en el comercio del opio......

Figure 6.5. Dramatic portrayal of Chinese drug-related violence. *Source:* José Angel Espinoza, *El ejemplo de Sonora* (Mexico, D.F.: n.p., 1932), 115.

Strategies and Tactics of the Anti-Chinese Movement

Leaders of the anti-Chinese movement disseminated their propaganda and recruited support among the larger Mexican population through the development of various clubs, organizations, and periodicals, as well as through the promotion of protests and boycotts.[56] According to José Angel Espinoza, President of the Comité Directivo Nacionalista de la Costa Occidental (Nationalist Board of the Occidental Coast), 215 anti-Chinese organizations existed throughout Mexico in 1932.[57] Dedicated to resisting the racial and economic influence of the Chinese immigrant community in Mexico, anti-immigrant groups such as the Junta Nacionalista

(Nationalist Council), the Liga Nacional Pro-Raza (National Pro-Race League), and El Club del Pueblo (the Club of the People) allegedly boasted a total membership of close to two million and maintained headquarters in many states and territories, including Sonora, Chihuahua, San Luis Potosí, Baja California Norte, Baja California Sur, Nayarit, Chiapas, Tamaulipas, Durango, Veracruz, and Sinaloa.[58]

Anti-immigrant propagandists also spread their message through the publication of various sinophobic periodicals. Publications such as *Pro-Patria* (Pro-Fatherland), *La Palabra* (the Word), *El Malcriado* (the Brat), *Nuevos Horizontes* (New Horizons), and *El Nacionalista* (the Nationalist) served as print vehicles for anti-Chinese rhetoric and afforded antichinistas the opportunity to articulate their concerns to a larger Mexican audience.[59] *El Nacionalista*, the "Organo del Antichinismo Nacional" (Organ of the National Anti-Chinese Movement), for example, printed articles admonishing the Mexican populace to boycott Chinese-owned stores, advising them to prohibit their children from entering Chinese business establishments for fear of contracting disease, and criticizing Chinese immigrants for their role in sponsoring vice activities.[60] In addition, *El Nacionalista* sought to advance the anti-Chinese movement by publishing judicial edicts and warnings, public interest announcements, and advertisements for Mexican merchants. Interested readers could purchase a three-month subscription of the newspaper for $1.50 (Mexican), a six-month subscription for $2.50, a one-year subscription for $4.00, or a sample copy for 10 cents.

In addition to the formation of clubs and juntas, and the publication of sinophobic periodicals, proponents of the anti-Chinese movement also sought to bring about the demise of the Chinese immigrant community through the organization of popular protests and commercial boycotts.[61] Appealing to revolutionary nationalism, anti-Chinese protesters condemned Chinese immigrants as exploiters of the Mexican people and chided the Mexican upper classes for their apathy and inaction in regard to the Chinese question. Further appealing to Mexican nationalism, leaders of the anti-Chinese movement admonished the Mexican populace to boycott Chinese commercial establishments. According to boycott advocates, the general public suffered from the mistaken belief that Chinese businessmen offered their merchandise at lower prices than their Mexican competitors, and the boycott offered one of the most effective means of empowering Mexican merchants and breaking the Chinese commercial stronghold.[62] Reflecting this perspective, and in a call to arms against the

Chinese mercantile monopoly, one editorial contributor to *El Nacionalista* proclaimed: "Onward children of the race, let us go triumphant; let us go showing the world that you know how to triumph, that you know how to overcome. . . . Nothing else matters when what you fight for is the life or death of our nationality. . . . I WHO AM A MEXICAN CHILD, SWEAR, BY THE BONES OF MY ANCESTORS THAT FROM TODAY ON I WILL NO LONGER PURCHASE EVEN ONE CENT FROM THE CHINESE STORES."[63]

As a final means of advancing their cause, leaders of the anti-Chinese movement promoted a wide assortment of invidious state legislation and discriminatory government circulars.[64] Through the passage of such laws, anti-chinistas sought to legally sanction their sinophobic perspectives and codify their comprehensive corpus of anti-Chinese rhetoric and propaganda. Anti-Chinese leaders sought to destroy the Chinese commercial stronghold in Sonora through the passage of state labor legislation in 1919 and 1931, requiring that at least 80 percent of the workforce of all commercial establishments consist of Mexican employees.[65] Chinese entrepreneurs tended to hire employees of their own ethnic community and/or to run the day-to-day operations of their businesses based upon the labor of active partners, and, through such legislation, Mexican activists hoped to create new employment opportunities for members of the Mexican working classes. In addition, the 80 percent labor laws also served as a means of courting the support of native Mexican workers for the anti-Chinese movement and, should the Chinese fail to obey such laws, provided a convenient excuse for the closure of Chinese businesses.

In a further attack upon the Chinese mercantile monopoly, anti-Chinese activists in Sonora secured the promulgation of discriminatory public health circulars targeting business practices that allowed the Chinese to outsell their Mexican competitors.[66] Chinese merchants saved on business overhead and living expenses (and presumably passed the savings on to their Mexican clients) in two major ways. First, they stored their unused stock in their business establishments rather than incurring further expense through the storage of such items in a separate warehouse location. Secondly, to lower their living expenses, Chinese merchants commonly lived in their stores. These two business practices allowed the Chinese to cut down on their overall expenses, thereby allowing them to offer their goods at low prices with which native Mexican merchants could not compete. Under the guise of public health considerations, Sonoran state public health director Dr. Antonio Quiroga promulgated, on November 12, 1930, a government circular targeting such business practices. His decree banned the Chinese practice of living in business establishments and ordered that all merchandise that blocked the entrance of sunlight and air, and which impeded the free flow of foot traffic, be removed from grocery store premises.

In addition to their use of legislation for the purpose of attacking the Chinese commercial monopoly, leaders of the anti-immigrant movement also lobbied for the creation of laws that codified their racist attitudes related to the proper bounds of Chinese–Mexican social interaction. On December 13, 1923, the Sonoran XXVII Legislatura Local passed two laws aimed at geographically isolating the Chinese immigrant community and ending the practice of intermarriage between Chinese immigrant males and native Mexican women. The first of these laws, "Ley 29" (Law 29), sought to segregate Chinese immigrants through the formation of residential ethnic barrios. As discussed in chapter 4, "Ley 31" (Law 31) prohibited interracial marriage between Mexican females and all Chinese males, barring even unions involving Chinese men who had become naturalized Mexican citizens. Violation of this miscegenation ban was to result in the payment of a fine ranging from $100 (Mexican) to $500.

In sum, through the promulgation of various types of invidious legislation and governmental circulars, such as Leyes 29 and 31, the 80 percent labor law, and Quiroga's public health circular of 1930, proponents of the anti-Chinese movement sought both to crush the Chinese commercial monopoly and to codify their racist perspectives pertaining to the proper bounds of Mexican–Chinese social interaction.

Chinese Legal Responses

In response to widespread public hostility and the legal assault waged against it by the leaders of the anti-Chinese movement, the Chinese immigrant community defended its legal and economic interests through the employment of top-flight Mexican attorneys known derisively as "chineros" or "Chinaman lovers." Through the hiring of such attorneys, Chinese immigrants challenged the constitutionality and application of invidious legislation aimed against them, sometimes even taking their cases all the way to the Mexican supreme court.

A review of Mexican Supreme Court cases from the years 1917, 1918, 1919, 1920, 1927, 1929, 1930, 1931, and 1932 revealed a total of twenty-five cases involving Chinese petitioners or participants.[67] Chinese immigrants sought legal protection from Mexico's highest court in regard to a wide range of criminal and civil legal matters, from homicide to violation of public health laws. Chinese legal petitions involved the following eclectic mix of subjects: violation of racial intermarriage laws; detention and deportation for violation of public health laws; the closure of a Chinese casino; the removal of a vendor's booth from a public sidewalk; criminal charges of battery, embezzlement, robbery, drug sales, and homicide; a Chinese soldier's challenge to a death penalty sentence for military insubordination; landlord–tenant contract law; a civil suit brought by the estate of a Chinese female domestic for thirty years of back pay; criminal prosecution for the smuggling of goods in the kitchen of a train; a restaurant owner's challenge of fines for violation of public health laws and the imprisonment of one of his employees for failure to pay this fine; violation of a 70 percent labor law in Baja California; labor law claims brought against a plantation owner by a Chinese union leader; and charges raised against Chinese merchants for illegal labor practices.

Jim Lim, Man Lim, Santiago Lee, Sam Tung, and Francisco Hing are just five of the Chinese immigrants who brought legal petitions before the Mexican Supreme Court in the early twentieth century.

Petition of Jim Lim and Man Lim

Jim Lim owned a restaurant in Mexicali, Baja California, called Tivoli.[68] Man Lim, presumably a close relative of Jim Lim, worked as an employee of the Tivoli restaurant.

According to the city public health delegate, on a visit to the restaurant, he observed a piece of rotting meat and decomposing lettuce that were destined for preparation and sale to the public. A fine of 100 pesos was subsequently levied against Man Lim but was not paid. In response, the Department of Public Health arrested Man Lim for failure to pay the fine and also pursued Jim Lim for nonpayment of the fine.

In their petition, the Lims challenged both the imposition of the fine and the imprisonment of Man Lim. They alleged that the public health official based his judgment about the rotting meat and lettuce not upon objective expert criteria, but only upon his own opinion. They also asserted that it was not proven that the lettuce and meat were going to be sold to the public. In addition, the Lims asserted that Man's imprisonment was completely arbitrary, because he had not committed any crime or made any mistake meriting incarceration.

The Mexican Supreme Court denied the Lims' petition with respect to the fine on procedural grounds, asserting that the Lims neglected to make use of a further recourse of appeal established in the sanitation code. The court granted Man Lim's petition with respect to the more serious issue of incarceration, arguing that the Department of Public Health did not legally possess the right to arrest people for violation of public health laws.

The Santiago Lee Case

Santiago Lee owned a bar in the city of Matamóros, Tamaulipas, and was charged by local police with the crime of selling drugs. As part of a sting operation, Lee gave heroin without charge to his Mexican chauffeur, Juan Pena. In return, Pena gave Lee five dollars for the drugs, stating that he was buying them for an American. In his confession to police, Lee asserted that he had found the drugs while cleaning his bar. The municipal court of Matamóros ruled that Lee was guilty of selling drugs and sentenced him to three years in prison, a fine of 500 pesos, and the closure of his bar. Following unsuccessful appeals to the state court of appeals and the Public Ministry, Lee's attorney, Guadalupe Jaramillo, filed a successful petition with the Mexican Supreme Court.

The court absolved Santiago Lee of all charges against him and all penalties associated with the case. Although Lee was caught by police in the possession of drugs with the intent to sell, the court held that state drug laws of Tamaulipas were incorrectly applied to him, because he never actually consummated a sale of drugs with his chauffeur. As a result, the only applicable laws in this case were federal drug laws. Since such federal laws were outside the jurisdiction of the state of Tamaulipas, this case represented a violation of Lee's procedural due process rights, and all charges were subsequently dropped.

The Sam Tung Case

Sam Tung was the owner of the Good Luck grocery store in Tijuana, Baja California. In winter of 1930, Nicandro Alfonso entered the Good Luck store, ordered some merchandise, and requested that he be given store credit because he did not have money to feed his family. After the denial of his request, Alfonso fled the store, taking the goods with him. Armed with a pistol in hand, Tung subsequently chased Alfonso down the street. After Tung caught up with him, Alfonso grabbed Tung by the throat. In response, Tung fired a shot, wounding Alfonso. Tung was subsequently arrested and jailed by local authorities on charges of criminal battery. Tung was denied bail, based upon the local court's determination that the charges against him warranted a jail sentence of more than five years. Tung subsequently appealed to the Mexican Supreme Court.

The court overturned and revoked the charges against Tung, in part, on grounds of self-defense. In summarizing its ruling, the court stated, "Tung was protecting what was legally his and was acting out of self-protection when he fired his pistol. The aggressor in this case is Nicandro. The judge should have considered this in his sentencing and should not have jailed Tung."

The Francisco Hing Case

Francisco Hing represents another example of a Chinese immigrant who took his legal claim all the way to the Mexican Supreme Court. In September of 1930, the Mexican Supreme Court ruled on the constitutionality of the Sonoran racial intermarriage prohibition as part of an appeal filed by Francisco Hing.[69] In violation of Ley 31, Hing entered into marriage with a Mexican woman in the state of Sonora, and, according to the provisions of the law, his marriage was ruled invalid by local authorities, even though he was a naturalized Mexican citizen. Upon review of the case, the Mexican Supreme Court affirmed the constitutionality of the Sonoran law and ruled Hing's marriage to be invalid. All but one justice, moreover, voted to uphold the validity of the Sonoran legislation and expressed sympathy toward the anti-Chinese movement. In the words of one Mexican federal legislator: "Although we find the opinion of one of the magistrates to be discouraging because he views the Chinese marital exception as hateful and repugnant, we find hope in the opinion of the other magistrates because they consider Chinese immigration undesirable and pernicious for our nation, and they also view as constitutional the Sonoran anti-Chinese law which prohibits intermarriage between Chinese and Mexicans."[70]

Mexican Judicial System as an Offensive Weapon

In addition to using the Mexican legal system as a means of defending its legal and economic rights, the Chinese community also utilized the Mexican judicial system as an offensive weapon against the leaders of the anti-Chinese movement. One poignant example involved the founder of the sinophobic movement in Sonora, José Maria Arana.[71] In October of 1916, shortly after the onset of the organized anti-Chinese campaigns, Arana ran for mayor of the town of Magdalena, Sonora. In an effort to legally disqualify Arana as a candidate in the municipal elections, wealthy Chinese businessman Juan Lung Tain filed a defamation lawsuit against Arana in the days leading up to the election. Tain was allegedly the richest Chinese merchant in all of Sonora, and he claimed that Arana had defamed him in a recent newspaper article by calling him "inhuman and egotistical" and accusing him of refusing to donate money to a local charity founded by General Plutarco Elias Calles.

Upon initial review of the case, local judge Jesús Gallo issued an arrest warrant against Arana. Consequently, state law disqualified Arana from running in the election pending the outcome of the lawsuit. Despite his disqualification, Arana went on to win the mayoral election by a landslide. What followed next was a confusing series of political maneuvers on the part of various state officials that ultimately left Arana bereft of political office. It seems clear from the historical record, moreover, that the Chinese of Sonora worked behind the scenes to broker deals with these state officials to ensure Arana's exclusion from the Magadalena city council.

Because the local court did not make a ruling upon Arana's defamation lawsuit by January 1, 1917, the date on which he was scheduled to take office, the Sonoran state legislature was forced to act. Upon review of the case, the legislature made the determination that another council member would be temporarily appointed to take Arana's place as mayor and also promised to organize a future mayoral election in which Arana would be allowed to run. On January 5, the state supreme court of Sonora subsequently revoked his arrest warrant and absolved him of all charges. This decision left Arana freed from jail and the legal charges against him, but still locked out of political office.

Sympathetic to his situation, a short time later, Magdalena council members appointed Arana to the post of secretary of the town council. The same day of his appointment, Arana was arrested by the state militia and incarcerated in the local jail. Several city councilmen who were supporters of Arana were also subsequently arrested and detained in the municipal jail. Following a period of incarceration in Magdalena, Arana and his colleagues were transferred to a prison in the state capital of Hermosillo for another sixteen days.

Arana's second imprisonment by the state militia was allegedly carried out at the behest of the governor of Sonora, Cesareo Soriano. Governor Soriano imprisoned Arana based upon accusations that the anti-Chinese campaigns had caused serious crimes to be committed against the Chinese of the state. Arana was accused of leading an armed insurrection in Magdalena that led to the murder of Chinese immigrants. Upon hearing these charges against him, Arana remained unrepentant. In a letter dated April 4, 1918, Arana responded to the charges:

> During war Generals and Majors commit crimes but the ideals of the revolutionary struggle should not be judged. If an individual commits a crime, an individual should pay for it. . . . Before I started my campaign there was murder of Chinese by Mexicans and vice versa and after I die it will be the same. If any Chinese was killed by my campaign, I am not personally responsible. . . . Why was I jailed? I don't know. They say that I had led an armed insurrection in Magdalena and beheaded the Chinese like Herods, that I am a destroyer of public peace and accuse me of having killed a Chinese person that was already dying. What grave charges these are. Then why set me free.

At the end of two weeks of imprisonment in Hermosillo, Arana was forced to appear before General Plutarco Elias Calles. Calles reprimanded Arana, pressured him to give up his appointed post of secretary, and subsequently freed him and his colleagues from prison.

Appeals to International Law—The Massacre of Torreón

In addition to hiring Mexican attorneys to represent their socioeconomic interests vis-à-vis local and state laws, the Chinese immigrant community also asserted its political and economic rights through appeals to international law. One such example involved the massacre of Torreón discussed earlier in this chapter.

As part of this ethnic pogrom, which occurred on May 15, 1911, more than three hundred Chinese immigrants were murdered by revolutionary soldiers of Francisco Madero.[72] In addition to the many lives that were claimed as part of the anti-Asian violence, Chinese merchants of Torreón and the neighboring vicinity suffered nearly $850,000 in financial losses as the result of robberies and looting perpetrated by marauding soldiers and civilian mobs.[73]

Following the massacre, the Chinese government hired the Anglo-American law firm of Wilfley and Bassett to investigate the crimes committed against the Chinese community of Torreón and to secure monetary indemnities from the Mexican government for its breach of treaty provisions guaranteeing the protection of Chinese residents.[74] Together with representatives of the Chinese and Mexican governments, the law firm launched an inquiry into the Torreón events within several days of the massacre. Drawing from the findings of this joint investigation, the law firm of Wilfley and Bassett subsequently appealed to the Mexican government for a large monetary indemnity based upon its failure to comply with both previous treaty stipulations and international law. Two years later, Mexico agreed to pay China $3,200,000 as compensation for the murder of Chinese citizens that took place during the massacre.[75] Notwithstanding this official diplomatic agreement, the indemnity remained unpaid as of December 1913.[76]

In sum, in the face of sinophobia, Chinese immigrants defended their legal and economic interests through the employment of top-flight Mexican lawyers. Through the hiring of such attorneys, Chinese immigrants challenged the constitutionality and application of invidious legislation aimed against them, and sometimes even raised their claims before the Mexican Supreme Court. The Chinese immigrant community also manipulated the Mexican legal system as an offensive weapon against the leadership of the anti-Chinese campaigns, and asserted its political and economic rights through appeals to international law.

The Triumph of the Anti-Chinese Movement: Chinese Expulsion from Sonora

The anti-Chinese movement in Sonora delivered the decisive blow against the Chinese immigrant community of that state on August 25, 1931. On that date, Sonoran governor Francisco S. Elias issued the following executive circular, authorizing local municipal authorities to order Chinese merchants to vacate their commercial establishments for noncompliance with the "80 percent labor law":[77]

TO C. MAYOR OF THE CITY COUNCIL.

Having observed that the Chinese merchants do not desire to comply with that laid out by revised Article 106 of the current Law of Labor and Social Precaution, which orders that in every company, workshop, or establishment, employers are required to ensure that 80 percent of their employees or workers are Mexican, instead preferring to close their businesses, and having knowledge that said merchants continue to retain stocks of warehoused merchandise, and who, in continuing this stated condition would cause as a natural consequence a scarcity of articles of primary necessity, this Executive, with the intent of preventing the stated wrongs from occurring which would result in serious harm to the inhabitants of that region, deem it appropriate to recommend that you mayors serve notification to the above-mentioned merchants located in that Jurisdiction who proceed to sell off the merchandise which they still have in their control, doing this as quickly as possible, advising them also to vacate the premises rented for their businesses or stores.

Undoubtedly, national commerce will soon surge following observance of the communicated measures, and those people who will work in these types of activities will have greater facility in finding their own business locations to set up.[78]

As described in the long-winded gubernatorial circular, prior to the issuance of this vacation order, Chinese merchants had unsuccessfully attempted to avoid compliance with the 80 percent labor law through a variety of legal, extralegal, and diplomatic tactics (see fig. 6.6). Chinese merchants tried to circumvent application of the laws through: the hiring of Mexican attorneys who spun creative legal arguments in support of noncompliance; the diplomatic intervention of the plenipotentiary minister of China and the Chinese secretary of legation; the voluntary closure of shops, depriving governmental authorities of large amounts of tax revenue; and, allegedly, through the attempted bribery of governmental officials, and blackmail involving the hoarding of foodstuffs and basic commodities.

In response to Chinese noncompliance with the 80 percent labor law, and specifically in reaction to Chinese hoarding of basic commodities and foodstuffs as part of a tactic dubbed by anti-chinistas "La Ley del Hambre" (The Law of Hunger), Governor Elias issued the vacation order of August 1931. Two months later in October, newly elected Sonoran governor Rodolfo Elias Calles, moreover, promulgated two more discriminatory circulars against the Chinese community.[79] Circulars no. 241 and no. 255, issued on October 14 and 21, respectively, targeted and penalized the attempts made by some Chinese merchants to reopen their businesses

......y el celo de "Las Guardias Verdes" era la prueba más evidente de que el pueblo respaldaba los actos del gobierno.

Figure 6.6. Cartoon depiction of popular enforcement of 80 percent labor law. Sign reads: "80% LAW, OR NO MORE SALES." *Source:* José Angel Espinoza, *El ejemplo de Sonora* (Mexico, D.F.: n.p., 1932), 121.

in both fixed and ambulatory forms, as well as the continuing trend of interracial marriage between Chinese immigrant males and native Mexican women in violation of existing antimiscegenation legislation. The gubernatorial circulars of Elias and Calles engendered the flight of the vast majority of Chinese immigrants of the state by the end of October. Some Chinese relocated to other parts of Mexico such as Sinaloa, Chihuahua, and Mexico City; others were deported by Mexican officials to the United States, presumably forced to illegally cross the international line into the custody of American border patrol officers. Some of the wealthiest of the Chinese colony returned to China, moreover, and some unemployed Chinese immigrants remained wandering in Sonora as vagabonds.[80] The expulsion of the Chinese from Sonora in 1931 represented the first such expulsion of any Chinese diasporic community anywhere in the world during the twentieth century.

Following the mass Chinese exodus from Sonora in 1931, the anti-Chinese movement continued fervently throughout Mexico, with 153 anti-Chinese organizations still in existence in various states and territories outside of Sonora in 1932.[81] Located in various states such as Sinaloa, Chiapas, Veracruz, Tamaulipas, Coahuila, Guanajuato, Durango, and Chihuahua, these organizations continued the assault begun in Sonora against the Chinese colony of Mexico. The ultimate success of these anti-immigrant organizations, and of the Mexican anti-Chinese campaigns in general, may perhaps be measured by the precipitous decline of the Chinese population in the years following the Great Depression. As discussed in chapter 3, based largely upon a numerically small but consistent yearly influx of Chinese immigrants during the second decade of the twentieth century, the Chinese population of Mexico grew to become the second-largest foreign ethnic community in Mexico in 1926, at a size of 24,218.[82] By 1940, however, following the intense persecutions of the organized anti-Chinese movement triggered by the economic downturn of the Great Depression, the number of registered Chinese nationals in Mexico plummeted to 4,856.[83] Based upon this close correlation between the precipitous decline of the Chinese population and the intensification of the anti-Chinese campaigns, as well as upon the documented mass Sonoran expulsions, it seems reasonable to assert that the organized anti-Chinese movement was a major factor contributing to the mass exodus of the Chinese from Mexico during the decade following the Great Depression. From the precipitous numerical decline of the Chinese colony of Mexico during these years, moreover, it appears that the lower-middle-class leaders of the anti-Chinese movement ultimately succeeded in their goal of breaking the Chinese commercial monopoly and eliminating the perceived socioeconomic and political threat posed by the Chinese immigrant community.

An Upper-Class Perspective: Industrial and Agricultural Elites of Frontier and Tropical Mexico

Whereas the Mexican lower middle classes condemned Chinese immigrants as unfair commercial competition and a major obstacle to national economic development, some members of the Mexican upper classes endorsed Chinese immigration as a necessary means of satisfying labor shortages in the commercial sectors of agriculture and industry.[84] As discussed in greater detail in chapters 2 and 3, large-scale Chinese migration to Mexico began after 1900, as a result of the successful governmental lobbying efforts and creative business negotiations of Mexican industrialists and agriculturalists of the lower coastal regions and underpopulated frontier zones. These Mexican capitalists touted Chinese immigration as an effective solution to the problem of regional labor shortages caused by the inability to recruit sufficient numbers of workers from surrounding cities and towns. As an early proponent of Chinese labor immigration, Mexican finance minister Matías Romero articulated this elite, pro-Chinese position in an article published by the Mexico City newspaper, the *Revista Universal*, in 1875: "It seems to me that the only colonists who could establish themselves or work on our coasts are Asians, coming from climates similar to ours, primarily China. The great population of that vast empire, the fact that many of them are agriculturalists, the relatively low wages they earn, and the proximity of our coast to Asia mean that Chinese immigration would be the easiest and most convenient for both our coasts."[85] Porfirian capitalists successfully secured this desired supply of Chinese emigrant workers by lobbying the federal government to negotiate a treaty of amity and commerce with China, and through collaboration with Chinese tong leaders of San Francisco who organized the recruitment and transportation of immigrant laborers to Mexico.

As reflected by the editorial of Matías Romero, moreover, large capitalists supported Chinese immigration because of the willingness of Chinese laborers to work for low wages as compared with native workers. In addition, they sought to promote such emigration because Chinese laborers were perceived to be skillful and persevering.[86] Arguing in defense of Chinese immigration, hacendados and industrialists of the tropics and frontier territories asserted that, in addition to labor shortages, the high cost of subsistence and rising worker salaries threatened to stymie Mexican national economic development. They maintained, moreover, that the inexpensive labor supplied by Chinese immigration provided an effective means of counteracting such destructive economic trends. Ostensibly, the recruitment and importation of Chinese emigrant workers allowed Mexican capitalists to both satisfy their burgeoning labor requirements and cut business expenses related to the payment of employee salaries.

Because of their support of Chinese labor migration, and because of their perceived apathy toward the anti-Chinese movement, large Mexican capitalists drew criticism from members of the lower socioeconomic classes and supporters of the sinophobic campaigns. The following editorial excerpt from the Sonoran newspaper *El Tráfico* (the Traffic), exemplifies lower-middle-class criticism of the pro-Chinese perspective articulated by elites such as Matías Romero. The columnist rejects the viewpoint that Chinese labor is necessary for agricultural and industrial expansion in the frontier regions as posited by large Mexican capitalists, and asserts that Chinese immigrants avoid employment as laborers contrary to the purposes of their initial recruitment:

> The defenders of the yellow race allege that we lack laborers for the growth of agriculture and mining, and, frankly, we would like them to prove to us that assertion, showing us the farm lands cultivated by the Chinese and the lands where the mongol has come to offer a portion of his labor. . . . They provide very isolated cases of some who work cultivating vegetables on a small scale and when they go to a mining camp it is only to set up a place for selling food, to establish a small restaurant, or to work in trade. Where then, is the need that we have for their labor?[87]

Leaders of the organized anti-Chinese movement, furthermore, chided the Mexican upper classes for their perceived antipathy toward the nationalistic campaigns. Anti-chinistas characterized the upper bourgeoisie as selfish, ambitious, and resistant to efforts of the anti-Chinese movement to eliminate the Chinese foreign economic threat. In his 1932 anti-Chinese treatise *El ejemplo de Sonora* (The example of Sonora), José Angel Espinoza decries the antipathy of the upper classes and evidences this lower-middle-class contempt for the Mexican economic elite:

> One of the most vivid and deplorable demonstrations of the antipathy directed towards the anti-Chinese struggle, on the part of almost all government officials and the egotistical and ambitious upper bourgeoisie who owns enormous interests, antipathy which consists of this pitiful truth: even the most insignificant abuse, not of a group, but of one or two overzealous individuals, always creates a great commotion in the columns of the newspapers that we consider such acts to be clearly intended to discredit the cause.[88]

In sum, agriculturalists and industrialists of the lower coastal regions and northern frontier embraced Chinese immigration as a means of filling labor quotas necessary for the expansion of their various commercial enterprises. They turned to Chinese immigration as a convenient and inexpensive solution to the problem of labor shortages caused by the inability to recruit sufficient numbers of native Mexican workers. In response to their support of Chinese labor migration, the Mexican upper classes attracted criticism by other members of Mexican society who opposed the continuing influx of Chinese immigrants. Leaders of the organized anti-Chinese movement, moreover, criticized the Mexican economic elite for their perceived antipathy toward the nationalistic campaigns and depicted them as enemies of "la causa" (the cause).

Perspectives and Policy Responses of the Mexican Federal Government: 1875–1931

This final section of chapter 6 examines various perspectives and policy responses of the Mexican federal government toward Chinese immigration and settlement in Mexico between 1875 and 1931. The analysis for this section is based primarily upon a review of three key governmental reports and publications that, together, trace the evolution of federal attitudes and policies toward Chinese immigration and the Chinese community of Mexico: *Comisión de inmigración; dictamen del vocal ingeniero José Maria Romero, encargado de estudiar la influencia social y económica de la inmigración asiática en Mexico* (*Report of Chairman, Expert José Maria Romero, in Charge of Examining the Social and Economic Influence of Asian Immigration in Mexico*)(1911),[89] *El Servicio de Migración en Mexico por Andrés Landa y Piña jefe del Departamento de Migración* (*The Migration Service in Mexico by Andrés Landa y Piña chief of the Department of Migration*) (1930),[90] and, Departamento de la Estadística Nacional, *Anuario de 1930* (*Department of National Statistics—Annual of 1930*).[91]

As described in the previous analysis of elite perspectives toward Chinese emigration, as well as in chapters 2 and 3, industrialists and hacendados of the northern frontier and tropics persuaded the government regime of Porfirio Díaz to negotiate a treaty of amity and commerce with China in 1899 with the intention of recruiting emigrant laborers for their various commercial enterprises. As evidenced by the writings of Mexican finance minister Matías Romero, as well as by the vigorous diplomatic negotiations leading up to the signing of the treaty between the two former colonial trading partners, the Mexican federal government in the late nineteenth century appeared persuaded as to the viability of Chinese immigration as a solution to the problem of regional labor shortages in the frontier and lower coastal regions.

In 1875 and 1876, Matías Romero publicly advocated for the recruitment of Chinese emigrant laborers in articles published by the *Revista Universal* and *El Correo del Comercio,* two Mexico City periodicals. In these articles, the minister of finance argued that Chinese immigration represented a convenient solution for labor shortages experienced by the coastal haciendas of the "tierra caliente" (hot lands), and he highlighted the economic benefits that would result from increased trade with China and Japan.[92]

Between the years of 1880 and 1899, Romero spearheaded Mexican governmental efforts aimed at establishing official diplomatic ties with China, promoting Chinese labor emigration, and developing increased trade relations between the two nations. Toward these ends, the Mexican government unsuccessfully initiated various efforts between 1882 and 1889. During these years, Romero failed at attempts to negotiate a commercial treaty with China, and the Mexican government achieved only moderate success in promoting increased commercial relations and labor migration between the two nations. Despite the appointment of a Mexican commercial agent at the port of Hong Kong, and the creation of a Mexican steamship company that was granted special privileges to transport goods and immigrants between Mexican and Asian ports, Mexico failed to significantly increase trade relations and promote labor migration from China during these years.

Notwithstanding the many efforts of the Mexican government, real progress toward significant diplomatic relations between the two countries was ultimately achieved at the instigation of the Chinese government in 1891. In that year, Qing imperial representatives called upon Romero to establish a commercial treaty, and in 1899, following another decade of sporadic negotiations, China and Mexico signed a treaty of amity and commerce. This diplomatic accord opened wide the floodgates of Chinese migration to Mexico, as it allowed for "free and voluntary" movement between the two nations. Because it removed all diplomatic impediments to Chinese immigration, this treaty served as the major legal impetus for the formation of the Chinese diasporic community of Mexico.

In sum, the vigorous and persistent diplomatic negotiations initiated by the Mexican government that led to the signing of the Treaty of Amity and Commerce, as well as the publications of Mexican finance minister Matías

Romero, strongly evidence a firm belief on behalf of the Porfirian regime as to the viability and, indeed, the critical importance of Chinese immigration as a solution to the problem of Mexican regional labor shortages.

The Romero Commission Report

Although the Mexican federal government during the late nineteenth century appeared strongly convinced as to the need for the recruitment of Chinese immigrant labor, just a few years after the signing of the Treaty of Amity and Commerce, the "científico" regime of Porfirio Díaz began to reevaluate its policy of promoting Chinese labor migration. In response to fears expressed by the Mexican citizenry related to wide-scale Chinese immigration, on October 17, 1903, President Díaz created a federal commission charged with investigating the socioeconomic impact caused by the massive influx of Chinese immigrants.[93] The commission consisted of five members, including one Lic. Genaro Raigosa, who served as president, Senator C. José Maria Romero, C. Dr. Eduardo Liceaga, C. Lic. Rafael Rebollar, and C. José Covarrubias. The blue ribbon commission focused its analysis on the following four issues:

1. Was it in the best interests of the nation to continue to allow the free immigration of Chinese and Japanese nationals to Mexico?

2. Did Chinese and Japanese immigration have the same effects upon Mexican society? Should the federal government develop different policies toward the two Asian groups?

3. The restriction of Asian immigration, should it not be agreed upon by the commission to permit the free and unfettered influx of immigrants from China and Japan.

4. The proposal of appropriate administrative measures and the development of various constitutional, legislative, and diplomatic reforms.

The federal commission summarized its findings in a 121-page report drafted by commission member José Maria Romero and published in 1911. Entitled *Comisión de inmigración; dictamen del vocal ingeniero José Maria Romero, encargado de estudiar la influencia social y económica de la inmigración asiática en Mexico,* the report concluded that it was not in the national interest to allow the continuance of free and unlimited Chinese immigration.[94] According to Romero, moreover, Chinese immigrants were undesirable both as a source of labor and for purposes of colonizing frontier Mexican territories. Romero summarized his position as follows: "It is not advisable for the national interests to permit the unlimited immigration of Chinese as an element of colonization, be it in group or individual form, free or contracted outside of our territory. . . . Neither is it advisable for the national interests to permit the unlimited and unrestricted immigration of Chinese as an element of manual labor, be it in group or individual form, free or by contracts formed outside of our territory."[95]

In support of his stance against the Chinese, Romero drew from Eurocentric Spencerian racial theory, then in vogue among leaders of the Porfirian government.[96] Consistent with such theory, Romero argued that the immigration of "desirable" ethnic groups facilitates national development, and that the influx of culturally distinct, impoverished emigrant groups, on the other hand, stunts socioeconomic development and thwarts the process of nation building. According to Romero, European immigrants played the most important role in the development of the Americas, both North and South. He credited Europeans for cultivating and colonizing the western U.S. frontier, the pampas of Argentina, the desert territories of Australia, and the rural agricultural lands of Brazil, and he asserted that Asian immigrants, by contrast, were recent arrivals who did not contribute substantially to the progress of the New World.[97]

Romero maintained, moreover, that Chinese immigrants were to be further distinguished from their Occidental counterparts because of their unwillingness to assimilate within their western host societies. According to Romero, Chinese did not emigrate with the intention of permanent settlement, but rather remained in their host countries only long enough to accumulate a sizable savings and return to China. As a consequence, they did not adopt the cultures of the nations to which they immigrated and did not participate within the sociopolitical mainstream of the societies in which they sojourned. In addition, whereas immigrants of various European origins blended easily within their countries of settlement because of cultural commonalities related to language, religion, and custom, Chinese immigrants, on the other hand, derived from a radically different ethnographic branch of the human family and, as a consequence of their distinctive cultural background, did not assimilate well into western society. According to Romero, assimilation was further impeded because of Chinese opposition to cultural mixture, a Chinese belief in the superiority of their civilization to that of Europeans, and their tendency to form secret societies based upon geographical origin. Because of the impossibility of assimilating Chinese immigrants into western civilization, Romero concluded, it was not in the national interest to allow the continuance of free and unlimited Chinese immigration to Mexico.

Romero also argued that wide-scale emigration from China was not in the best interests of Mexico because a massive influx of Chinese immigrants would hinder the socioeconomic advancement and integration of the country's indigenous population. Consistent with the racial theory of "indigenísmo" (nascent among policy makers of the Porfirian regime and fully developed and embraced by ideologues of the postrevolutionary Mexican government), Romero sympathized with the plight of Mexico's indigenous peoples and believed that the solution to their socioeconomic marginalization lay in their noncoercive integration into the Mexican mainstream.[98] According to Romero, the Indians of Mexico exhibited many admirable qualities, including strict morality, great sobriety, obedience, military prowess, and courage; furthermore, they contributed significantly to national development through their participation as laborers in government infrastructural projects related to railway and road construction, and various public works. Despite their many virtues, Romero asserted, the indigenous population remained poor and marginalized, because of their exploitation at the hands of landowners and industrialists, their lack of education, and their isolation from the Mexican mainstream. Consistent with his "indigenísta" perspective, Romero argued that improvement for the Indian community would result from education, modernization, and integration within Creole Mexican society.

According to Romero, wide-scale Chinese immigration would hinder this process of integration and the socioeconomic advancement of the indigenous population. Chinese laborers posed unfair economic competition for Indian laborers and represented a negative cultural influence for the indigenous lower classes. Should Chinese immigrants be recruited en masse, they would be exploited by Mexican industrialists as cheap labor, and, because of their willingness to work for depressed wages, would steal employment from Indian workers. Extensive contact between Chinese immigrants and native Indians, moreover, would pollute indigenous culture, exposing the latter to "the contagion of depraved customs" and engendering "disastrous degeneration."

In sum, the Romero Commission Report of 1911 represents a radical shift in the perspective of the Mexican federal government toward Chinese labor migration. Although the Porfirian government appeared strongly persuaded as to the need for the recruitment of Chinese emigrant laborers during the late nineteenth century, as evidenced by the writings of Matías Romero, and the various diplomatic efforts of the Mexican government that culminated in the signing of the Treaty of Amity and Commerce in 1899, by 1911 the federal government viewed wide-scale Chinese immigration as a threat to the socioeconomic advancement and integration of Mexico's indigenous population. According to the *Comisión de inmigración; dictamen del vocal ingeniero José Maria Romero*, Chinese immigration was not in the best interests of the country, because Chinese immigrants represented both unfair economic competition and a degenerative cultural influence on the indigenous lower classes.

Landa y Piña Report of 1930

Despite this shift in perspective of the Mexican federal government toward Chinese immigration, Chinese movement to Mexico increased substantially during the second and third decades of the twentieth century. Although the Chinese population of Mexico numbered just over a thousand in 1895, by 1926, at a total of 24,218, Chinese immigrants had come to form the second-largest foreign ethnic community in all of Mexico.[99] In 1930, the Mexican Secretaría de Gobernación (secretary of the interior) published a report describing contemporary trends of immigration and emigration, and summarizing federal government perspectives toward Chinese immigration. The federal report, entitled *El Servicio de Migración en Mexico por Andrés Landa y Piña jefe del Departamento de Migración*, continued the critique of the earlier Romero Commission Report and described Asian immigration to Mexico as "an invasion as in a conquered nation."[100] In its comparison of Asian settlement in Mexico with that of a military invasion, the report declared: "In a short period of time, the coastal towns of the Pacific have become invaded by an enormous number of Asians, and from there they came to the towns in the center of the Republic, settling themselves as in a conquered nation, without requirements of any kind, in the places most convenient to them."[101]

In addition, the report portrayed Chinese immigrants as a grave public health threat and as an important cause of Mexican migration to the United

States. According to Landa y Piña, Chinese and other foreign elements brought infectious diseases such as trachoma, bubonic plague, and beriberi into Mexico. Infected immigrants entered Mexico through the bribery of port health inspectors, and by evading health inspection through illicit lifeboat drop-offs on Mexican coasts. In addition to posing a serious public health threat, such foreigners were also a substantial financial burden on the Mexican government, which was forced to support them as a consequence of their inability to secure employment. According to Landa y Piña, these infected emigrants who immigrated to Mexico from China and other parts of the Orient represented the "true scum of humanity."[102]

In addition to depicting Chinese movement to Mexico as a major source of public health problems, Landa y Piña decried the influx of Chinese and other foreigners as an important cause of Mexican migration to the United States. Between the years of 1908 and 1928, approximately 853,038 native Mexicans emigrated from their homeland, with the vast majority, 769,113, settling in the United States. According to Landa y Piña, foreign immigration to Mexico by Chinese and others harmed the Mexican lower classes and served as a major precipitating factor for Mexican emigration. In his view, factors such as the urban nature of immigrant settlement, the paternal protection of the federal government extended toward resident foreigners, immigrant concentration in small-scale commerce and modest employment positions, and the irregular form of foreign integration within Mexican society combined to hurt the Mexican proletariat. Humble Mexicans, as a consequence, were forced to migrate from the cities to rural areas in search of employment. In rural settlements, however, they encountered various types of abuse and exploitation that led them eventually to migrate to the United States. In the countryside they were paid low wages, treated harshly by hacienda managers, drafted into the military, and forced to travel constantly in search of employment. In response to such horrible treatment, Landa y Piña asserts, Mexican workers immigrated to the United States, where they were welcomed and provided with high-paid employment opportunities.

The Landa y Piña report, therefore, like the Romero Commission Report of 1911, presents a negative view of the Mexican federal government toward Chinese immigration and settlement in Mexico. Whereas José Maria Romero depicted the Chinese as an obstacle to the integration and socioeconomic improvement of the indigenous community, Landa y Piña highlighted the public health threat posed by wide-scale Chinese immigration to Mexico and criticized the influx of Chinese for being an important cause of Mexican flight to the United States. Both reports strongly evidence a dramatic shift in the perspective of the Mexican federal government toward Chinese migration as compared with the favorable Porfirian view of the late nineteenth century.

Federal Government Policy Responses, 1908–1931

In response to the perceived Chinese socioeconomic threat, the Mexican federal government during the early twentieth century enacted a series of legislative and public policy measures aimed at eliminating the Chinese public health nuisance and at extending economic protection to the native working classes. On December 22, 1908, following the publication of various essays that raised concern about the public health threat posed by foreign immigration and which criticized Mexico's free immigration policies, the Mexican federal government passed La Ley de Inmigración de los Estados Unidos Mexicanos (the Immigration Law of the United Mexican States).[103] This legislation created two new government agencies—the Servicio de Migración (Migration Service) and the Servicio de Inspeccion de Inmigrantes (Immigrant Inspection Service)—the latter being charged with the task of inspecting incoming immigrants and preventing the entrance of those infected with disease or deemed morally unfit.[104] According to the Landa y Piña report, the agency was ultimately unsuccessful in its efforts to restrict the entrance of undesirable foreign nationals because of the vague restriction criteria established by the 1908 legislation. The law barred entry to those of "notoria incapacidad en el órden moral y en el sanitario" (obvious moral and medical incapacity), and examiners found it difficult to evaluate the moral fitness of incoming immigrants. As a consequence of these vague requirements, according to Landa y Piña, Mexico attracted heterogeneous and undesirable immigrants who had earlier been denied entrance into other countries.

The Ley de Inmigración of 1908 was also viewed as a failure by the federal government, because it did not possess provisions for the suspension or limitation of the entrance of foreign laborers.[105] As a consequence, allegedly, the Mexican working classes were hurt by the unfair competition of immigrant laborers, who worked for depressed wages. Moreover, as previously discussed, according to Landa y Piña, this foreign economic competition represented an important cause of widespread Mexican emigration.

In response to the perceived failures and limitations of the Ley de Inmigración, special remedial legislation drafted by officials of the Servicio de Inspeccion de Inmigrantes was delivered to the Mexican congress in September of 1923.[106] Following the presentation of the proposed legislation, instead of passing the relevant immigration laws, the Mexican congress granted special legislative authority to the executive branch to create the new legislation. The result was the promulgation of La Ley de Migración de Los Estados Unidos Mexicanos (the Migration Law of the United Mexican States), in 1926. The law, drafted by a commission approved by both President Plutarco Elias Calles and the Secretaría de Gobernación, sought to more closely regulate foreign immigration, to control the problem of Mexican emigration, and to extend greater protections to native and immigrant laborers. Toward these ends, the Ley de Migración mandated that all incoming immigrant laborers be required to possess a labor contract, established a registry for nationals and foreigners seeking to leave or enter the country, and implemented the use of standardized identification cards for both immigrants and emigrants. In addition, the 1926 legislation granted the Secretaría de Gobernación special powers to establish temporary prohibitions on the entry of foreign laborers in the event of future national labor shortages, and authority to institute policies aimed at preventing Mexican workers from illegally entering the United States. The Ley de Migración, also required the Secretaría de Gobernación to establish immigration/emigration surveillance offices throughout Mexico and left ultimate authority over the admission or rejection of newly arrived immigrants in the hands of the Servicio de Salubridad (Public Health Service) and special "Delegados Sanitarios" (Sanitation Agents). The Ley de Migración was brought into effect on June 1, 1926.

In July of 1931, the Mexican federal government issued further policy rulings targeting the Chinese and other foreign immigrant groups, which sought to extend greater economic protection to the Mexican lower classes. Drawing upon the special powers granted by article 50 of the 1926 Ley de Migración, on July 14, 1931, the Ejecutivo Federal (Federal Executive), through the Secretaría de Gobernación, issued a disposition temporarily barring the entrance of immigrant laborers into the country.[107] Seeking to protect the Mexican working classes in the face of depressed labor markets, the federal decree denied admission to, and defined as laborers, all foreign emigrants possessing less than 10,000 pesos of investment capital.

Potential immigrants in possession of at least 10,000 pesos could gain legal entrance into Mexico based upon a special commercial investment exemption, provided that they invest their capital within six months after entering the country, and only if the financial returns from such investments would be sufficient to cover the living expenses of the immigrant investor and those of his household. The restriction order also provided exemption for professionals, technical specialists, travel agents, landlords, minors under the age of eighteen entering for educational purposes, and immigrants hailing from nations with which Mexico had entered contrary diplomatic agreements. According to the provisions of the disposition, the immigration ban was to remain in effect until decided by the Secretaría de Gobernación, and in accordance with the goals of the 1926 Ley de Migración.

On July 21, 1931, just one week after the decree of the Secretaría de Gobernación barring foreign immigrant laborers from admission to Mexico, the Mexican Cámara de Diputados (House of Representatives) approved national labor legislation requiring commercial employers to hire at least 90 percent native Mexican employees.[108] In striking similarity to the 80 percent labor law of Sonora, this federal legislation mandated that at least 90 percent of the employees of every business establishment, regardless of the national origins of its owners, be native-born Mexicans, in both skilled and unskilled labor positions. Based upon the similarity of the federal labor law to that of the Sonoran state legislation, as well as in view of the fact that the organized anti-Chinese movement was at its height during the summer of 1931, it would appear that this federal legislation targeted Chinese merchants of Sonora, and of other states throughout the nation, whose common business practice it was to employ little or no non-Chinese help. This 90 percent labor requirement was included as part of larger federal labor legislation known collectively as the Ley de Trabajo (the Labor Law).

In sum, the Mexican federal government enacted various legislative and public policy measures against the Chinese and other foreign immigrants during the first three decades of the twentieth century. Through such major federal legislation as the 1908 Ley de Inmigración, the 1926 Ley de Migración, and the 1931 Ley de Trabajo, Mexican federal authorities sought to eliminate the perceived public health and economic threat posed by foreign groups such as the Chinese. Such anti-immigrant legislation further evidences the radical shift in the perspective of the Mexican

federal government toward Chinese immigration and settlement as compared with the pro-Chinese Porfirian view of the late nineteenth century.

Conclusion

The anti-Chinese campaigns represent a dark and forgotten chapter of
Mexican history. Accounts of the massacre of Torreón and the organized
sinophobic campaigns are conspicuously absent from traditional historical narratives of the Mexican Revolution. According to "official" Mexican
history, the Revolution was a heroic and patriotic social and political
movement that expunged oppressive American and European capitalist
interests from Mexico. As this chapter has endeavored to show, Chinese
immigrants were also condemned by certain factions of the Revolution
as foreigners who had grown rich based upon the exploitation of the
Mexican people. As a result, sinophobia developed into a patriotic expression of the Mexican Revolution, and the Chinese became open targets
for murder, robbery, looting, boycotts, invidious legislation, and ultimate
expulsion from the state of Sonora in 1931. The persecution experienced
by the Chinese in Mexico equaled or surpassed that of any other Chinese
diasporic community anywhere in the world during the twentieth century.

The organized anti-Chinese campaigns were spearheaded by disgruntled Mexican merchants and embraced by members of the working class
of northern Mexico. To garner broad-based support for their movement,
anti-chinistas couched their complaints against the Chinese in terms of
revolutionary economic nationalism. They asserted that the Chinese had
become rich at the expense of humble Mexicans, blamed the Chinese for
the depreciation of Mexican currency and rising food costs, and chided
Chinese immigrants for their occupation of categories of employment
traditionally reserved for Mexican women. In addition, they decried
Chinese-Mexican racial intermarriage as engendering the downfall of
the Mexican "race," portrayed the Chinese as a serious public health
nuisance, and alleged that Chinese immigrants were a major source of
vice and crime. Notwithstanding the elaborate and well-developed body
of sinophobic rhetoric and propaganda, the true motivation of lower-
middle-class sinophobes like Arana and Espinoza was much more selfish—through the anti-Chinese campaigns they sought to end the Chinese
commercial monopoly and eliminate the Chinese small businessman,
with whom they could not effectively compete.

Contrary to popular conception, the Chinese were not passive victims of revolutionary sinophobia. In resistance to widespread public hostility and racist laws, the Chinese immigrant community hired top-flight Mexican attorneys known derisively as "chineros." Through the hiring of such attorneys, Chinese immigrants challenged the constitutionality and application of invidious legislation aimed against them, sometimes taking their cases all the way to the highest court in the land. The Chinese immigrant community also utilized the Mexican legal system as an offensive weapon against leaders of the anti-Chinese movement and asserted its political and economic rights through appeals to international law.

In contradistinction to both the lower middle and subaltern classes, some members of the Mexican economic elite advocated for Chinese immigration and settlement. Mexican industrialists and plantation owners of frontier northern Mexico and the lower coastal regions embraced Chinese immigration as a means of solving regional labor shortages caused by the inability to recruit sufficient numbers of native Mexican workers.

In the late nineteenth century, the Porfirian government appeared to be in agreement with members of the Mexican upper classes who viewed Chinese emigrant labor recruitment as a viable means of filling industrial and agricultural worker shortages. Toward the end of promoting free and unlimited Chinese labor migration to Mexico, in 1899 the Mexican federal government signed a treaty of amity and commerce with China. Just several years after entering into this diplomatic agreement with China, which opened wide the floodgates of Chinese immigration to Mexico, however, the federal government began to reevaluate its official policy towards the Chinese.

The first three decades of the twentieth century evidenced a radical shift in the attitudes and perspectives of the Mexican federal government toward Chinese immigration. Whereas earlier writings of the late nineteenth century favorably portrayed Chinese movement to Mexico as beneficial for the health of the national economy, the Romero Commission Report of 1911, and the later Landa y Piña report of 1930, present negative governmental views toward Chinese immigration and settlement in Mexico. According to the report of José Maria Romero, free and unlimited Chinese migration to Mexico was not in the best interests of the country, because such immigration represented a grave threat to the socioeconomic advancement and integration of Mexico's indigenous population.

In agreement with Romero, Landa y Piña also viewed Chinese immigrants as undesirable. For Landa y Piña, however, Chinese immigrants posed a threat to the nation because they represented a serious public health threat and because their economic competition was an important cause of Mexican flight to the United States.

Consistent with this change of perspective toward the Chinese, the Mexican federal government promulgated a series of legislative and policy measures in the early twentieth century aimed at eliminating the perceived Chinese socioeconomic threat. Through the passage of national legislation such as the 1908 Ley de Inmigración, the 1926 Ley de Migración, and the 1931 Ley de Trabajo, the Mexican federal government attempted to more closely regulate Chinese immigration, eliminate the alleged Chinese public health nuisance, and extend greater economic protection to the native Mexican working classes.

7
Conclusion
Re-envisioning Mestizaje and "Asian-Latino" Studies

This book has endeavored to tell and to preserve the forgotten history of Pablo Chee, Ricardo Cuan, Alejandro Chan, and the thousands of Chinese who immigrated to Mexico during the late nineteenth and early twentieth centuries. It has attempted to trace their stories and to recreate, however humbly, a picture of daily life within the Chinese immigrant community of Mexico during these years. Beyond such academic aims, it is hoped that this book will dignify the memory of these immigrants by capturing, in a small but significant way, the beauty of their corporate perseverance and resilience in the face of overwhelming historical, socioeconomic, and political circumstances.

Together with Chee, Cuan, and Chan, tens of thousands of Chinese immigrants traversed the Chinese transnational commercial orbit of the Americas during the late nineteenth and early twentieth centuries in search of economic opportunity. Fleeing great socioeconomic and political instability in southern China, many of these immigrants traveled to Big Lusong in search of employment opportunities within the developing Mexican economy. As demonstrated by the life story of Alejandro Chan, many also entered Mexico with an eye to crossing into the United States—legally or illegally—after a brief sojourn in Mexico.

Prior to the passage of the Chinese Exclusion Act of 1882, Mexico was not a primary destination for immigrants of the Chinese diaspora. Although small numbers of Chinese began to settle in Mexico in the 1860s and '70s, the United States represented the main receiving country of Chinese immigrants in the Americas during the mid-nineteenth century. Drawn by the allure of the California gold rush and employment opportunities in railroad construction, industry, and agriculture, more than 300,000 Cantonese immigrants journeyed to the United States between the years of 1848 and 1882. Following the passage of the Chinese Exclusion Act of 1882, which barred the immigration of Chinese laborers to the United States, many Chinese turned their sights to Mexico as a new land of economic opportunity.

Wide-scale Chinese migration to Mexico after 1882 was made possible by the development of the "Chinese transnational commercial orbit." In resistance, and adaptation, to the Chinese Exclusion Laws, entrepreneurial Chinese of San Francisco and Latin America created the transnational commercial orbit to facilitate the lucrative businesses of immigrant smuggling and contract labor recruitment. As a means of circumventing the legal restrictions on Chinese settlement in the United States, Chinese merchants and capitalists "invented" undocumented immigration from Mexico to the United States and developed a highly sophisticated transnational immigrant smuggling network involving representatives in China, Mexico, Cuba, and various cities throughout the United States. As part of their efforts to expand their business in illicit human trafficking, they devised a multiplicity of schemes, procedures, and techniques, which utilized "coyotes," corrupt immigration officials, insider connections in the transportation industry, and legal loopholes in immigration policy. Chinese immigrant smuggling comprised the first important economic activity of the transnational commercial orbit.

Transnational Chinese merchants of San Francisco also partnered with the Mexican government to recruit Chinese contract laborers for the haciendas, ranchos, and mines of northern Mexico. Following the failure to attract substantial numbers of European immigrants to facilitate its plan of economic modernization and fill labor shortages in the farming and mining territories of the northern frontier, the Mexican government looked to Chinese immigration as an alternative. As part of its efforts to promote Chinese immigration, the Mexican government negotiated a treaty of amity and commerce with China in 1899 and turned to Chinese merchants of San Francisco to assist in the recruitment of Chinese immigrant laborers. Together, they created a profitable and effective scheme of transnational labor contracting. This contract labor recruitment represented a second important activity of the transnational Chinese commercial orbit. Immigrant smuggling and contract labor recruitment operated within the same transnational commercial network and involved many of the same key financial business interests and players.

Although the Chinese were initially recruited to Mexico under contract, and significant numbers earned their livelihoods as agricultural laborers and urban unskilled employees, many Chinese immigrants transitioned into employment as merchants and skilled artisans, who comprised the privileged, wealthier, and more assimilated social class of the Chinese overseas community. Their greater privilege, wealth, and access

to lucrative employment opportunities were often shaped by kinship connections to other, more established immigrants residing in Mexico.

Chinese borderlands merchants were highly successful and generally
fell into one of four distinct categories: the immigrant merchant magnate,
the medium-sized merchant, the small merchant, and the sole proprietor. Membership in one of these specific categories was determined by
various factors such as diversification of investments, capitalization, and
participation in transnational commerce. Each of these merchant types
served a vital function in the development and day-to-day operations of
the Chinese transnational commercial orbit.

Chinese commercial success was made possible by unique business
practices and various "class" and "ethnic" resources. Transnational capital
recruitment and transnational wholesaling represent two distinct business
practices and "class resources" that allowed Chinese borderlands merchants to thrive vis-à-vis their aspiring Mexican counterparts. Nepotistic
hiring patterns and sojourner attitudes are examples of "ethnic resources"
that allowed Chinese merchants to maximize commercial profits through
the minimization of expenditures related to business overhead, room, and
board. Because of the great economic prosperity experienced by Chinese
immigrants, by the 1920s Mexico became a central hub of the Chinese
diaspora in the Americas.

Chinese mercantile success engendered jealousy and resentment on
the part of lower-middle-class Mexican merchants of Sonora and led to
the development of the organized anti-Chinese campaigns. José Maria
Arana and other leaders of the sinophobic movement plainly delineated
their goals to be: (1) the promotion of the interests of the Mexican businessman through all possible means, and (2) the use of all measures
allowed by law to bring about the extinction of the Chinese merchant
class. Unfortunately, contrary to the stated goals of Arana and his cronies,
anti-Chinese sentiment frequently expressed itself in extralegal acts of
violence, robbery, and murder. Such sinophobic violence rivaled, and
in many cases exceeded, that experienced by any Chinese diasporic
community in the world during the twentieth century. Between 1911 and
1919 alone, more than five hundred Chinese were killed by disgruntled
revolutionary soldiers and Mexican civilians. During the early years of the
Mexican Revolution, Chinese immigrants filed more than six hundred
property claims, totaling more than one million dollars in economic
losses. The most horrendous outbreak of violence against the Chinese
occurred in 1911, during the massacre of Torreón. As part of this two-day

revolutionary massacre, more than three hundred Chinese and Japanese immigrants were murdered by Maderista soldiers in the city of Torreón in Coahuila, Mexico.

Anti-chinistas couched their complaints against the Chinese in a rhetoric of economic nationalism. Revolutionary activists associated Chinese merchants with U.S. and European capitalist interests, which they blamed for the downturn of the national economy and the commercial exploitation of the Mexican populace. They claimed that the Chinese had become rich at the expense of humble Mexicans, and that they took away jobs traditionally reserved for Mexican women. They also blamed the Chinese for rising food costs and the depreciation of Mexican currency.

As part of their larger body of propaganda against the Chinese, leaders of the anti-Chinese movement also condemned the Chinese as a public health nuisance and alleged that they were a major source of vice and crime. An important touchstone issue of the anti-Chinese campaigns was the topic of Chinese-Mexican intermarriage. Interracial marriage with prosperous Chinese merchants was scornfully depicted as a shameless shortcut by which slothful Mexican women avoided the need to work and secured lives of material comfort. Such women were shunned as "dirty," "wretched," "lazy," and disloyal to the Mexican nation. Chinese-Mexican offspring, moreover, were rejected by leaders of the sinophobic move-ment as subhuman, racially degenerate, and unworthy of full inclusion within the postrevolutionary Mexican nation-state. As a matter of fact, many Chinese male immigrants did intermarry with Mexican women, and some, like Pablo Chee, maintained transnational marriages with their Mexican wives and children who lived overseas in China.

Contrary to popular belief, the Chinese were not passive victims of the sinophobic campaigns. Chinese immigrants defended their socioeco-nomic and political interests through the development of transnational community organizations such as the Chee Kung Tong and the Guo Min Dang. In addition, they contested a wide assortment of anti-Chinese laws by hiring first-rate Mexican attorneys who represented them in local, state, and federal courts. Large numbers of Chinese even brought suc-cessful legal claims before the Mexican Supreme Court. Beyond using the Mexican legal system for defensive purposes, the Chinese also utilized the court system aggressively as a means of legally and politically paralyzing the anti-Chinese campaign of José Maria Arana.

In the end, the anti-Chinese movement won out, and the Chinese were expelled from the state of Sonora. On August 25, 1931, Sonoran governor

Francisco S. Elias issued an executive order that authorized city officials to order Chinese merchants to vacate their commercial establishments for failing to comply with the 80 percent labor law. In response to this gubernatorial order and related orders issued two months later, most Chinese fled the state of Sonora by the end of October 1931. Some relocated to friendlier states and localities in Mexico, such as Sinaloa, Chihuahua, and Mexico City; others were forced to cross into the United States, where they were apprehended by the Immigration and Naturalization Service and deported to China at the expense of the American government; some of the wealthiest members of the Chinese Sonoran community returned to China. This Chinese mass exodus from Sonora in 1931 represents the first expulsion of any Chinese diasporic community in the world during the twentieth century. As a consequence of the Sonoran expulsions and the intense persecution of the sinophobic campaigns, by 1940 the Chinese population, which once constituted the second-largest immigrant community in all of Mexico, plummeted to less than five thousand. To this day, the Chinese immigrant community of Mexico has never recovered.

Re-envisioning Mestizaje

Beyond presenting a social history of the Chinese in Mexico, this book challenges traditional notions of "mestizaje." Despite the historical presence of tens of thousands of Chinese in Mexico, Mexican culture is most frequently depicted as resulting from the racial mixture, or mestizaje, of only two races—the indigenous and European. This limited view of Mexican mestizaje is prevalent within both popular and academic discourse, and is the dominant view articulated by scholars of Latin American studies and of my own field of Chicana/o studies.

Since its inception in the early 1970s, the academic discipline of Chicana/o studies has largely embraced this faulty racial model of mestizaje, emphasizing the dual cultural contributions of the Spanish and the indigenous peoples of Mexico. Drawing on the Mexican post-revolutionary writings of José Vasconcelos, Manuel Gámio, and Alfonso Caso, most existing Chicana/o studies scholarship describes Mexico as a mestizo society resulting from the collision of Spanish and indigenous cultural elements. Emblematic of this dominant view, "El Plan Espiritual de Aztlán," an important manifesto of the Chicano movement, states: "With our heart in our hands and our hands in the soil, we declare the independence of our *mestizo* nation. We are a bronze people with a bronze culture. Before the world, before all of North America, before all our brothers in the bronze continent, we are a nation, we are a union of free pueblos, we are *Aztlán*."[1]

One of the central implications of this book is that such traditional notions of mestizaje must be revisited and revised to account for the significant cultural contributions made by the Chinese to Mexican society and to the process of postrevolutionary Mexican racial formation. Since their physical expulsion from Sonora in 1931, the Chinese have also experienced ideological exile from popular and academic notions of Mexican mestizaje. In light of the hundredth anniversary of the Mexican Revolution, it is time for the Chinese to return from intellectual exile and become fully integrated into "Aztlán" and the racial theorization of Latin American and Chicano/Latino studies.

In addition to its theoretical contributions related to the theory of mestizaje, this book also provides important historical context for understanding the contemporary Asian-Latino community of the United States, Asian-Latino relations, and Asian-Latino coalition building. The 2000 U.S. census recorded the presence of more than 300,000 individuals of Asian-Latino ancestry. These individuals fell into two categories: (1) Latino persons of full Asian ancestry, presumably ethnic Asians who immigrated from Mexico and other parts of Latin America to the United States, and (2) persons of mixed Latino and Asian ancestry. There is scant research on this huge community of Asian-Latinos, and the discipline of Chicano/Latino studies needs to wrestle with how to incorporate these individuals within the existing racial theory of the field. This book on Chinese immigration and settlement in Mexico provides important historical context for understanding this contemporary phenomenon. Indeed, many Asian-Latinos of the United States can trace their ancestry to Chinese immigrants who first settled and intermarried in Mexico during the early twentieth century.

In addition to the secondary migration of large numbers of Asians from Latin America to the United States, "Chino-Chicano" communities are rapidly developing in Los Angeles. Within the past twenty years, cities of the San Gabriel Valley such as Alhambra, Monterey Park, Hacienda Heights, Rosemead, and El Monte have been transformed into Asian-Latino communities in which Chinese-ancestry and Mexican-ancestry populations make up the majority. With the development of these interracial communities have come Chinese–Mexican racial tensions and conflict in the educational and political arenas. Although few may realize it, these racial tensions are not new and have deep historical roots: the two groups have met before. Fortunately, in addition to the conflict that has resulted from the recent development of Chino-Chicano communities, efforts have also begun to build Asian-Latino coalitions.

Toward a Perspective on "Chino-Chicano"/ Asian-Latino Studies

Finally, this monograph also suggests the need for the creation of a new intellectual space within the disciplines of Latin American, Latino, and Chicano studies that explores the historical and contemporary interactions between Asians and Latinos in both Latin America and the United States. Such an intellectual program might be termed, "Asian-Latino Studies" or, more playfully, "Chino-Chicano Studies," and would fuse the research agendas of Latin American studies, Chicano/Latino studies, and Asian American studies. This new field of research would examine the historical trajectory of Latino–Asian and Chino–Chicano relations in the United States, Mexico, and Latin America from the sixteenth century to the present. In addition, it would uncover and analyze the often-overlooked Asian contributions to Latin American and Chicano/ Latino culture and identity.

As a further topic of inquiry, Chino-Chicano studies would examine the historical and sociological experiences of Chicanos/Latinos of Chinese, Asian, and partial Asian ancestry living in the United States. As specific topics of research, it would analyze their experiences of cultural adaptation in the United States as well as the variations of ethnic/cultural identity possessed by this unique segment of the Chicano/Latino community. Insofar as this book offers an analysis of Chinese immigration and settlement in Mexico during the early twentieth century, it provides the historical context for understanding contemporary Chino-Chicano identity and cultural relations, and represents a small but important step toward the development of the new field of Asian-Latino, or Chino-Chicano, studies.

Notes

files, Record Group 85, National Archives,
Chee, file no. 2295/7 (hereafter cited as NA
Laguna, Pablo Chee).

2. C. Luther Fry, "Illegal Entry of Orientals into the United States between 1910 and 1920," *Journal of the American Statistical Association* 23 (June 1928): 176.

3. As is discussed further in chapter 2, the immigration restrictions of the Chinese Exclusion Act of 1882 were extended by federal legislation in 1892 and 1904. This bar to Chinese immigration was not officially lifted until 1943.

4. At a size of 48,558, Spaniards formed the largest ethnic minority group.

5. The Chinese expulsion from Mexico represented the first such expulsion of any Chinese diasporic community in the world during the twentieth century.

6. Madeline Hsu, *Dreaming of Gold, Dreaming of Home: Transnationalism and Migration between the United States and South China, 1882–1943* (Stanford: Stanford University Press, 2000), 7.

7. Erika Lee, *At America's Gates: Chinese Immigration during the Exclusion Era, 1882–1943* (Chapel Hill: University of North Carolina Press), 158.

8. For more on the Chinese transnational commercial orbit, see Robert Chao Romero, "Transnational Commercial Orbits," in *A Companion to California History,* ed. William Deverell and David Igler (Malden, Mass.: Blackwell, 2008).

9. Chinese Exclusion Act case files, Record Group 85, National Archives, Laguna Niguel, California, Cuan Sun (Ricardo Cuan), file no. 14036/88 (hereafter cited as NA Laguna, Cuan Sun [Ricardo Cuan]); Chinese Exclusion Act case files. Record Group 85. National Archives, Laguna Niguel, California, Federico Cham, no. 25100/38 (hereafter cited as NA Laguna, Federico Cham).

10. NA Laguna, Pablo Chee; NA Laguna, Cuan Sun (Ricardo Cuan); NA Laguna, Federico Cham; Laguna Niguel, California, National Archives, Ley Chip or Rodolfo Ley, Chinese Exclusion Act Case File no. 4067/728 (hereafter cited as NA Laguna, Lee Chip [Rodolfo Ley]).

11. Laurence J. C. Ma and Carolyn L. Cartier, *The Chinese Diaspora: Space, Place, Mobility, and Identity* (Lanham, Md.: Rowman & Littlefield, 2003), 8.

12. Based upon data compiled from *International Migrations,* vol. 1, *Statistics, Compiled on Behalf of the International Labour Office, Geneva,* ed. Walter F. Wilcox (New York: National Bureau of Economic Research, 1929), 149; Mexico, Secretaría de la Economía Nacional, *Quinto censo de población 1930, resúmen general* (Mexico, D.F.: Dirección General de Estadistica); Mexico, Secretaría de la Economía Nacional, *Anuário estadístico de la República Mexicana 1930* (Mexico, D.F.: Dirección General de Estadística).

13. The "tong" in "tong wars" is "tang" in Modern Chinese. This term literally means "hall," but by extension it is commonly used to mean "family lineage." Before, during, and after the Qing dynasty (1644–1911), family lineage organizations were extremely powerful, especially in southern/southeastern Chinese provinces like Guangdong and Fujian. Some entire villages were essentially controlled by some of the more powerful lineages, which were often run like corporate units, holding property, investing capital, and performing charity in the name of a huge extended lineage. Lineages sometimes even engaged in dramatic feuds with other lineages. By the end of the eighteenth century, famous illicit organizations, like the Heaven and Earth Society (often called by the catch-all name the Triads) began using the organizing principles of the "tang" lineage to found their own groups dedicated to both legal and illegal corporate activities. For a definitive work on the topic of family lineage organizations, see Zheng Zhenman, *Family Lineage Organization and Social Change in Ming and Qing Fujian* (Honolulu: University of Hawaii Press, 2001).

14. José Jorge Gómez Izquierdo, *El movimiento antichino en Mexico: Problemas del racismo y del nacimiento durante la Revolución Mexicana* (Mexico City: Instituto Nacional de Antropología e Historia, 1991); Juan Puig, *Entre el río Perla y el Nazas: La China decimónonica y sus braceros emigrantes, la colonia china de Torreón y la matanza de 1911* (Mexico City: Consejo Nacional para la Cultura y las Artes, 1993); Ota Mishima, ed., *Destino Mexico: Un estudio de las migraciones asiáticas a Mexico, siglos XIX y XX* (Mexico City: El Colegio de México, Centro de Estudios de Asia y Africa, 1997); Maricela Gonzáles Félix, *El proceso de aculturación de la población de origen chino en la ciudad de Mexicali* (Mexicali: Universidad Autónoma de Baja California, Instituto de Investigaciones Sociales, 1990); José Luis Trueba Lara, *Los chinos en Sonora: Una historia olvidada* (Hermosillo: Instituto de Investigaciones Historicas, Universidad de Sonora, 1990); For a community history written from the perspective of a Chinese-Mexican intellectual and artist, see Eduardo Auyón Gerardo, *El dragón en el desierto: Los pioneros chinos en Mexicali* (Mexicali: Instituto de Cultura de Baja California, 1991).

15. Evelyn Hu-DeHart, "Immigrants to a Developing Society: The Chinese in Northern Mexico, 1875–1932," *Journal of Arizona History* 21 (Autumn 1980):

275–312, and "Racism and Anti-Chinese Persecution in Sonora, Mexico, 1876–1932," *Amerasia* 9 (1982): 1–28; Gerardo Benigue, "Race, Region, and Nation: Sonora's Anti-Chinese Racism and Mexico's Postrevolutionary Nationalism, 1920s–1930s," in *Race and Nation in Modern Latin America*, ed. Nancy Applebaum, Anne S. MacPherson, and Karin Alejandra Rosemblatt (Chapel Hill: University of North Carolina Press), 211–36; Grace Delgado, "At Exclusion's Southern Gate: Changing Categories of Race and Class among Chinese Fronterizos, 1882–1904," in *Continental Crossroads: Remapping U.S.–Mexico Borderlands History*, ed. Samuel Truett and Elliott Young (Durham: Duke University Press, 2004); Julia Camacho, "Traversing Boundaries: Chinese, Mexicans, and Chinese Mexicans in the Formation of Gender, Race, and Nation in the Twentieth-Century United States–Mexican Borderlands" (PhD diss., University of Texas, El Paso, 2006).

16. For a general background on transnationalism, consult the following pioneering anthropological studies: Roger Rouse, "Mexican Migration and the Social Space of Postmodernism," *Diaspora* 1 (Spring 1991): 8–23; Linda Basch, Nina Glick Schiller, and Cristina Szanton Blanc, eds., *Towards a Transnational Perspective on Migration: Race, Class, Ethnicity, and Nationalism Reconsidered* (New York: New York Academy of Sciences, 1992).

17. See Sucheng Chan, ed., *Chinese American Transnationalism: The Flow of People, Resources, and Ideas between China and America during the Exclusion Era* (Philadelphia: Temple University Press, 2006); Hsu, *Dreaming of Gold, Dreaming of Home*; Lee, *At America's Gates*; Adam McKeown, *Chinese Migrant Networks and Cultural Change: Peru, Chicago, Hawaii, 1900–1936* (Chicago: University of Chicago Press, 2001); Yong Chen, *Chinese San Francisco, 1850–1943: A Transpacific Community* (Stanford: Stanford University Press, 2000).

18. For more on the claim that transnationalism is a postmodern phenomenon, see Aihwa Ong and Donald M. Nonini, eds., *Ungrounded Empires: The Cultural Politics of Modern Chinese Transnationalism* (New York: Routledge, 1997); Akhil Gupta and James Ferguson, eds., *Culture, Power, Place: Explorations in Critical Anthropology* (Durham, N.C.: Duke University Press, 1997).

19. The term *cuarta raíz* means "fourth root." It is used to distinguish Asian immigrants of Latin America from Latin Americans of European, indigenous, or African descent. A growing body of historical research has emerged in recent years related to the African "third root" of Latin America. For example, see Herman L. Bennett, *Africans in Colonial Mexico: Absolutism, Christianity, and Afro-Creole Consciousness, 1570–1640* (Bloomington: Indiana University Press, 2003); Marco Polo Hernandez Cuevas, *African Mexicans and the Discourse on Modern Nation* (Dallas: University Press of America, 2004).

Migrants to the British West Indies, 1838–1918 (Baltimore: Johns Hopkins University Press, 1993); Armando Choy, Gustavo Chui, and Moisés Sio Wong, *Our History Is Still Being Written: The Story of Three Chinese-Cuban Generals in the Cuban Revolution* (New York: Pathfinder Press, 2005).

21. Jeffrey Lesser, *Negotiating National Identity: Immigrants, Minorities, and the Struggle for Ethnicity in Brazil* (Durham, N.C.: Duke University Press, 1999); Daniel Masterson, *The Japanese in Latin America* (Urbana: University of Illinois Press, 2004); Steven M. Ropp, "Japanese Ethnicity and Peruvian Nationalism in the 1990s: Transnational Imaginaries and Alternative Hegemonies" (PhD diss., UCLA, 2003).

Chapter 2. The Dragon in Big Lusong

1. Composed between the years of 1910 and 1940, this poem is a translation of a Chinese-language poem written on the walls of Angel Island immigrant detention center, San Francisco, California. Between 1910 and 1940, Chinese immigrants entering the United States from the port of San Francisco were detained for questioning by immigration authorities at Angel Island. During their stays upon the island, which sometimes lasted weeks, Chinese immigrants expressed their frustrations through poetry that they wrote upon the walls of the detention center. This poem and others inscribed by Chinese immigrants of Angel Island were compiled and published as an anthology titled, *Island: Poetry and History of Chinese Immigrants on Angel Island, 1910–1940*, ed. Him Mark Lai, Genny Lim, and Judy Yung (Seattle: University of Washington Press, 1991), 167.

2. Mexico and the Philippines were both Spanish colonies in the seventeenth century. Mexico did not gain its political independence from Spain until 1821, and the Philippines did not overthrow Spanish colonial rule until 1898.

called "Da (Big) Lusong," and the Philippines became "Xiao (Small) Lusong." "Lusong" is still used by Chinese Americans as a colloquial expression to refer to persons of Mexican ancestry.

6. Mike Tom, interview with author, August 24, 2001, San Bruno, California. Mike Tom is the grandson of Lee Kwong Lun.

7. Like Lee Kwong Lun, some Chinese immigrated to Arizona during the early twentieth century after first sojourning in Sonora, Mexico. As in California, Chinese immigrants were recruited to Arizona as railroad laborers. Following the completion of their work on the railroads, many stayed on and became cooks, waiters, and grocery merchants. For more on the Chinese of Arizona, see Grace Peña Delgado, "In the Age of Exclusion: Race, Region, and Chinese Identity in the Making of the Arizona–Sonora Borderlands, 1863–1943" (PhD diss., UCLA, 2000), and, "At Exclusion's Gate: Changing Categories of Race and Class among Chinese Fronterizos, 1890–1900," in *Continental Crossroads: Frontiers, Borders, and Transnational History*, ed. Samuel J. Truett and Elliott Young (Durham: Duke University Press, 1999); Lawrence Michael Fong, "Sojourners and Settlers: The Chinese Experience in Arizona," *Journal of Arizona History* 21, no. 3 (Autumn 1980): 227–53; Heather S. Hatch, comp., "The Chinese in the Southwest: A Photographic Record," " *Journal of Arizona History* 21, no. 3 (Autumn 1980): 257.

8. Ma and Cartier, *Chinese Diaspora*, 8. For further readings on the theoretical model of "diaspora" within the field of Asian American studies, see Shirley Hune, "Rethinking Race: Paradigms and Policy Formation," *Amerasia Journal* 21 (1995): 29–40; L. Ling-Chi Wang, "The Structure of Dual Domination: Toward a Paradigm for the Study of the Chinese Diaspora in the United States, *Amerasia Journal* 21 (1995): 149–160; Jonathan Okamura, *Imagining the Filipino American Diaspora: Transnational Relations, Identities, and Communities* (New York: Garland, 1998).

9. Lynn Pan, *Sons of the Yellow Emperor* (Boston: Little, Brown, 1990), 43.

10. Brazilian planters and politicians first imported Chinese contract laborers during the second half of the nineteenth century in response to international pressure to abolish African slavery, and after failed attempts at recruiting central European workers to replace black workers. For more on early Chinese immigration to Brazil, see Lesser, *Negotiating National Identity*.

Between 1847 and 1874, some 125,000 Chinese immigrated to Cuba as plantation contract laborers. Chinese immigrant "coolies" were recruited to fill labor shortages in Cuban sugar plantations engendered by the abolition of African slavery. For a detailed examination of Chinese immigration to Cuba during the late nineteenth and early twentieth centuries, see López, "Migrants between Empires and Nations." For further readings on Chinese "coolie" migration to Cuba, see Evelyn Hu-DeHart, "Chinese Coolie Labour in Cuba in the Nineteenth Century: Free Labour or Neo-Slavery?" *Slavery and Abolition* (April 1993): 67–83; Mary Turner, "Chinese Contract Labor in Cuba, 1847–1874," *Caribbean Studies* 14, no. 2 (July 1974): 66–78; Ching Chich Chang, "The Chinese in Latin America: A Preliminary Geographical Survey with Special Reference to Cuba and Jamaica" (PhD diss., University of Maryland, 1956); Eugenio Chang-Rodriguez, "Chinese Labor Migration into Latin America in the Nineteenth Century," *Revista de Historia de America* 46 (December 1958): 375–97. For insight into the experience of the Chinese community of Cuba during the nineteenth century from the perspective of the immigrants themselves, see *The Cuba Commission Report: A Hidden History of the Chinese in Cuba*, intro. by Denise Helly (Baltimore: Johns Hopkins University Press, 1993). *The Cuba Commission Report* provides English-language translations of hundreds of interviews of Chinese "coolies" conducted by the government of China in 1873 and originally published in 1876. Esteban Montejo's *The Autobiography of a Runaway Slave* (ed. Miguel Barnet [New York: Pantheon Books, 1968]) offers an African slave's perspective of Chinese immigrant laborers. For western travel accounts describing the treatment and experience of Chinese coolies in Cuba, see Richard Henry Dana, *To Cuba and Back* (Carbondale: University of Illinois Press, 1966); Julia Ward Howe, *A Trip to Cuba* (New York: Praeger, 1969); Richard J. Lewis, *Diary of a Spring Holiday in Cuba* (Philadelphia: Porter and Coates, 1872).

Between 1847 and 1874, about 100,000 Chinese immigrated to Peru to serve as laborers in guano mines, cotton and sugar plantations, and railroad construction. See Michael J. Gonzales, "Chinese Plantation Workers and Social Conflict in Peru in the Late Nineteenth Century," *Journal of Latin American Studies* 21, no. 3 (October 1989): 385; Hu-DeHart, "Coolies, Shopkeepers, Pioneers:

The Chinese of Mexico and Peru"; Chang-Rodriguez, "Chinese Labor Migration into Latin America in the Nineteenth Century." For an examination of contemporary Chinese assimilation patterns in Peru, see Bernard Wong, "A Comparative Study of the Assimilation of the Chinese in New York City in Lima, Peru," *Comparative Studies in Society and History* 20 (1978): 335–58.

11. This figure was calculated based upon statistics from the following sources: Wilcox, *International Migrations*, vol. 1, 149; Mexico, Secretaría Economía Nacional, *Quinto censo de poblacion 1930, resumen general N Secretaría de la Economia Nacional, Anuario estadístico de la República cana 1930.*

12. Wilcox, *International Migrations*, 150–60.

13. "June Mei, "Socioeconomic Origins of Emigration: Guangdo fornia, 1850–1882," *Modern China* 5: 474–75; Wilcox, *International Migrations,* 149; Shih-shan Henry Tsai, *China and the Overseas Chinese in the United States, 1868–1911* (Fayetteville: University of Arkansas Press, 1983), 14; Pan, *Sons of the Yellow Emperor,* 43.

14. This revolt involved the rebellion of three Chinese generals—Wu Sangui, Geng Jingzhong, and Shang Kexi—against the foreign Qing dynasty of the Manchus. The Manchus conquered China in 1644 and held power in China until the fall of the Qing dynasty in 1912.

15. John King Fairbank, *China: A New History* (Cambridge: Belknap Press of Harvard University Press, 1992), 168–69.

16. Ibid., 170; Conrad Schirokauer, *A Brief History of Chinese Civilization* (San Diego: Harcourt Brace Gap College), 266; Cuba Commission Report, 18.

17. *Cuba Commission Report,* 18–19.

18. Mei, "Socioeconomic Origins of Emigration," 468–69, 492–93, 497.

19. Schirokauer, *Brief History,* 262.

20. Mei, "Socioeconomic Origins of Emigration," 469; Schirokauer, *Brief History,* 262, 265.

21. Mei, "Socioeconomic Origins of Emigration," 470–72.

22. Ibid., 472–73; Schirokauer, *Brief History,* 267–71; *Cuba Commission Report,* 19.

23. Mei, "Socioeconomic Origins of Emigration," 473.

24. Stanford Lyman, *Chinese Americans* (New York: Random House, 1974), 4; Mei, "Socioeconomic Origins of Emigration," 493. For further reading on Asian labor migration to the United States during the late nineteenth and early twentieth centuries, see *Labor Immigration under Capitalism: Asian Workers in the United States before World War II,* ed. Edna Bonacich and Lucie Cheng (Berkeley: University of California Press, 1984).

25. Wilcox, *International Migrations*, 149–50.

26. The 1877 emigration ban, as well as its subsequent diplomatic extension, likely resulted from China's desire to protect its citizens from the abuses of the "coolie" trade. As part of the coolie trade, Chinese immigrants were deceptively recruited, transported overseas in former slave ships, and subjected to living and working conditions similar to those of African slaves.

27. Townsend Walker, "Gold Mountain Guests: Chinese Migration to the United States, 1848–1882" (PhD diss., Stanford University, 1976), 1.

28. Ibid., 30–31.

29. Sucheng Chan, *Asian Americans: An Interpretive History* (Boston: Twayne, 1991), 27–28; Mei, "Socioeconomic Origins of Emigration," 475; Walker, *Chinese Migration*, 25–28, 30–31.

30. Mei, "Socioeconomic Origins of Emigration," 486; Chan, *Asian Americans*, 28.

31. Mei, "Socioeconomic Origins of Emigration," 464–65, 476.

32. Alexander Saxton, *The Indispensable Enemy* (Berkeley and Los Angeles: University of California Press, 1971), 258.

33. Bill Ong Hing, *Making and Remaking Asian America through Immigration Policy, 1850–1890* (Stanford: Stanford University Press, 1993), 20–21.

34. Saxton, *Indispensable Enemy*, 259–65.

35. Ibid., 90–91.

36. Hing, *Making and Remaking Asian America*, 22–26.

37. "Gold Mountain" was the name given by Chinese immigrants to California and the western region of North America. This term is a translation of the Cantonese "Gum Saan" and the Mandarin "jīn shān."

38. Robert M. Buffington and William E. French, "The Culture of Modernity," in *The Oxford History of Mexico*, ed. Michael C. Meyer and William H. Beezley (New York: Oxford University Press, 2000), 398–400; Raymond B. Craib, "Chinese Immigrants in Porfirian Mexico: A Preliminary Study of Settlement, Economic Activity and Anti-Chinese Sentiment," LAII Research Paper Series no. 28 (Albuquerque: Latin American and Iberian Institute at the University of New Mexico, May 1996); Kennet Cott, "Mexican Diplomacy and the Chinese Issue, 1876–1910," *Hispanic American Historical Review* 67, no. 1 (February 1987): 63–64; Thomas E. Skidmore and Peter H. Smith, *Modern Latin America* (New York: Oxford University Press, 1997), 231–33.

39. Craib, "Chinese Immigrants," 2; Cott, "Mexican Diplomacy," 64.

40. David Bushnell and Neill Macaulay, *The Emergence of Latin America in the Nineteenth Century* (New York: Oxford University Press), 208–9; Cott, "Mexican Diplomacy," 64; Craib, "Chinese Immigrants," 5.

41. Cott, "Mexican Diplomacy," 64; Craib, "Chinese Immigrants," 5.

42. Craib, "Chinese Immigrants," 6.

43. *Estatutos de la Compañía de Colonización Asiática* (Mexico: Imprenta de J. M. Lara, 1866), Bancroft Library, University of California, Berkeley, 154–57.

44. Cott, "Mexican Diplomacy," 64–70.

45. Ibid., 66–70.

46. José Angel Espinoza, *El ejemplo de Sonora* (Mexico, D.F.: n.p., 1932), 16.

47. Romero, "Transnational Commercial Orbits," 13.

48. Mexico, Secretaría de la Economía Nacional, *Quinto censo de población 1930, resúmen general.*

49. Mexico, Secretaría de Agricultura y Fomento, *Tercer censo de población de los Estados Unidos Mexicanos, verificado el 27 de octubre 1910* (Mexico: Dirección General de la Estadística).

50. Mexico, Secretaría de Gobernación, *El Servicio de Migración en México por Andrés Landa y Piña jefe del Departamento de Migración* (Mexico, D.F.: Talleres Gráficos de la Nación, 1930), Bancroft Library, University of California, Berkeley, 38–39.

Chapter 3. Transnational Journeys

1. Chinese Exclusion Act case files, Record Group 85, Laguna Niguel, National Archives, Francisco Rios, file no. 1000/1.

2. Customs Bureau Special Agents Reports and Correspondence, ca. 1865–1915, Record Group 36, National Archives, Washington, D.C. (hereafter cited as NA D.C.), Hudgins to Carlisle, San Antonio, Texas, 18 July 1896, 2; Ralph Izard, Special Inspector of Customs, to Col. W. P. Hudgins, Laredo, Texas, 12 January 1895, box no. 276; Clifford A. Perkins, *Border Patrol, with the U.S. Immigration Service on the U.S.–Mexico Boundary, 1910–1954* (El Paso: Texas Western Press, University of Texas, El Paso, 1978), 12.

3. The official name of the organization was the Chinese Consolidated Benevolent Association. The name Six Companies was given to the organization by Anglo-American observers. William Hoy, *The Chinese Six Companies* (San Francisco: Chinese Consolidated Benevolent Association, 1942), 9–12.

4. NA D.C., Hudgins to Carlisle, San Antonio, Texas, 18 July 1896, 2; Ralph Izard, Special Inspector of Customs, to Col. W. P. Hudgins, Laredo, Texas, 12 January 1895; Izard to Hudgins, Laredo, Texas, 26 September 1896, box no. 276.

5. For more on Chinese immigration to Cuba, see chapter 2, n. 10.

6. Wilcox, *International Migrations*, vol. 1, 149.

7. NA D.C., Izard to Hudgins, Laredo, Texas, 26 September 1896, enclosed in letter from Hudgins to Carlisle Secretary of the Treasury, San Antonio, Texas, 28 September 1896, box no. 276.

8. Chin's name might belie another important transnational connection that he may have possessed. *Pinoy* means "Filipino" and therefore might be indicative of his roots as part of the Chinese diasporic community of the Philippines.

9. Perkins, *Border Patrol*, 11–13.

10. NA D.C., Stokes to Secretary of the Treasury, El Paso, Texas, 12 August 1897, box no. 392; Chinese Exclusion Act case files, Record Group 85, National Archives, Laguna Niguel, California, Hui Tong Ping, file no. 494/28 (hereafter cited as NA Laguna, Hui Tong Ping).

11. NA D.C., McEnery to Hon. J. J. Crowley, New Orleans, 4 May 1894, box 314.

12. NA D.C., Wicker to the Honorable Charles Foster Secretary of the Treasury, 24 May 1891; Wicker to Foster, 29 May 1891; Wicker to Foster, 6 June 1891; U.S. Attorney Wm. Grant to Wicker, 6 June 1891, enclosed in previous letter, box no. 424.

13. NA D.C., Stokes to Secretary of the Treasury, El Paso, Texas, 12 August 1897; Stokes to Collector of Customs San Francisco, El Paso, 12 August 1897, box no. 392.

14. NA D.C., Stokes to Carlisle, 13 March 1896; H. E. Tippett, Chinese Inspector, to Honorable John G. Carlisle, Secretary of the Treasury, Plattsburgh, N.Y., 12 March 1896, box no. 392.

15. NA D.C., Datus E. Coon, Chinese Inspector, to Collector of Customs of San Francisco, San Diego, 2 August 1890, marked "Exhibit B"; Coon to Honorable William Windom, Secretary of the Treasury, San Diego, 13 October 1890; "Prisoner for Prisoner," "The Alameda Jail Trouble," newspaper articles attached to October 13 letter and marked as "Exhibit A."

16. NA D.C., Richard Rule, Special Inspector, to Mr. W. P. Hudgins, Special Agent in Charge, El Paso, 1 April 1897, enclosed with letter from Hudgins to Honorable L. J. Gage, Secretary of the Treasury, 28 April 1897, box no. 276.

17. NA D.C., Hudgins to Honorable L. J. Gage, Secretary of the Treasury, 28 April 1897, box no. 276.

18. Ibid.; NA D.C., Izard to Hudgins, 24 April 1897, enclosed in Hudgins to Honorable L. J. Gage, Secretary of the Treasury, 28 April 1897, box no. 276.

19. NA D.C., F. N. Wicker, Special Inspector, to O. L. Spaulding, Assistant Secretary of the Treasury, 6 August 1891, box no. 424; W. F. Norman, Chinese Inspector, to Honorable J. G. Carlisle, Secretary of the Treasury, 25 July 1895; Norman to Hon. C. S. Hamlin, Assistant Secretary of the Treasury, 24 July 1895, box no. 353; E. T. Stokes, Special Agent, to Mr. Chas. Davis, Collector of Port at El Paso, Eagle Pass, Texas, 19 May 1897, box no. 392; Richard Rule, Special Inspector Acting in Charge, to Mr. George W. Whitehead, Special Agent, El Paso, Texas, 15 March 1897, box no. 374.

20. NA D.C., F. N. Wicker Special Inspector to O. L. Spaulding Assistant Secretary of the Treasury, 6 August 1891, box no. 424.

21. NA D.C., McEnery to C. S. Hamlin Assistant Secretary of the Treasury, New Orleans, 4 July 1894; McEnery to Honorable John G. Carlisle Secretary of the Treasury, New Orleans, 25 July 1894, box no. 314.

22. NA D.C., Special Agent McEnery to Hon. C. S. Hamlin, Ass't Sec. Of Treasury, 3 May 1894; McEnery to Hamlin, New Orleans, 29 May 1894, box no. 314; Izard to Hudgins, New Orleans, 14 May 1894; "List of Chinamen naturalized at New Orleans La.," enclosed with 14 May 1894 letter from Izard to Hudgins; Acting Secretary of the Treasury Department to Mr. J. A. McEnery Special Agent, enclosed with above 14 May 1894 letter from Izard to Hudgins; Acting Secretary to Mr. W. P. Hudgins, 28 May 1894, enclosed with May 14 letter, box no. 2786.

23. NA D.C., Richard Rule Special Inspector Acting in Charge to Mr. George W. Whitehead Special Agent, El Paso, Texas, 15 March 1897, box no. 374; E. T. Stokes Special Agent Office of Treasury Department to Honorable John G. Carlisle Secretary of the Treasury, Plattsburgh, N.Y., 2 January 1894; E. T. Stokes Special Agent to Hon. John G. Carlisle, Plattsburgh, 2 January 1894; sworn statement of Adelbert F. Miles before Wendell A. Anderson, Consul General of the United States of America at Montreal, 30 December 1893, enclosed with above letter of Stokes to Carlisle from 2 January 1894, box 391.

24. John MacDonald and Leatrice MacDonald, "Chain Migration, Ethnic Neighborhood Formation, and Social Networks," *Milbank Memorial Fund Quarterly* 42, no. 1 (January 1964): 82–97, 82–83.

25. Jose Maria Romero, *Comisión de inmigración; dictamen del vocal ingeniero José Maria Romero, encargado de estudiar la influencia social y económica de la inmigración asiática en Mexico* (Mexico: Imprenta de A. Carranza e hijos, 1911), Bancroft Library, University of California, Berkeley, 21; Espinoza, *Ejemplo de Sonora*, 21.

26. Espinoza, *Ejemplo de Sonora*, 16.

27. Ibid.; Mexico, Secretaría de Gobernación, *Servicio de Migración*, 6.

28. Romero, *Comisión de inmigración*, 4; Espinoza, *Ejemplo de Sonora*, 21.

29. Minister of China to Sr. Alberto J. Pani, Mexico, 29 July 1921; Claude I. Dawson to the Honorable Secretary of State, Mexico City, 11 September 1922, attached "Memorandum re Case of 'New China,'" microfilm roll "Chinese Question in Mexico, 1910–1930," Record Group 59, General Records of the Department of State, Decimal File 312.93, 1910–1929, 1930–1939; 704.9312, 1910–1929, 1930–1939, University of Arizona Main Library (hereafter cited as "Chinese Question in Mexico").

30. George Seltzer to the Honorable Secretary of State, Salina Cruz, Mexico, 8 March 1922, 2; K. T. Ouang Chinese Minister to Raymond C. Hafey, Esq., Mexico, 28 November 1921, 2, "Chinese Question in Mexico."

31. Raymond C. Hafey, American Vice Consul to the Honorable K. T. Ouang, Chinese Minister, Salina Cruz, Mexico, 4 December 1921, "Chinese Question in Mexico," 2, 3.

32. "Attested protest of Secundino Mendezona," 15 November 1921, 1; "Memorandum re Case of 'New China,'" 1, "Chinese Question in Mexico."

33. Raymond G. Hafey, American Vice Consul in Charge, to Secretary of State, Salina Cruz, Mexico, 8 November 1921; "Memorandum re Case of 'New China,'" 1, "Chinese Question in Mexico."

34. "Memorandum re Case of 'New China,'" 1; K. T. Ouang, Chinese Minister, to Monsieur Chargé d'Affaires, Mexico, 12 December 1921, 2, "Chinese Question in Mexico."

35. Raymond C. Hafey to the Honorable K. T. Ouang, Chinese Minister, Salina Cruz, Mexico, 4 December 1921, 5, "Chinese Question in Mexico."

36. K. T. Ouang, Chinese Minister, to Raymond C. Hafey, Esq., Mexico, 28 November 1921, "Chinese Question in Mexico," 1.

37. George Seltzer, American Vice Consul, to the Honorable Secretary of State, Salina Cruz, Mexico, 7 August 1922, 2; George Seltzer to The Honorable Secretary of State, Salina Cruz, Mexico, 26 August 1922, 1; George Seltzer to the Honorable Secretary of State, Salina Cruz, 22 March 1922, 1, "Chinese Question in Mexico."

38. Claude I. Dawson, American Consul-General, to the Honorable Secretary of State, Mexico City, 11 September 1922, "Chinese Question in Mexico."

39. It is unclear from the historical record how B. C. Wong came to form his coolie transportation company with the assistance of a Spaniard—Secundino Mendezona—and why he chose to name his company the Spain and China Navigation Company. One possibility is that Wong first organized his coolie smuggling operation in the Philippines during the years of Spanish colonial rule. Though Wong served as manager of the Canton Bank of Hong Kong, it is possible that he himself hailed from the Philippines or that he possessed familial or business ties to the large Chinese community of the Philippines. Based upon any of these possible connections to the Philippines, Wong may have come into contact with Spaniard Mendezona. The latter likely possessed his own ties to the Philippines, based upon the colonial relationship between Spain and the Philippines that ended in 1898, just a few years prior to the "New China" incident. Wong may have first organized the Spain and China Navigation Company and formed his business relationship with Mendezona in the Philippines during

the final years of Spanish colonial rule. This would explain Wong's hiring of a Spanish manager and the inclusion of the word *Spain* as part of his company's name. Moreover, this would also explain the fact that the majority of the officers of the *New China* steamship were citizens of the Philippines.

40. MacDonald, "Chain Migration," 82 (emphasis original).

41. NA Laguna, Cuan Sun (Ricardo Cuan).

42. Chinese Exclusion Act case files, Record Group 85, National Archives, Laguna Niguel, California, Chong Chin (José Chong), file no. 14036/47 (hereafter cited as NA Laguna, Chong Chin (José Chong).

43. Translation from Chinese; ibid., 2.

44. Chinese Exclusion Act case files. Record Group 85. National Archives, Laguna Niguel, California, José Chong Cuy, file no. 4067/492 (hereafter cited as NA Laguna, José Chong Cuy).

45. The existing historiography neglects significant discussion of the various migration mechanisms utilized by Chinese immigrants to Mexico. Although providing analysis of the initial recruitment of Chinese laborers by Mexican capitalists, the current literature ignores the important role played by familial chain migration as part of Chinese movement to Mexico. In addition, the historiography fails to provide detailed discussion of both Chinese "coolie" smuggling to Mexico during the early twentieth century and Chinese immigrant smuggling to the United States via Mexico and Cuba. The following analysis of Chinese migration mechanisms fills this conspicuous void of the immigration literature.

46. Chinese Exclusion Act case files, Record Group 85, National Archives, Laguna Niguel, California, Santiago Wong Chao, file no. 29160/9 (hereafter cited as NA Laguna, Santiago Wong Chao).

47. Matías Romero, *Geographical and Statistical Notes on Mexico, 1837–1898* (New York: G. P. Putnam's Sons, 1898).

48. Mexico, Secretaría de la Economía Nacional, *Anuario estadístico de la República Mexicana 1901* (Mexico, D.F.: Dirección General de Estadística) (hereafter cited as AE 1901).

49. Mexico, Secretaría de la Economía Nacional, *Anuario Estadístico de la República Mexicana 1907* (Mexico, D.F.: Dirección General de Estadística) (hereafter cited as AE 1907).

50. See chapter 3 for detailed discussion of Chinese transnational immigrant smuggling.

51. Louis Kaiser to Herbert H. D. Peirce, Mazatlán, Mexico, 26 March 1903, U.S. Consular Reports, Mazatlán, Mexico, University of California at Irvine Main Library (hereafter referred to as U.C.I. Consular Reports).

52. Mexico, Secretaría de la Economía Nacional, *Anuario estadístico de la Republica Mexicana 1905* (Mexico, D.F.: Dirección General de Estadística).

53. As in the case of the shift toward Pacific port arrivals, the popularity of the "in transit" procedure was likely, in part, tied to the immigrant smuggling trade. As discussed in greater detail earlier in this chapter, the "in transit" procedure was closely tied to a smuggling technique known as "substitution." See chapter 3 for more on the "substitution" smuggling procedure.

54. NA Laguna, Chong Chin (José Chong).

55. Mexico, Secretaría de Economía, *Estadísticas sociales del Porfiriato: 1877–1910* (Mexico, D.F.: Dirección General de Estadística, 1956), 190.

56. Ibid., 184–85.

57. Willard to Department of State, Guaymas, Mexico, 26 September 1885, U.C.I. Consular Reports.

58. Willard to Department of State, Guaymas, Mexico, 18 September 1889, U.C.I. Consular Reports.

59. Mexico, Ministerio de Fomento, *Censo general de la República Mexicana verificado el 20 de octubre de 1895, resúmen del censo de la República* (Mexico, D.F.: Dirección General de Estadística); Mexico, Secretaría de la Economía Nacional, *Quinto censo de población 1930, resúmen general.*

60. Lucy Salyer, *Laws Harsh as Tigers: Chinese Immigrants and the Shaping of Modern Immigration Law* (Chapel Hill: University of North Carolina Press, 1995).

61. Perkins, *Border Patrol,* 49.

62. Mexico, Secretaría de la Economia Nacional, *Anuario estadistico de la Republica Mexicana 1930.*

63. Mexico, Secretaría de la Economia Nacional, *Anuario estadistico de la Republica Mexicana 1913* (Mexico, D.F.: Direccion General de Estadistica); Mexico, Secretaría de la Economia Nacional, *Anuario estadistico de la Republica Mexicana 1930.*

64. Perkins, *Border Patrol,* 49.

65. Mexico, Secretaría de Gobernación, *El Servicio de Migración en México por Landa y Pina jefe del Departamento de Migración* (Mexico, D.F.: Talleres Gráficos de la Nación, 1930), Bancroft Library, University of California, Berkeley, 38–39.

66. Mexico, Secretaría de la Economía Nacional, *Sexto censo de población 1940, resúmen general* (Mexico, D.F.: Dirección General de Estadística, 1943), 9.

67. Circular Num. 194, Sección de Gobernación, Referencia: 58–15, Hermosillo, Sonora, 25 August 1931, Espinoza, *Ejemplo de Sonora,* 119.

68. Espinoza, *Ejemplo de Sonora,* 63–72.

69. Ibid., 138–40; Humberto Monteón González, José Luis Trueba Lara, *Chinos y antichinos en Mexico: Documentos para su estudio* (Guadalajara, Jalisco: Gobierno de Jalisco, Secretaría General, Unidad Editorial, 1988), 134; Bartley F. Yost to the Honorable Secretary of State, Nogales, Mexico, 21 March 1932, "Chinese Question in Mexico"; Hu-DeHart, "Immigrants to a Developing Society," 305.

70. Mexico, Secretaría de la Economía Nacional, *Censo de población 1895, resúmen general* (Mexico, D.F.: Dirección General de Estadística), 24, 25.

71. Mexico, Secretaría de la Economía Nacional, *Censo de población 1910, resúmen general* (Mexico, D.F.: Dirección General de Estadística) 42, 43.

72. Samuel Truett, *Fugitive Landscapes: The Forgotten History of the U.S.-Mexico Borderlands* (New Haven: Yale University Press, 2006), 90, 121.

73. Ibid., 120, 124–25.

74. Mexico, *Servicio de Migración*, 36–38.

75. Much of the increase of the Chinese population of the Pacific states was the result of wide-scale Chinese movement to northern Baja California in response to the Mexicali cotton boom of the early twentieth century. Initially recruited to fill labor shortages in the developing cotton economy of Mexicali, Chinese immigrants branched out into a variety of commercial endeavors, becoming tenant farmers, merchants, hotel owners, and restaurant proprietors. Representing only 5 percent of the population of northern Baja in 1910, by 1927 the Chinese had come to comprise 14 percent of the district's entire population. Home to only 851 Chinese in 1910, the Chinese population of Baja California increased to 5,889 by 1926. For more on Chinese immigration and settlement in Baja California during the early twentieth century, see Evelyn Hu-DeHart, "The Chinese of Baja California Norte, 1910–1934," *Proceedings of the Pacific Coast Council on Latin American Studies: Baja California and the North Mexican Frontier* 12 (1985–1986): 9–28; Robert H. Duncan, "The Chinese and the Economic Development of Northern Baja California, 1889–1929," *Hispanic American Historical Review* 74 (1994); Eugene Keith Chamberlain, "Mexican Colonization versus American Interests in Lower California," *Pacific Historical Review* 20 (1951): 43–55; James R. Curtis, "Mexicali's Chinatown," *Geographical Review* 85, no. 3 (July 1995): 335–48; Celso Aguirre Bernal, *Compendio histórico-biográfico de Mexicali, 1539–1966* (Mexicali, B. CFA.: 1966). For discussion and treatment of contemporary Chinese cultural adaptation patterns in Mexicali, Mexico, see Gonzáles Felix, *Proceso de aculturación de la población de origen chino en la ciudad de Mexicali;* and Gerardo, *Dragón en el desierto*. For interesting memoir reflections upon Mexicali's Chinatown, see Antonio Gastélum Gámez, *Mi viejo Mexicali: Remembranzas* (Mexicali: A. Gastélum Gámez, 1991).

Chapter 4. Gender, Interracial Marriage, and Transnational Families

1. Chinese Exclusion Act case files, Record Group 85, National Archives, Laguna Niguel, California, Ramon Wong Fong Song, file no. 14036/262 (hereafter cited as NA Laguna, Ramon Wong Fong Song).

2. Mexico, Secretaría de la Economía, *Anuário estadístico de la República Mexicana 1930*.

3. Mexico, Ministerio de Fomento, *Censo general de la República Mexicana verificado el 20 de octubre de 1895*.

4. Mexico, Secretaría de la Economía Naciónal, *Quinto censo de población 1930*.

5. Mexico, Secretaría de Gobernación, *Servicio de Migración en Mexico*, 36–38.

6. Mexico, Dirección General de Estadística, *Censo de población del municipio de Chihuahua, Chihuahua, 1930* (Salt Lake City: Filmado por la Sociedad Genealógica de Utah, 1987)(hereafter cited as Chihuahua Manuscripts 1930); *Censo de población del municipio de Hermosillo, Sonora* (Salt Lake City: Filmado por la Sociedad Genealógica de Utah, 1988)(hereafter referred to as Hermosillo Manuscripts 1930), Mormon Family History Center, West Covina, California.

7. In 1910, the Chinese female population of Mexico reportedly consisted of 85 persons; by 1930, this number had increased to 2,711.

8. This same general rule was also found to apply to the case of Mexican-born women married to immigrant husbands from Europe, Japan, the United States, and the Middle East

9. For more on race and the Mexican census of 1930, see Kif Augustine-Adams, "Making Mexico: Legal Nationality, Chinese Race, and the 1930 Population Census," *Law and History Review* 27, no. 1, 2009.

10. A similar trend is revealed in the Chihuahua City municipal census manuscripts related to children born to immigrant fathers of other nationalities. Children born in Mexico to Mexican-born mothers and fathers who were foreign nationals of Europe and the Middle East were counted as being of the same nationality as their fathers; children born in Mexico to two European parents who had not become naturalized citizens were not considered Mexican nationals, but rather were assigned the same national status as their parents.

11. NA Laguna, Cuan Sun (Ricardo Cuan).

12. Luis Chong provides another example. Born in the Xingning District of south China, Mexican farm laborer Luis Chong traveled by steamship from Hong Kong to Manzanillo, Mexico, in December of 1912 at the age of fourteen. From Manzanillo, Chong moved to Tampico, where he lived for four years before relocating to Mexicali. In an interview with Immigration and

Naturalization Service agent W. A. Brazie in September of 1917, Chong stated that his father Chin Shew Gin resided in the Hai Ping Jong village of Sunning, China, and that he had relatives neither in Mexico nor in the United States. Chong, like Wong and Cuan, immigrated to Mexico at a young age as a single bachelor, presumably to find employment to provide financially for his father and other family members left behind in China. Chinese Exclusion Act case files, Record Group 85, National Archives, Laguna Niguel, California, Luis Chong alias Leon Chong, file no. 5528/619.

13. As was the case for internal migrants of early modern Japan and sojourning Italian male immigrants of the early twentieth century, Chinese international migration was a "family strategy" for socioeconomic survival. These high numbers of transnational marriages strongly suggest that Chinese males did not choose to emigrate for selfish and individualistic reasons, but that they turned to emigration as a means of securing both their personal and familial economic livelihoods. For more on Japanese "family" migration strategies, see Mary Louise Nagata, "Labour Migration, Family and Community in Early Modern Japan," in *Women, Gender, and Labour Migration: Historical and Global Perspectives*, ed. Pamela Sharpe (London: Routledge, 2001), 60–84. Like Italian immigrants in the United States and Argentina, moreover, the Chinese of Mexico formed "transnational family economies." As part of these international family economies, Chinese males earned wages in Mexico that were likely higher than those available in their native lands, and their wives and family members left behind in China were able to spend these earnings where subsistence costs were relatively low. For more detailed discussion of Italian transnational family economies, see Donna Gabaccia, "When the Migrants Are Men: Italy's Women and Transnationalism as a Working-Class Way of Life," in *Women, Gender, and Labour Migration: Historical and Global Perspectives*, ed. Pamela Sharpe, 190–208 (London: Routledge, 2001). For a transnational comparative study of Italian immigration to the United States and Latin America, see Samuel L. Baily, *Immigrants in the Lands of Promise: Italians in Buenos Aires and New York City, 1870–1914* (Ithaca: Cornell University Press, 1999).

14. For a detailed examination of the transnational connections maintained by Chinese immigrants of the United States and their kinsmen who remained in China, see Hsu, *Dreaming of Gold, Dreaming of Home*.

15. Chihuahua Manuscripts 1930.

16. Hermosillo Manuscripts 1930.

17. NA Laguna, Lee Chip (Rodolfo Ley); NA Laguna, Pablo Chee.

18. NA Laguna, Federico Cham; National Archives, Laguna Niguel, California, Enrique Chong, file no. 25100/38 (hereafter cited as NA Laguna, Enrique Chong).

19. Immigration interviews provide conflicting information as to whether Cham truly had a daughter. In an interview of 1922, he claimed to have had one daughter; in a later interview, of 1934, he denied ever having a daughter. These conflicting interview responses would seem to evidence a common method of circumventing U.S. immigration laws known as the "paper sons" technique. According to a loophole in immigration legislation, the children of Chinese merchants or U.S. citizens were legally entitled to immigrate to the United States from China. As part of the "paper sons" method of circumventing immigration restrictions, some Chinese merchants and citizens of the United States falsely alleged that they had children in China and, based upon this claim, brought children over to the United States who were not their true offspring. Judy Yung, *Unbound Feet: A Social History of Chinese Women in San Francisco* (Berkeley and Los Angeles: University of California Press, 1995), 3, 23, 106, 309. For further reading on the creation of fictitious immigration families as a method of circumventing the Chinese Exclusion Act, see Lee, *At America's Gates*.

20. Although Chinese laborers were barred from the United States based upon the Chinese Exclusion Act, Chinese merchants were allowed to immigrate to Mexico according to the Section 6 merchant exemption.

21. For an interesting comparison of Mexican-Punjabi marriages in the Imperial Valley of California, see Karen Leonard, *Making Ethnic Choices: California's Punjabi Mexican Americans* (Philadelphia: Temple University Press, 1992).

22. Netty Rodriguez and Jesus Rodriguez, "El chino," Vocalion, Brunswick Record Corporation, 1937, in the UCLA Frontera Digital Archive. This recording and the following corrido, "Los chinos," were identified and researched utilizing the UCLA Frontera Digital Collection. This digital archive and audio clips of these two recordings may be accessed via the Web at http://digital .library.ucla.edu/frontera/. For more on the Frontera Collection, see Robert Chao Romero, "*Musica de la Frontera*: Research Note on the UCLA Frontera Digital Archive," *Aztlan: A Journal of Chicano Studies* 30 (Spring 2005).

23. The author wishes to thank Leonard Melchor for his assistance in translating the poem and Frontera Collection sources used in this article. All other translations are the work of the author.

24. This cartoon and the following sketches are from José Angel Espinoza, *El ejemplo de Sonora* (Mexico, D.F.: n.p., 1932). In prose and cartoon, *El ejemplo de Sonora* chronicles the organized anti-Chinese movement of the state of Sonora during the early twentieth century.

25. "El destierro de los chinos: Que se pongan a llorar de lo a gusto que han vivido y el tronido que han de har." Undated broadside. Item xfPQ7260 C6, no. 376. Bancroft Library, University of California, Berkeley.

26. This "braid" worn by Chinese immigrant males refers to the "queue" that all Chinese men were required to grow. The wearing of a queue was originally a Manchurian cultural practice among men of the ruling Qing dynasty. The creation of the policy requiring all Chinese to wear the queue was designed to produce cultural uniformity. After the collapse of the Qing dynasty in 1919, the queue fell out of use.

27. GRDS (General Records of the Department of State). [U.S. consular agent] Wilson to Secretary of State, Mexico City, 2 November 1911; Wilson telegram, Mazatlán, 16 March 1912; Wilson telegram, Mazatlán, no. 115, 21 October 1912.;U.S. consul William Alger to Secretary of State, Mazatlán, Sinaloa, 17 March 1912; Alger to Secretary of State, San Diego, Cal., December 10, 1913; Hamm to Secretary of State, Durango, Mexico, 18 September 1913, "Chinese Question in Mexico."

28. For further reading on the fusion between masculinity and postrevolutionary nationalism, see Ilene O'Malley, *The Myth of the Revolution: Hero Cults and the Institutionalization of the Mexican State, 1920–1940* (New York: Greenwood Press, 1986); Ana Maria Alonso, *Thread of Blood: Colonialism, Revolution, and Gender on Mexico's Northern Frontier* (Tucson: University of Arizona Press, 1995); and, Robert McKee Irwin, *Mexican Masculinities* (Minneapolis: University of Minnesota Press, 2003).

29. The following discussion of spousal repatriation includes details that were not part of the original "Aztlan" publication.

30. Julia Schiavone Camacho, "Ni que me den un palacio alla, prefiero Mexico: The Transpacific Journeys of the Mexican Chinese and the 'Mexican Diaspora.'" Unpublished paper.

31. Original Spanish text reads: "Aunque vayamos a escarbar camotes amargos a la sierra, queremos México." Ibid.

32. Although these children were legally classified as Mexican nationals, they were not treated as "Mexican" in society.

33. *Mestizaje* refers to the cultural mixture that has taken place in Mexico and other countries of Latin America since the Spanish conquest of the sixteenth century. *Mestizo* refers to a person of mixed Spanish and indigenous ancestry.

34. Renique, "Race, Region, and Nation," 218. See also Gerardo Renique, "Anti-Chinese Racism, Nationalism and State Formation in Post-Revolutionary Mexico, 1920s–1930s," *Political Power and Social Theory* 14 (2000): 91–140.

35. José Vasconcelos, *La raza cósmica*, trans. Didier T. Jaen (Baltimore: Johns Hopkins University Press, 1997), 20.

36. Renique, "Race, Region, and Nation," 223–24.

37. Ibid., 215–18.

38. Espinoza, *Ejemplo de Sonora*, 35.

39. José Maria Arana, "Al margen del informe del C. Gobernador del Estado Dr. Cesareo G. Soriano," Magdalena, Mexico, April 4, 1918, José Maria Arana Papers, University of Arizona Library Special Collections, Tucson.

40. Espinoza, *Ejemplo de Sonora,* 37–38.

41. "Intervenciones de los diputados Walterio Pesqueira, Juan de Díos Batiz, Francisco Trejo y Julio Bustillos, Cámara de Diputados. Martes 30 de septiembre de 1930," in *Chinos y antichinos en Mexico: Documentos para su estudio,* ed. Humberto Monteón Gonzáles and José Luis Trueba Lara (Guadalajara, Jalisco, Mexico: Gobierno de Jalisco, Secretaría General, Unidad Editorial, 1988), 95–97.

Chapter 5. Employment and Community

1. NA Laguna, Santiago Wong Chao.

2. The existing literature asserts that Chinese immigrants, although initially recruited by Mexican capitalists as laborers, eventually transitioned into entrepreneurial roles to the exclusion of working-class positions. Evelyn Hu-DeHart, pioneer historian of Chinese immigration to Mexico, for example, states, "[Chinese] in northern Mexico did not take up laboring jobs, which were filled by Mexicans, but rather entered commerce as small independent entrepreneurs, and occasionally in partnership with American mine and railroad owners in the company towns." Hu-DeHart, "Coolies, Shopkeepers, Pioneers," 91–116, 97. For further examples from the existing historiography that emphasize the role of the Chinese as merchants and entrepreneurs, see Hu-DeHart, "Racism and Anti-Chinese Persecution in Sonora, Mexico, 1876–1932," 1–28; Leo M. Jacques, "Have Quick More Money than Mandarins: The Chinese in Sonora," *Journal of Arizona History* 17 (1976): 208–18; Jacques Dambourges, "The Anti-Chinese Campaigns in Sonora, Mexico, 1900–1931" (PhD diss., University of Arizona, 1974); Kennett Cott, "Mexican Diplomacy and the Chinese Issue," *Hispanic American Historical Review* 67 (1987): 63–84.

3. Insofar as the Chinese immigrant community of Mexico consisted of two distinct socioeconomic tiers of merchants and artisans on the one hand, and rural and urban unskilled laborers on the other, Chinese immigration to Mexico shared characteristics of both "Huashang" and "Huagong" patterns of migration. Typical of Chinese movement to Southeast Asia, and possessing historical roots tracing back to the Song dynasty, the "Huashang" pattern of immigration refers to the emigration of merchants, artisans, and other skilled workers. The "Huagong" pattern, on the other hand, common during the nineteenth and early twentieth centuries, was characterized by Chinese "coolie" migration to places such as the United States, Australia, Cuba, and other countries founded upon plantation economies. For more on the "Huashang" and

"Huagong" patterns of Chinese migration, see Wang Gungwu, *China and the Overseas Chinese* (Singapore: Times Academic Press, 1991). For further reading on Chinese immigration and settlement in Southeast Asia and Australia, see Wang Gungwu, *Community and Nation: China, Southeast Asia, and Australia* (Kensington, Australia: Asian Studies Association of Australia in association with Allen & Unwin, 1992); *Sojourners and Settlers: Histories of Southeast Asia and the Chinese*, ed. Anthony Reid (Australia: Allen and Unwin, 1996); Victor Purcell, *The Chinese in Southeast Asia* (London: Oxford University Press, 1951); and Mary F. Somers Heidhues, *Southeast Asia's Chinese Minorities* (Hong Kong: Longman Australia, 1974).

4. The available census data do not distinguish between those who were employed in the domestic sphere as wage-earning servants and those who served in the domestic sphere as non-wage-earning housewives, mothers, etc.

5. Mexico, Dirección General de Estadística, *Censo de población del municipio de Chihuahua, Chihuahua, 1930* (Salt Lake City: Filmado por la Sociedad Genealógica de Utah, 1987) (hereafter referred to as Chihuahua Manuscripts 1930); Mexico, Dirección General de Estadística, *Censo de población del municipio de Hermosillo, Sonora* (Salt Lake City: Filmado por la Sociedad Genealógica de Utah, 1988)(hereafter cited as Hermosillo Manuscripts 1930), Mormon Family History Center, Los Angeles.

6. Chinese Exclusion Act case files, Record Group 85, National Archives, Laguna Niguel, California, Alejandro Chan, alias Chan On, file no. 5528/636-A.

7. Profile based upon comprehensive samplings of Chihuahua and Hermosillo Manuscripts 1930 conducted by author.

8. NA Laguna, Santiago Wong Chao.

9. NA Laguna, Chong Chin (José Chong).

10. Although speaking much in general terms about the Chinese mercantile monopoly in northern Mexico, the existing historiography provides limited insight into the demographic profiles of immigrant merchants and the functioning and organization of their commercial organizations. As stated by pioneering Chinese immigration historian Evelyn Hu-DeHart, "Little is known about the small Chinese businesses that seemed to proliferate throughout Sonora and the north during the *Porfiriato*, but whenever urbanization and population growth appeared, Chinese could be found participating actively in the local economy." Hu-DeHart, "Immigrants to a Developing Society," 275–312, 282. The following discussion of merchant demographics and borderlands merchant types contributes substantially to this gap in the historical literature related to the ubiquitous Chinese merchants of Sonora and northern Mexico.

11. NA Laguna, Cuan Sun (Ricardo Cuan).

12. Chihuahua and Hermosillo Manuscripts 1930.

13. Macdonald and Macdonald, "Chain Migration, Ethnic Neighborhood Formation, and Social Networks," 82–97, 82.

14. Ibid., 90.

15. Statement by Mexican bookkeeper and bill collector of the Tijuana Chamber of Commerce, Eugenio Bereau, NA Laguna, Santiago Wong Chao.

16. NA Laguna, Ley Chip (Rodolfo Ley); NA Laguna, Pablo Chee.

17. Although the Chinese Exclusion Act of 1882 and its subsequent legislative reenactments barred the immigration of Chinese laborers to the United States, Section 6 provided an exception for Chinese immigrants who could prove that they were bona fide merchants.

18. Macdonald and Macdonald, "Chain Migration, Ethnic Neighborhood Formation," 113.

19. Chihuahua and Hermosillo Manuscripts 1930.

20. NA Laguna, Cuan Sun (Ricardo Cuan).

21. Macdonald and Macdonald, "Chain Migration, Ethnic Neighborhood Formation," 82–83.

22. NA Laguna, Enrique Chong.

23. Chinese merchants residing in the U.S. border cities of Calexico and Nogales are included in this discussion because of the close relationship existing between Chinese borderlands merchants of Mexico and the United States. Substantial numbers of Chinese merchants residing in U.S. cities such as Calexico previously got their start as emigrant merchants in Mexico; Chinese merchants residing in the United States also traveled to Mexico to sell merchandises to their compatriots living and working on the other side of the border; some even journeyed to Mexico to purchase grocery items such as vegetables for their own businesses; friendship relationships, moreover, were maintained between Chinese emigrant merchants residing on both sides of the national line.

24. The following profile is drawn from biographical data of Chinese merchant Pablo Chee. NA Laguna, Pablo Chee.

25. NA Laguna, Pablo Chee.

26. This mid-level merchant profile is based upon biographical data related to Chinese merchants Ricardo Cuan and José Chong Cuy. NA Laguna, Cuan Sun (Ricardo Cuan); NA Laguna, José Chong Cuy.

27. In 1942, one peso was worth approximately twenty cents in U.S. currency. NA Laguna, Ramon Wong Fong Song. Cuan possessed his 15,000-peso interest in Rafael Chan and Company as of 1943. This peso-to-dollars conversion is based upon the 1942 conversion rate.

28. The 1943 salary converted to U.S. dollars based upon 1942 monetary conversion rate.

29. NA Laguna, Ricardo Cuan.

30. Value of stock on hand as of 1943; conversion to U.S. currency based upon conversion rate of 1942.

31. Cuan's initial investment was made in 1927. Currency conversion rate unavailable for this year.

32. Small merchant profile based upon biographical data found in NA Laguna, Pablo Chee; NA Laguna, Ramon Wong Fong Song; NA Laguna, Federico Cham; NA Laguna, Chong Chin (José Chong); NA Laguna, Santiago Wong Chao; Chinese Exclusion Act case files, Record Group 85, National Archives, Laguna Niguel, California, Wong Chaun Fay, file no. 495/35; and NA Laguna, Enrique Chong.

33. NA Laguna, Federico Cham.

34. Based upon case studies from NA Laguna, Rodolfo Ley; NA Laguna, Hui Tong Ping; Chinese Exclusion Act case files, Record Group 85, National Archives, Laguna Niguel, California, Lee Bing Foon, file no. 494/52.

35. NA Laguna, Rodolfo Ley.

36. According to Chinese Exclusion Act case file records, Maria Refugio helped out with her husband's business by assisting customers and watching the store. Her active involvement in the day-to-day administration of El Progreso provides a rare example of female employment activity within the public sphere. In contrast to Maria's example, the wives of Chinese immigrants (both Chinese and Mexican), as recorded in the Hermosillo and Chihuahua manuscripts, remained relegated exclusively to the domestic sphere in accordance with traditional Chinese patriarchal values. Out of a comprehensive sampling of seventy-four wives and free-union partners of Chinese immigrants from these two municipal districts in 1930, all were registered as "domestics." By contrast, however, out of five female Chinese offspring over the age of sixteen recorded in these municipal manuscripts, three were cited as possessing employment outside of the domestic sphere. Of these three, one was a teacher, or "profesora," another was a dressmaker, or "costurera," and the third was a commercial employee, or "empleado particular." These latter findings suggest a certain measure of generational employment mobility for the female offspring of Chinese male immigrants. For more on Chinese patriarchy and patterns of Chinese female immigrant involvement in the public sphere of American life during this time period, see Yung, *Unbound Feet*.

37. Excerpted from Immigration and Naturalization Service description of El Progreso store. NA Laguna, Rodolfo Ley.

38. Value of stock of merchandise in 1939. In this year, one peso was worth approximately twenty cents in U.S. currency. NA Laguna, Rodolfo Ley.

39. Ivan Light and Edna Bonacich, *Immigrant Entrepreneurs: Koreans in Los Angeles, 1965–1982* (Berkeley and Los Angeles: University of California Press, 1988).

40. NA Laguna, Rodolfo Ley.

41. NA Laguna, Cuan Sun (Ricardo Cuan).

42. Gerardo, *Dragón en el desierto,* 89–102.

43. Ibid., 100, 101. Although the lineage structure was common throughout China prior to the mid-twentieth century, the lineage organizational system was further developed in South China as compared with the rest of the country. Although representatives of various familial lineages scattered themselves throughout the world in places such as Mexico, they maintained close transnational connections with their home villages and their kinsmen living abroad. For further reading on patrilineal kinship patterns in South China during the early to mid-twentieth century and their relationship to international emigration, see Yuen-fong Woon, *Social Organization in South China, 1911–1949: The Case of the Kuan Lineage in K'ai-p'ing County* (Ann Arbor: Center for Chinese Studies, University of Michigan, 1984); James L. Watson, *Emigration and the Chinese Lineage: The Mans in Hong Kong and London* (Berkeley and Los Angeles: University of California Press, 1975).

44. Gerardo, *Dragón en el desierto,* 99; "Carta de Francisco L. Yuen al Presidente Alvaro Obregon, 20 de julio de 1922"; "Manifiesto del Partido Nacionalista chino en que se refutan los cargos lanzados por la Sociedad Chee Kung Tong, octubre de 1922," Monteón González and Trueba Lara, *Chinos y antichinos en Mexico,* 68, 71, 73.

45. José Luis Trueba Lara, *Los Chinos en Sonora: Una historia olvidada* (Hermosillo: Instituto de Investigaciones Historicas, Universidad de Sonora, 1990), 73.

46. Espinoza, *Ejemplo de Sonora,* 229, 244.

47. "Carta de Francisco L. Yuen al Presidente Alvaro Obregon, 20 de julio de 1922"; "Manifiesto del Partido Nacionalista chino en que se refutan los cargos lanzados por la Sociedad Chee Kung Tong, octubre de 1922," in Monteón González and Trueba Lara, *Chinos y antichinos en Mexico,* 68, 71.

48. Trueba Lara, *Los Chinos en Sonora,* 72.

49. "Manifiesto del Partido Nacionalista," in Monteón González and Trueba Lara, *Chinos y antichinos en Mexico,* 71–72; Espinoza, *Ejemplo de Sonora,* 245.

50. Translation mine. The original Spanish text reads: "En Estados Unidos, en China, en Japón, en Mexico y en general en todo país en que haya un miembro de la CHEE KUNG TONG, habrá opio, habrá juego y habrá inmoralidad."

51. Espinoza, *Ejemplo de Sonora,* 319–24.

52. Translation mine. The original Spanish text reads: "El Supremo Consejo de México, que es la más alta autoridad masónica en nuestro país, y con el cual estoy directamente relacionado actualmente, el año próximo pasado giró circular a todas las Potencias Masónicas (Grandes Logias) de la República, dando a conocer un acuerdo reciente Congreso Masónico Internacional de Laussane, en el que se da una lista de las falsas sociedades Masónicas, y entre ellas figuraba y sigue figurando la 'Chee Kung Tong,' que será una asociación tan Antigua y bien organizada como Uds. dicen, pero no es Masónica, según el sentir de todos los masones del Universo, representados debidamente en dicho Congreso."

53. Espinoza, *Ejemplo de Sonora*, 242–44.

54. Trueba Lara, *Los Chinos en Sonora*, 75–78.

55. Espinoza, *Ejemplo de Sonora*, 303–5. The Spanish text, translated from Chinese in *Ejemplo de Sonora*, reads as follows:

"Hoy, al desear la adquisición, únicamente debemos de obrar el asesinato secretamente, por que así no provocará la complicidad general, y de tal suerte, se aprobarán en todas partes esta forma de asesinar: SECRETAMENTE. . . . Mientras tanto, esperáramos el asunto del Diablo HAU; si puede hacer, hágalo; si debe suspender, suspéndalo; pero lo principal y lo importante es de buscar el bienestar general." Translation from Chinese to Spanish. Translation to English from Spanish is mine.

56. Trueba Lara, *Los Chinos en Sonora*, 74; Article 33 of the Mexican Constitution granted the president the exclusive right to "[remove] from the national territories without any preliminary hearing/trial, any foreigner whose stay is deemed inconvenient" (77).

57. Ibid., 75.

Chapter 6. Mexican Sinophobia and the Anti-Chinese Campaigns

1. J. B. Moore to Mr. Chang Kang-jen, Chinese Chargé d'Affaires, Washington, D.C., 27 June 1913; Frederick Simpich, American Consul to the Honorable Secretary of State, Nogales, Sonora, 24 June 1913; A. L. Gustetter to Honorable Frederick Simpich, American Consul, Nogales, Arizona, 25 June 1913; Frederick Simpich to the Honorable Secretary of State, Nogales, Mexico, 27 February 1914, "Chinese Question in Mexico."

2. Frederick Simpich American Consul to the Honorable Secretary of State, Nogales, Sonora, 24 June 1913, "Chinese Question in Mexico."

3. Wilfley and Bassett, "Memorandum Showing Extent of Destruction of Life and Property of Chinese Subjects during the Recent Revolution in Mexico

and Mexico's Responsibility Therefor, Together with Citation of Authorities," *Memorandum on the Law and the Facts in the Matter of the Claim of China against Mexico for Losses of Life and Property Suffered by Chinese Subjects at Torreón on May 13, 14, 15, 1911* (Mexico, D.F.: American Book & Printing, 1911)(hereafter cited as "Memorandum Showing Extent of Destruction"), 3; "Note," Index Bureau 312.93/172–312.93/181, "Chinese Question in Mexico."

4. William C. Burdett, American Consul, to the Honorable Secretary of State, Ensenada, B.C., 30 April 1921; "Protection of Chinese in Mexico . . . Note," Index Bureau 312.93/46; Frederick Simpich, American Vice Consul in Charge, to the Honorable Secretary of State, Nogales, Mexico, 29 October 1914; W. J. Bryan to Mr. Kai Fu Shah, Chinese Minister, Washington, D.C., 25 March 1915; Frederick Simpich, American Consul, to the Honorable Secretary of State, Nogales, Mexico, 21 April 1915; Homer G. Coen, American Vice Consul, to the Honorable Secretary of State, Durango, Mexico, 19 April 1915; [John R.] Silliman, care American Consul, to Department of State (Telegram), Guadalajara, Mexico, 3 March 1916; "Note," Index Bureau 312.93/161, "Chinese Question in Mexico."

5. For example, although the infamous Los Angeles Chinese Massacre of 1871 claimed the lives of some twenty individuals, more than three hundred Chinese were killed as part of the little-known Mexican massacre of Torreón.

6. Chas. L. Montague, American Consular Agent, to Honorable Frederick Simpich, American Consul, Cananea, Sonora, 30 August 1915, "Chinese Question in Mexico."

7. Louis Hostetler, American Consul, to the Honorable Secretary of State, Hermosillo, Sonora, 21 May 1915, "Chinese Question in Mexico."

8. W. J. Bryan to Mr. Kai Fu Shah, Chinese Minister, Washington, D.C., 25 March 1915, "Chinese Question in Mexico."

9. Chas. L. Montague, Acting American Consular Agent, to Honorable Frederick Simpich, American Consul, Cananea, Sonora, 4 May 1915, "Chinese Question in Mexico."

10. "List of Personal Property Sam Wah, Piedras Negras, Coahuila," enclosed in Luther I. Illsworth, American Consul, to the Honorable Secretary of State, Ciudad Porfirio Díaz, Coahuila, 23 July 1913; "List of Personal Propert [*sic*] at P. Negras Coah., of Foon Chuck," enclosed in Luther I. Illsworth, American Consul, to the Honorable Secretary of State, Ciudad Porfirio Díaz, Coahuila, 23 July 1913; "List of Personal Property Foon Chuck and Sam Wah, located at Fuente Coahuila"; "List of Personal Property—Foon Chuck and Sam Wah," enclosed in Luther I. Illsworth, American Consul, to the Honorable Secretary of State, 23 July 1913, "Chinese Question in Mexico."

11. American Consular Agent Chas. L. Montague to Honorable Frederick Simpich, American Consul, Cananea, Sonora, 30 August 1915, "Chinese Question in Mexico."

12. Wilfley and Bassett, "Memorandum Showing Extent of Destruction," 3.

13. "Report of Investigation of Chinese Massacre That G. C. Carothers, American Consular Agent, Torreón, Coahuila, Mexico, Made June 7, 1911," enclosed in American Consul Charles M. Freeman to the Honorable Secretary of State, Durango, Mexico, 10 June 1911, "Chinese Question in Mexico" (hereafter cited as "Report of Investigation of Chinese Massacre").

14. Wilfley and Bassett, "Memorandum Showing Extent of Destruction," 3.

15. "Report of Investigation of Chinese Massacre," "Chinese Question in Mexico," 3; Wilfley and Bassett, "Report of Messrs. Owyang King and Arthur Bassett Representatives of His Excellency, Minister Chang Yin Tang in an Investigation Made in Conjunction with Licenciado Antonio Ramos Pedrueza, Representative of His Excellency, Francisco L. De la Barra, President of Mexico, of the Facts Relating to the Massacre of Chinese Subjects at Torreón on the 15th of May, 1911," *Memorandum on the Law and the Facts in the Matter of the Claim of China against Mexico for Losses of Life and Property Suffered by Chinese Subjects at Torreón on May 13, 14, 15, 1911* (Mexico, D.F.: American Book & Printing, 1911)(hereafter cited as "Report of Messrs. Owyang King and Arthur Bassett"), 10.

16. Wilfley and Bassett, *Memorandum on the Law and the Facts*, 4, "Report of Messrs. Owyang King and Arthur Bassett," 7.

17. Wilfley and Bassett, "Report of Messrs. Owyang King and Arthur Bassett," 10 (emphasis original).

18. Wilfley and Bassett, *Memorandum on the Law and the Facts*, 4–5.

19. Wilfley and Bassett, "Report of Messrs. Owyang King and Arthur Bassett," 10–11, *Memorandum on the Law and the Facts*, 5, "Report of Investigation of Chinese Massacre," 3–5.

20. Wilfley and Bassett, *Memorandum on the Law and the Facts*, 5, "Report of Messrs. Owyang King and Arthur Bassett," 11.

21. Wilfley and Bassett, "Report of Messrs. Owyang King and Arthur Bassett," 11–13, *Memorandum on the Law and the Facts*, 5–6.

22. Wilfley and Bassett, "Report of Messrs. Owyang King and Arthur Bassett," 12.

23. Wilfley and Bassett, *Memorandum on the Law and the Facts*, 5, "Report of Messrs. Owyang King and Arthur Bassett," 12.

24. "Report of Investigation of Chinese Massacre," 5.

25. Wilfley and Bassett, *Memorandum on the Law and the Facts*, 6.

26. Ibid., 3, "Memorandum Showing Extent of Destruction," 3.

27. Wilfley and Bassett, *Memorandum on the Law and the Facts*, 6.

28. Ibid., 2, 6–7.

29. Ibid., 6, "Report of Messrs. Owyang King and Arthur Bassett," 13.

30. Wilfley and Bassett, *Memorandum on the Law and the Facts*, 3, "Report of Messrs. Owyang King and Arthur Bassett," 1, 3.

31. Wilfley and Bassett, "Memorandum Showing Extent of Destruction," 1–10, *Memorandum on the Law and the Facts*, 1–22.

32. J. Earuie to Mr. Clark, Mexico City, 30 January 1913, "Chinese Question in Mexico." In this letter to Mr. Clark, J. Earuie states that he was not sure of the accuracy of this amount and uncertain as to whether this amount was in dollars or pesos.

33. Telegram no. 662, Mexico, 3 December 1913, Index Bureau 312.93/54, "Chinese Question in Mexico."

34. Wilfley and Bassett, *Memorandum on the Law and the Facts*, 4, "Report of Messrs. Owyang King and Arthur Bassett," 7, 10; American Consul Wm. E. Alger to the Honorable Secretary of State, Mazatlán, Sinaloa, 17 March 1912; Simpich to Secretary of State (telegram), Nogales, Arizona, 24 February 1914; American Vice Consul in Charge Frederick Simpich to the Honorable Secretary of State, Nogales, Mexico, 27 February 1914, "Chinese Question in Mexico."

35. This speech was never actually presented, as the scheduled rally was cancelled by Mexican authorities as a consequence of U.S. diplomatic intervention. American Consul Wm. E. Alger to the Honorable Secretary of State, Mazatlán, Sinaloa, 17 March 1912, "Chinese Question in Mexico."

36. American Vice Consul in Charge Frederick Simpich to the Honorable Secretary of State, Nogales, Mexico, 27 February 1914, "Chinese Question in Mexico."

37. Ibid.; Wilfley and Bassett, "Report of Messrs. Owyang King and Arthur Bassett," 10; "Mensaje de Quong Sang Lung y Fong Fo Qui al Gobernador del Estado de Sonora, el 27 de junio de 1906," in Monteón Gonzalez and Trueba Lara, *Chinos y antichinos en Mexico*, 57.

38. In 1916, this perceived collusion between Chinese immigrants and U.S. interests was further cemented in the minds of certain Mexicans as a consequence of Chinese support of U.S. military forces sent to Mexico as part of a punitive expedition against Pancho Villa. In retaliation against Villa for his military attack against the community of Columbus, New Mexico, President Wilson ordered General John Pershing to pursue and capture Villa. While in Mexico, Pershing's troops were aided by Chinese merchants, laborers, laundrymen, and cooks. Following the withdrawal of Pershing's expeditionary force,

Pershing successfully lobbied Congress for the granting of U.S. permanent residence status for those Chinese immigrants who assisted him and his troops. For more on the Pershing incident, see Edward Eugene Briscoe, "Pershing's Chinese Refugees: An Odyssey of the Southwest" (master's thesis, St. Mary's University, San Antonio, 1947).

39. American Vice Consul in Charge Frederick Simpich to the Honorable Secretary of State, Nogales, Mexico, 27 February 1914; Robert Lansing to Mr. Kai Fu Shah, Chinese Minister, Washington, D.C., 10 February 1915, "Chinese Question in Mexico."

40. American Consul Louis Hostetler to the Honorable Secretary of State, Hermosillo, Sonora, 21 May 1915, "Chinese Question in Mexico." As an example of the decrease in wages that occurred during the years of the Porfiriato, Aurora Gómez-Galvarriato asserts that real wages for Mexican industrial workers declined by almost 18 percent between 1907 and 1911. Moreover, from 1914 to 1916, hyperinflation engendered by revolutionary political instability produced a decrease in purchasing power and a reduction of real wages for industrial workers. For an econometric examination of the effects of the Mexican Revolution upon real wage earnings, see Aurora Gómez-Galvarriato, "The Evolution of Prices and Real Wages in Mexico from the Porfiriato to the Revolution," in *Latin America and the World Economy since 1800,* ed. James H. Coatsworth and Alan M. Taylor (Cambridge: Harvard University Press, 1998).

41. American Consul Alexander V. Dye to the Honorable Secretary of State, Nogales, Sonora, 19 May 1911, "Chinese Question in Mexico."

42. American Consul Louis Hostetler to the Honorable Secretary of State, Hermosillo, Sonora, 25 May 1915, "Chinese Question in Mexico."

43. Wilfley and Bassett, *Memorandum on the Law and the Facts,* 4, "Report of Messrs. Owyang King and Arthur Bassett," 10.

44. "Al margen del informe del C. Gobernador del Estado Dr. Cesareo G. Soriano," Magdalena, 4 April 1918; Manifesto of "Junta Comercial y de Hombres de Negocios," ca. February 1916, José Maria Arana Papers, University of Arizona Special Collections (hereafter cited as Arana MSS).

45. Manifesto of "Junta Comercial y de Hombres de Negocios," ca. February 1916, Arana MSS.

46. Espinoza, *Ejemplo de Sonora,* 50–52.

47. Ibid., 62; *El Nacionalista,* November 22, 1925, Arana MSS.

48. Luis León to Sr. D. José Maria Arana, Hermosillo, 23 October 1918, Arana MSS.

49. Ibid. Original Spanish text reads: "Creo yo que un verdadero nacionalismo, encaminado a destruir, no tan sólo el eminente monopolio chino, sino

aún también, el monopolio de las Fuentes de riqueza del Estado por otros extranjeros, como algunas compañías norteamericanas, no sólo nos dará una fuerte simpatía en toda la República." Translation into English, mine.

50. Junta Central Nacionalista to Presidente de la República Mexicana, Culiacán, 25 October 1920; Manifesto of "Junta Comercial y de Hombres de Negocios," ca. February 1916; "Carísimos niños, amigos nuestros," *El Nacionalista*, November 22, 1925, 3; supporter of anti-Chinese campaigns to José Maria Arana, Pilares de Nacozari, Arana MSS.

51. Rafael C. Silves to José Ma. Arana, Calexico, California, 18 August 1919; José F. Barifel to Señor Director de "Pro-Patria," Magdalena, 12 September 1917; *El Nacionalista*, November 22, 1925, Arana MSS. The experience of the Chinese of Mexico parallels that of Jewish and Japanese immigrants of Brazil during this same time period. Similar charges, founded upon a rhetoric of economic nationalism, were also leveled against the Jewish community of Brazil. Brazilian nativists scapegoated Jewish immigrants for both the economic downturn engendered by the Great Depression and the decline of Brazil's coffee economy. In addition, like the Chinese of Mexico, the Jews of Brazil were criticized for being culturally unassimilable, financially oriented, and urban. During the first quarter of the twentieth century, Brazilian elites spearheaded a xenophobic public movement against the Japanese known as the "Campanha Anti-Niponica." This anti-Japanese campaign reached its height in the 1920s, and proponents of the movement condemned Japanese immigrants as biologically inferior, unassimilable, and agents of economic expansion sent by the Japanese government. For more on the Jewish and Japanese experiences in Brazil, see Jeffrey Lesser, *Welcoming the Undesirables: Brazil and the Jewish Question* (Berkeley and Los Angeles: University of California Press, 1995).

52. Espinoza, *Ejemplo de Sonora*, 33, 77, 172; José F. Barifel to Señor Director de "Pro-Patria," Magdalena, 12 September 1917; Reynaldo Villalobos to José M. Arana, Culiacán, 4 May 1919; Junta Central Nacionalista to Presidente de la República Mexicana, Culiacán, 25 October 1920; Ramón Garcia to José Maria Arana, Arana MSS.

53. Espinoza, *Ejemplo de Sonora*, 46, 67, 69, 91, 102; José F. Barifel to Señor Director de "Pro-Patria," Magdalena, 12 September 1917; Junta Central Nacionalista to Presidente de la República Mexicana, Culiacán, 25 October 1920, Arana MSS.

54. The expression "lopa pa'laval" was used to mock the inability of many Chinese immigrants to pronounce the letter "r." The proper expression should have been "ropa pa'lavar." Espinoza, *Ejemplo de Sonora*, 39, 46, 228, 270. For a detailed history of vice along the U.S.–Mexico border, see Eric Michael Schantz,

"From the Mexicali Rose to the Tijuana Brass: Vice Tours of the United States–Mexico Border, 1910–1965" (PhD diss., UCLA, 2001).

55. Espinoza, *Ejemplo de Sonora*, 115, 231–32, 241–318. For further discussion regarding Chinese immigrant organizations and the "tong wars," please see chapter 5.

56. Ibid., 177, 120–23, 57, 97; "Extracto de una comunicación de Vito Aguirre, Presidente de la Alianza Nacionalista de Chihuahua y Comités adherentes, al Presidente Abelardo L. Rodriguez, dirigida desde Chihuahua, Chihuahua, el 17 de junio de 1933"; "Extracto de un telegrama de Manuel Romero, miembro del Comité Nacionalista Pro-Raza dirigido al Presidente de la República desde Santiago Ixcuintla, Nayarit, el 22 de noviembre de 1933"; "Extracto de un telegrama de José Angel Espinoza dirigido al Secretario particular del presidente de la República, fechado en la ciudad de México, el 28 de noviembre de 1933"; Espinoza, *Ejemplo de Sonora*, 121; "Al margen del informe del C. Gobernador del Estado Dr. Cesareo G. Soriano," Magdalena, 4 April 1918; "Carísimos niños, amigos nuestros," *El Nacionalista*, 3; "Pocas palabras y mucha acción," *El Nacionalista*, November 22, 1925; "Actas de la 2a Gra: Convención Antichina," *El Nacionalista*, November 22, 1925, Arana MSS.

57. Espinoza, *Ejemplo de Sonora*, 165–66, 177.

58. L. Villareal, Silvano B. Figueroa to Sr. José Ma. Arana, Tuxpan, Nayarit, 1 January 1921; José Ma. Arana to H. Junta Nacionalista de Culiacán, Magdalena, 24 November 1920; El Club del Pueblo to H. Congreso del Estado, Magdalena, 12 September 1918; "Carísimos niños, amigos nuestros," 3, Arana MSS.

59. *El Nacionalista*, November 22, 1925; "Al margen del informe del C. Gobernador del Estado Dr. Cesareo G. Soriano," Magdalena, 4 April 1918, Arana MSS.

60. "Carísimos niños, amigos nuestros," 3; "La vida del comercio nacional," *El Nacionalista*, November 22, 1925, 2; "Historia del tubo de una lámpara," *El Nacionalista*, Sonora, November 22, 1925, 2; "Grito de . . . ," *El Nacionalista*, November 22, 1925, 4; "Son más de 200 los fumaderos de opio en la República," *El Nacionalista*, November 22, 1925, 1, 4, Arana MSS.

61. Espinoza, *Ejemplo de Sonora*, 97; "Organicemos a los trabajadores chinos," in Gonzáles Monteón and Trueba Lara, *Chinos y antichinos*, 100; "Carísimos niños, amigos nuestros," 3; "Pocas palabras y mucha acción," Arana MSS.

62. "La vida del comercio nacional," 2; "Pocas palabras y mucha acción," Arana MSS.

63. "Carísimos niños, amigos nuestros," 3, Arana MSS. Original Spanish text reads: "Adelante niños de la raza, vamos triunfado; vamos demostrando al mundo que sabéis triunfar, que sabéis vencer. . . . Que importa cuando lo que se pelea es la vida o la muerte de nuestra nacionalidad. . . . YO QUE SOY

UN NINO MEXICANO, JURO, POR LOS HUESOS DE MIS ANTEPASADOS
QUE DESDE HOY YA NO COMPRARE NI UN CENTAVO EN LAS TIENDAS
DE CHINOS." Translation to English, mine.

64. Espinoza, *Ejemplo de Sonora*, 50–51, 74–79.

65. Ibid., 51, 74–75.

66. Ibid., 63–68.

67. Mexico, *Semanario judicial de la Federación*, 1917, 1918, 1919, 1920, 1927, 1929, 1930, 1931, 1932 (Mexico: Antigua Imprenta de Murguia).

68. "Lim Jim y coag.," 25 de octubre de 1930, *Semanario judicial de la Federación*, vol. 30, pt. 1, 1132–36.

69. "Intervenciones de los diputados," in Monteón Gonzalez and Trueba Lara, *Chinos y antichinos en Mexico*, 95, 97.

70. The original Spanish text reads: "Contra el desaliento que causa la opinión de uno de los señores magistrados, en el sentido de que es odiosa y repugnante la excepción que se hace de los chinos, nos trae una esperanza la opinión de otros de los señores magistrados que consideran indeseable y perniciosa para nuestra nacionalidad la inmigración china y que consideran también Constitucional la ley que llamamos antichina, del Estado de Sonora, en la parte que prohíbe el matrimonio de chinos con mexicanos." Ibid., 95.

71. "Al margen del informe del C. Gobernador del Estado Dr. Cesareo G. Soriano," Magdalena, 4 April 1918, Arana MSS.

72. "Report of Investigation of Chinese Massacre."

73. Wilfley and Bassett, "Memorandum Showing Extent of Destruction," 3.

74. Wilfley and Bassett, *Memorandum on the Law and the Facts*, 1–22, "Memorandum Showing Extent of Destruction," 1–10, "Report of Messrs. Owyang King and Arthur Bassett," 1–14; J. Earuie to Mr. Clark, Mexico City, 30 January 1913, "Chinese Question in Mexico."

75. J. Earuie to Mr. Clark, Mexico City, 30 January 1913, " Chinese Question in Mexico."

76. Telegram no. 662, Mexico, 3 December 1913, Index Bureau 312.93/54, "Chinese Question in Mexico."

77. Espinoza, *Ejemplo de Sonora*, 119–20.

78. Ibid., 119 (emphasis mine). Translation to English, mine. *Circular Num. 194; Sección de Gobernación (Department of the Governor). Referencia (Reference): 58–15.* The original Spanish text reads:

AL C. PRESIDENTE DEL CONCEJO MUNICIPAL.

Habiéndose observado que los comerciantes chinos no queriendo acatar lo dispuesto por el Articulo 106 reformado de la Ley de Trabajo y Previsión

Social vigente, que ordena que en toda empresa, taller o establecimiento, los patronos están obligados a ocupar al 80 percentil de mexicanos como empleados u obreros prefrieron cerrar sus negocios, y teniendo conocimiento de que dichos comerciantes continúan reteniendo existencias de mercancías almacenadas, las cuales de continuar en la citada condición provocarían como consecuencia natural la escasez de artículos de primera necesidad, este Ejecutivo, con el propósito de prevenir que lleguen a presentarse los males indicados que desde luego causarían serios perjuicios a los vecinos de esa región, estima conveniente recomendar a usted se sirva notificar a los aludidos comerciantes, radicados en esa Jurisdicción que procedan a realizar las mercancías que todavía tengan en su poder, haciéndolo dentro del menor tiempo posible, advirtiéndolos también que *desocupen* los locales que tuvieron alquilados para sus comercios o almacenes.

Indudable que con la observancia de las medidas que se le comunican surgirá prontamente el comercio nacional y las personas que vayan a dedicarse a este género de actividades, tendrán mayores facilidades para encontrar locales propios para establecerse.

79. Ibid., 134–37.

80. Ibid., 138–40; Gonzáles Monteón and Trueba Lara, *Chinos y antichinos*, 134; Bartley F. Yost to the Honorable Secretary of State, Nogales, Mexico, 21 March 1932, "Chinese Question in Mexico."

81. Espinoza, *Ejemplo de Sonora*, 177–78.

82. Mexico, Secretaría de Gobernación, *Servicio de Migración* , 38–39.

83. Mexico, Secretaría de la Economía Nacional, *Estados Unidos Mexicanos: Sexto censo de población, 1940*.

84. Romero, *Comisión de inmigración*, 12–15; "El sol chino III," in Monteón Gonzáles and Trueba Lara, *Chinos y antichinos*, 50.

85. Cott, "Mexican Diplomacy and the Chinese Issue," 65.

86. Romero, *Comisión de inmigración*, 14–15.

87. "El sol chino III," 50. Translation mine. Original Spanish text reads:

Los defensores de la raza amarilla alegan que nos faltan brazos para el fomento de la agricultura y de la minería y francamente, quisiéramos que nos probarán esa aserción señalándonos las sementeras cultivados por chinos y las mismas donde el mongol se ha ido a ofrecer el contingente de sus brazos. . . . Se dan casos muy aislados de que algunos se dediquen al cultivo de las verduras en pequeña escala y cuando van a un campo minero es solo para sentar plaza de cocineros, para establecer una fonda o para dedicarse al comercio. Donde esta, pues, esa necesidad que tenemos de sus brazos?

88. Ibid., 179. Translation mine. Original Spanish text reads:

Una de las manifestaciones más vivas y más lamentables de la antipatía perfectamente localizada hacia la lucha anti-chinista, parte de casi la totalidad de los hombres del gobierno y de la alta burguesía egoísta, ambiciosa y dueña de inmensos intereses, antipatía que consiste en esta verdad lastimosa: hasta el más insignificante abuso, no de un grupo, sino de uno o dos exaltados, ha repercutido siempre con gran revuelo en las columnas de los periódicos y nos ha sido posible anotar esos hechos como una marcada idea intencional de desprestigiar la causa.

89. See n. 87 above.

90. See n. 85 above.

91. Mexico, Secretaría de la Economia Nacional, *Anuário estadístico de la República Mexicana 1930.*

92. Cott, "Mexican Diplomacy and the Chinese Issue."

93. Romero, *Comisión de inmigración,* v, 2.

94. Ibid., 121.

95. Ibid. Translation mine. Original text states:

No es conveniente a los intereses nacionales permitir la inmigración ilimitada de chinos como elemento de colonización, sea en forma colectiva o individual, libre o contratada fuera de nuestro territorio. . . . Tampoco conviene a los intereses nacionales permitir la inmigración ilimitada ni restringida de chinos como elemento de trabajo manual, sea en forma colectiva o individual, libre o por contratos celebrados fuera de nuestro territorio.

96. Ibid., 77; *The Idea of Race in Latin America, 1870–1940,* ed. Richard Graham (Austin: University of Texas Press, 1990), 78.

97. Romero, *Comisión de inmigración,* 12, 76, 77.

98. Graham, *Idea of Race,* 77–83.

99. Mexico, Secretaría de Gobernación, *Servicio de Migración,* 38–39; Mexico, Ministerio de Fomento, *Censo general de la República Mexicana verificado el 20 de octubre de 1895, resúmen del censo de la República.*

100. The original Spanish text reads: "una invasion como en país conquistado."

101. Mexico, Secretaría de Gobernación, *Servicio de Migración,* 5. Translation mine. Original Spanish text reads: "En breve tiempo se vieron invadidos por una enorme cantidad de asiáticos las poblaciones costeñas del Pacífico, y por ellas llegaron a las del centro de la República, estableciéndose como en un país conquistado, sin requisitos de ninguna clase, en el lugar que mas les convenía."

102. The original Spanish text reads: "la verdadera escoria humana."

103. Ibid., 12–13.

104. Ibid., 8–9; Mexico, Secretaría de la Economia Nacional, *Anuário estadístico de la República Mexicana 1930*, 144.

105. Mexico, Secretaría de Gobernación, *Servicio de Migración*, 12–17.

106. Mexico, Secretaría de la Economía Nacional, *Anuário estadístico de la República Mexicana 1930*, 144.

107. "Mexico restringe la entrada de inmigrantes trabajadores," *Excelsior* (Mexico City), July 15, 1931, 1.

108. "La Cámara de Diputados aprobó ayer ochenta y tres artículos de la ley del Trabajo y entre ellos los que se refieren al contrato colectivo," *Excelsior*, July 22, 1931, 1.

Chapter 7. Conclusion

1. "El Plan Espiritual de Aztlán" was adopted by the First National Chicano Liberation Youth Conference in Denver, Colorado, in March 1969.

Bibliography

Primary Sources

Manuscript and Archival Collections

Bancroft Library, University of California, Berkeley. Various governmental reports and publications as cited in the listing of governmental publications below.

"Chinese Question in Mexico, 1910–1930." Microfilm roll. Record Group 59, General Records of the Department of State, Decimal File 312.93, 1910–1929, 1930–1939; 704.9312, 1910–1929, 1930–1939, University of Arizona Main Library.

Customs Bureau Special Agents Reports and Correspondence, ca. 1865–1915. Record Group 36. National Archives, Washington, D.C.

Chinese Exclusion Act case files. Record Group 85. National Archives, Laguna Niguel, California.

Chinese Partnership case files, Certificate of Identity books. Record Group 85. National Archives, San Bruno, California.

José Maria Arana Papers. Special Collections Department, University of Arizona, Tucson.

Mexican municipal census manuscripts for Hermosillo, Magdalena, Guaymas, Arizpe, Moctezuma, Nogales, Chihuahua City. Mormon Family History Centers of Los Angeles and West Covina, California.

United States consular reports for Ensenada, Guaymas, Mazatlan, Mexico City, Monterrey, Nogales, Nuevo Laredo, Tampico, Veracruz, circa 1830–1906. Main Library, University of California, Irvine.

Government Publications and Reports

Estatutos de la Compañía de Colonización Asiática. Mexico: Imprenta de J. M. Lara, 1866. Bancroft Library, University of California, Berkeley.

Mexico. Ministerio de Fomento. Censo general de la República Mexicana verificado el 20 de octubre de 1895, resúmen del censo de la República. Mexico: Dirección General de Estadística, 1899.

Mexico. Secretaría de Agricultura y Fomento. *Tercer censo de población de los Estados Unidos Mexicanos, verificado el 27 de octubre 1910*. Mexico: Dirección General de la Estadística, 1911.

Mexico. Secretaría de Economía. *Estadísticas sociales del Porfiriato: 1877–1910*. Mexico, D.F.: Dirección General de Estadística, 1956.

Mexico. Secretaría de Gobernación. *El Servicio de Migración en Mexico por Andrés Landa y Pina jefe del Departamento de Migración*. Mexico, D.F.: Talleres Gráficos de la Nación, 1930. Bancroft Library, University of California, Berkeley.

Mexico. Secretaría de la Economía Nacional. *Anuário estadístico de la República Mexicana 1901*. Mexico, D.F.: Dirección General de Estadística, 1902.

Mexico. Secretaría de la Economía Nacional. *Anuario Estadístico de la Republica Mexicana 1905*. Mexico, D.F.: Dirección General de Estadística, 1906.

Mexico. Secretaría de la Economía Nacional. *Anuário estadístico de la República Mexicana 1907*. Mexico, D.F.: Dirección General de Estadística, 1908.

Mexico. Secretaría de la Economía Nacional, *Anuário estadístico de la República Mexicana 1913*. Mexico, D.F.: Dirección General de Estadística, 1914.

Mexico. Secretaría de la Economía Nacional, *Anuário estadístico de la República Mexicana 1930*. Mexico, D.F.: Dirección General de Estadística.Mexico. Secretaría de la Economía Nacional. *Censo de población 1910, resúmen general*. Mexico: Dirección General de la Estadística, 1918–1920.

Mexico. Secretaría de la Economía Nacional. *Quinto censo de población, 1930, resúmen general*. Mexico: Dirección General de la Estadística, 1932–1936.

Mexico. Secretaría de la Economía Nacional. *Estados Unidos Mexicanos: Sexto censo de población 1940, resúmen general*. Mexico, D.F.: Dirección General de Estadística, 1943.

Mexico. *Semanario judicial de la Federación, 1917, 1918, 1919, 1920, 1927, 1929, 1930, 1931, 1932*. Mexico: Antigua Imprenta de Murguia.

Monteón González, Humberto, and José Luis Trueba Lara. *Chinos y antichinos en Mexico: Documentos para su estudio*. Guadalajara, Jalisco: Gobierno de Jalisco, Secretaría General, Unidad Editorial, 1988.

Romero, José M. *Comisión de inmigración; dictamen del vocal ingeniero José Maria Romero, encargado de estudiar la influencia social y económica de la inmigración asiática en Mexico*. Mexico: Imprenta de A. Carranza e hijos, 1911. Bancroft Library, University of California, Berkeley.

Romero, Matías. *Geographical and Statistical Notes on Mexico, 1837-1898*. New York: G. P. Putnam's Sons, 1898.

Wilfley and Bassett. *Memorandum on the Law and the Facts in the Matter of the Claim of China against Mexico for Losses of Life and Property Suffered by Chinese Subjects at Torreon on May 13, 14, 15, 1911*. D.F., Mexico: American Book & Printing, 1911.

Newspapers

Excelsior (Mexico City), 1931
El Nacionalista, 1925
El Tráfico, 1899

Oral Histories

Rodriguez, Pablo [pseud.]. Interview with author, May 30, 2002.
Tom, Mike. Interview with author, August 24, 2001.

Travelers' Accounts, Memoirs

Dana, Richard H. *To Cuba and Back*. Carbondale: University of Illinois Press, 1966.
Espinoza, José Angel. *El ejemplo de Sonora*. Mexico, D.F.: n.p., 1932.
Gamez, Antonio G. *Mi viejo Mexicali: Remembranzas*. Mexicali: A. Gastelum Gamez, 1991.
Howe, Julia W. *A Trip to Cuba*. New York: Praeger, 1969 (reprint of 1860 ed.).
Lewis, Richard J. *Diary of a Spring Holiday in Cuba*. Philadelphia: Porter & Coates, 1872.
Montejo, Estéban. *The Autobiography of a Runaway Slave*, edited by Miguel Barnet. New York: Pantheon Books, 1968.
Perkins, Clifford A. *Border Patrol, with the U.S. Immigration Service on the U.S.–Mexico Boundary, 1910–1954*. El Paso: Texas Western Press, University of Texas, El Paso, 1978.

Secondary Sources

Augustine-Adams, Kif. "Making Mexico: Legal Nationality, Chinese Race, and the 1930 Population Census." *Law and History Review* 27, no. 1, 2009.
Baily, Samuel L. *Immigrants in the Lands of Promise: Italians in Buenos Aires and New York City, 1870–1914*. Ithaca, N.Y.: Cornell University Press, 1999.
Basch, Linda, Nina Glick Schiller, and Cristiana Szanton Blanc. *Nations Unbound: Transnational Projects, Postcolonial Predicaments, and Deterritorialized Nation-States*. United States: Gordon and Breach, 1994.
——, eds. *Towards a Transnational Perspective on Migration: Race, Class, Ethnicity, and Nationalism Reconsidered*. New York: New York Academy of Sciences, 1992.
Bennett, Herman L. *Africans in Colonial Mexico: Absolutism, Christianity, and Afro-Creole Consciousness, 1570–1640*. Bloomington: Indiana University Press, 2003.
Bernal, Celso A. *Compendio histórico-biográfico de Mexicali, 1539–1966*. Mexicali: B.C.F.A., 1966.

Blalock, Hubert. *Toward a Theory of Minority Group Relations*. New York: John Wiley, 1967.

Bonacich, Edna. "Middleman Minorities and Advanced Capitalism." *Ethnic Groups* 2 (1980): 211–19.

———. "A Theory of Middleman Minorities." *American Sociological Review* 38 (1973): 583–94.

Bonacich, Edna, and Lucie Cheng Hirata. *Labor Immigration under Capitalism: Asian Workers in the United States before World War II*. Berkeley and Los Angeles: University of California Press, 1984.

Briscoe, Eugene. "Pershing's Chinese Refugees: An Odyssey of the Southwest." MA thesis, St. Mary's University at San Antonio, 1947.

Buffington, Robert M., and William E. French. "The Culture of Modernity." In *The Oxford History of Mexico*, edited by Michael C. Meyer and William H. Beezley. New York: Oxford University Press, 2000.

Bushnell, David, and Neill Macaulay. *The Emergence of Latin America in the Nineteenth Century*. New York: Oxford University Press, 1994.

Camacho, Julia. "Traversing Boundaries: Chinese, Mexicans, and Chinese Mexicans in the Formation of Gender, Race, and Nation in the Twentieth-Century United States–Mexican Borderlands." PhD diss., University of Texas, El Paso, 2006.

Chamberlain, Eugene K. "Mexican Colonization versus American Interests in Lower California." *Pacific Historical Review* 20 (1951): 43–55.

Chan, Sucheng. *Asian Americans: An Interpretive History*. Boston: Twayne, 1991.

———, ed. *Chinese American Transnationalism: The Flow of People, Resources, and Ideas between China and America during the Exclusion Era*. Philadelphia: Temple University Press, 2006.

———, ed. *Entry Denied: Exclusion and the Chinese Community in America, 1882–1943*. Philadelphia: Temple University Press, 1991.

Chang, Ching Chich. "The Chinese in Latin America: A Preliminary Geographical Survey with Special Reference to Cuba and Jamaica." PhD diss., University of Maryland, 1956.

Chang-Rodriguez, Eugenio. "Chinese Labor Migration into Latin America in the Nineteenth Century." *Revista de Historia de America* 46 (December 1958): 375–97.

Chen, Ta. *Emigrant Communities in South China: A Study of Overseas Migration and Its Influence on Standards of Living and Social Change*. Shanghai: Kelly and Walsh, 1939.

Chen, Yong. *Chinese San Francisco, 1850–1943: A Transpacific Community*. Stanford: Stanford University Press, 2000.

Cheng, Lucie, Liu Yuzun, and Zheng Dehua. "Chinese Emigration, the Sunning Railway and the Development of Toisan." *Amerasia* 9, no. 1 (1982): 59–74.

Choy, Armando, Gustavo Chui, and Sio Wong, Moisés. *Our History Is Still Being Written: The Story of Three Chinese-Cuban Generals in the Cuban Revolution.* New York: Pathfinder Press, 2005.

Cott, Kennet. "Mexican Diplomacy and the Chinese Issue, 1876–1910." *Hispanic American Historical Review* 67, no. 1 (February 1987): 63–84.

Craib, Raymond B. "Chinese Immigrants in Porfirian Mexico: A Preliminary Study of Settlement, Economic Activity and Anti-Chinese Sentiment." LAII Research Paper Series no. 28. Albuquerque: Latin American and Iberian Institute at the University of New Mexico, May 1996.

The Cuba Commission Report: A Hidden History of the Chinese in Cuba: The original English-language text of 1876. Introduction by Denise Helly. Baltimore: Johns Hopkins University Press, 1993.

Cumberland, Charles C. "The Sonora Chinese and the Mexican Revolution." *Hispanic American Historical Review* 40 (1960): 191–205.

Curtis, James R. "Mexicali's Chinatown." *Geographical Review* 85, no. 3 (July 1995): 335–48.

Delgado, Grace Peña. "At Exclusion's Southern Gate: Changing Categories of Race and Class among Chinese Fronterizos, 1882–1904." In *Continental Crossroads: Remapping U.S.–Mexico Borderlands History,* edited by Samuel Truett and Elliott Young. Durham, N.C.: Duke University Press, 2004.

———. "In the Age of Exclusion: Race, Region, and Chinese Identity in the Making of the Arizona–Sonora Borderlands, 1863–1943." PhD diss., UCLA, 2000.

Dennis, Philip A. "The Anti-Chinese Campaigns in Sonora, Mexico." *Ethnohistory* 26, no. 1 (1979): 65–80.

Dubs, Homer. "The Chinese in Mexico City in 1635." *Far Eastern Quarterly* 1 (1941–42): 387–89.

Duncan, Robert H. "The Chinese and the Economic Development of Northern Baja California, 1889–1929." *Hispanic American Historical Review* 74, no. 4 (November 1994): 615–47.

Fairbank, John K. *China: A New History.* Cambridge: Belknap Press of Harvard University Press, 1992.

Fong, Michael L. "Sojourners and Settlers: The Chinese Experience in Arizona." *Journal of Arizona History* 21, no. 3 (Autumn 1980): 227–53.

Fry, C. Luther. "Illegal Entry of Orientals into the United States between 1910 and 1920." *Journal of the American Statistical Association* 23 (June 1928): 173–77.

Gabaccia, Donna. "When the Migrants Are Men: Italy's Women and Transnationalism as a Working-Class Way of Life." In *Women, Gender, and Labour*

Migration: Historical and Global Perspectives, edited by Pamela Sharpe, 190–208 (London: Routledge, 2001).

Gerardo, Eduardo A. *El dragón en el desierto: Los pioneros chinos en Mexicali.* Mexicali: Instituto de Cultura de Baja California, 1991.

Gomez-Galvarriato, Aurora. "The Evolution of Prices and Real Wages in Mexico from the Porfiriato to the Revolution." In *Latin America and the World Economy since 1800,* edited by James H. Coatsworth and Alan M. Taylor. Cambridge: Harvard University Press, 1998.

Gómez Izquierdo, José Jorge. *El movimiento antichino en Mexico: Problemas del racismo y del nacimiento durante la Revolución Mexicana.* Mexico City: Instituto Nacional de Antropología e Historia, 1991.

Gonzales, Michael J. "Chinese Plantation Workers and Social Conflict in Peru in the Late Nineteenth Century." *Journal of Latin American Studies* 21, no. 3 (October 1989): 385.

González Félix, Maricela. *El proceso de aculturación de la población de origen chino en la ciudad de Mexicali.* Cuadernos de Ciencias Sociales 7. Mexicali: Universidad Autónoma de Baja California, Instituto de Investigaciones Sociales, 1990.

———. *Viaje al corazón de la peninsula: Testimonio de Manuel Lee Mancilla.* Mexicali: Instituto de Cultura de Baja California, 2000.

Graham, Richard, ed. *The Idea of Race in Latin America, 1870–1940.* Austin: University of Texas Press, 1990.

Gungwu, Wang. *China and the Overseas Chinese.* Singapore: Times Academic Press, 1991.

———. *Community and Nation: China, Southeast Asia, and Australia.* Kensington, Australia: Asian Studies Association of Australia in association with Allen & Unwin, 1992.

Gupta, Akhil, and James Ferguson, eds. *Culture, Power, Place: Explorations in Critical Anthropology.* Durham: Duke University Press, 1997.

Hatch, Heather, comp. "The Chinese in the Southwest: A Photographic Record." *Journal of Arizona History* 21, no. 3 (Autumn 1980): 257.

Heidhues, Mary F. Somers. *Southeast Asia's Chinese Minorities.* Hong Kong: Longman Australia, 1974.

Helmrich, Stefan. "Kinship, Nation, and Paul Gilroy's Concept of Diaspora." *Diaspora* 2, no. 2 (1992): 243–49.

Hernandez Cuevas, Marco Polo. *African Mexicans and the Discourse on Modern Nation.* Dallas: University Press of America, 2004.

Hing, Bill Ong. *Making and Remaking Asian America through Immigration Policy, 1850–1990.* Stanford: Stanford University Press, 1993.

Hoy, William. *The Chinese Six Companies.* San Francisco: Chinese Consolidated Benevolent Association, 1942.

Hsu, Madeline Y. *Dreaming of Gold, Dreaming of Home: Transnationalism and Migration between the United States and South China, 1882–1943*. Stanford: Stanford University Press, 2000.

Hu-DeHart, Evelyn. "Chinese Contract Labor in Cuba, 1847–1874." *Caribbean Studies* 14, no. 2 (July 1974).

———. "Chinese Coolie Labour in Cuba in the Nineteenth Century: Free Labour or Neo-Slavery?" *Slavery and Abolition* (April 1993): 67–83.

———. "The Chinese of Baja California Norte, 1910–1934." *Proceedings of the Pacific Coast Council on Latin American Studies: Baja California and the North American Frontier* 12 (1985–86): 9–28.

———. "Coolies, Shopkeepers, Pioneers: The Chinese of Mexico and Peru, 1849–1930." *Amerasia* 15, no. 2 (1989): 91–116.

———. "From Area Studies to Ethnic Studies: The Study of the Chinese Diaspora in Latin America." In *Asian Americans: Comparative and Global Perspectives*, edited by Shirley Hune. Pullman: Washington State University Press, 1991.

———. "Immigrants to a Developing Society: The Chinese in Northern Mexico, 1875–1932." *Journal of Arizona History* 21 (Autumn 1980): 275–312.

———. "Latin America in Asia-Pacific Perspective." In *What Is in a Rim? Critical Perspectives on the Pacific Region Idea*, edited by Arif Dirlik, 251–83. Boulder, Colo.: Westview Press, 1993.

———. "Race Construction and Race Relations: Chinese and Blacks in Nineteenth Century Cuba." Unpublished paper.

———. "Racism and Anti-Chinese Persecution in Sonora, Mexico, 1876–1932." *Amerasia* 9, no. 2 (1982): 1–28.

Hu-DeHart, Evelyn, and Kathleen Lopez, guest eds. *Afro-Hispanic Review* 27 special issue, "Afro-Asia" (Spring 2008).

Hune, Shirley. "Expanding the International Dimension of Asian American Studies." *Amerasia* 15, no. 2 (1989): xix–xxiv.

———. "Rethinking Race: Paradigms and Policy Formation," *Amerasia Journal* 21 (1995): 29–40

Jacques, Leo M. "The Anti-Chinese Campaigns in Sonora, Mexico, 1900–1931." PhD diss., University of Arizona, 1974.

———. "The Chinese Massacre in Torreon (Coahuila) in 1911." *Arizona and the West* 16, no. 3 (1974): 233–46.

———. "Have Quick More Money than Mandarins." *Journal of Arizona History* 17 (Summer 1976): 208–18.

Jiménez Pastrana, Juan. *Los chinos en la historia de Cuba, 1847–1930*. Havana: Editorial de Ciencias Sociales, 1983.

Krutz, Gordon. "Chinese Labor, Economic Development, and Social Reaction." *Ethnohistory* 18, no. 4 (1971): 321–33.

Lai, Him Mark, Genny Lim, and Judy Yung, eds. *Island: Poetry and History of Chinese Immigrants on Angel Island, 1910–1940*. Seattle: University of Washington Press, 1991.

Lai, Walton Look. *Essays on the Chinese Diaspora in the Caribbean*. Trinidad and Tobago: Printcom, 2006.

——. *Indentured Labor, Caribbean Sugar: Chinese and Indian Migrants to the British West Indies, 1838–1918*. Baltimore: Johns Hopkins University Press, 1993.

Lee, Erika. *At America's Gates: Chinese Immigration during the Exclusion Era, 1882–1943*. Chapel Hill: University of North Carolina Press.

Lesser, Jeffrey. *Negotiating National Identity: Immigrants, Minorities, and the Struggle for Ethnicity in Brazil*. Durham: Duke University Press, 1999.

——. *Welcoming the Undesirables: Brazil and the Jewish Question*. Berkeley: University of California Press, 1995.

Light, Ivan, and Edna Bonacich. *Immigrant Entrepreneurs: Koreans in Los Angeles, 1965–1982*. Berkeley and Los Angeles: University of California Press, 1988.

Liu, Haiming. "The Trans-Pacific Family: A Case Study of Sam Chang's Family History." *Amerasia* 18, no. 2 (1992): 1–34.

Lopez, Kathy. "Migrants between Empires and Nations: The Chinese in Cuba, 1874–1959." PhD diss., University of Michigan, 2005.

Lyman, Stanford. *Chinese Americans*. New York: Random House, 1974.

Ma, Laurence J. C., and Carolyn L. Cartier. *The Chinese Diaspora: Space, Place, Mobility, and Identity*. Lanham, Md.: Rowman & Littlefield, 2003.

MacDonald, John, and Leatrice MacDonald. "Chain Migration, Ethnic Neighborhood Formation, and Social Networks." *Milbank Memorial Fund Quarterly* 13, no. 42 (1964): 82–97.

Masterson, Daniel. *The Japanese in Latin America*. Urbana: University of Illinois Press, 2004.

McKeown, Adam. *Chinese Migrant Networks and Cultural Change: Peru, Chicago, Hawaii, 1900–1936*. Chicago: University of Chicago Press, 2001.

Mei, June. "Socioeconomic Origins of Emigration: Guangdong to California, 1850–1882." *Modern China* 5, no. 4 (1979): 463–500.

Mishima, Ota, ed. *Destino Mexico: Un estudio de las migraciones asiáticas a Mexico, siglos XIX y XX*. Mexico City: El Colegio de México, Centro de Estudios de Asia y Africa, 1997.

Morales, Catalina V. *Los inmigrantes chinos en Baja California, 1920–1937*. Mexicali: Universidad Autónoma de Baja California, 2001.

Moya, José. *Cousins and Strangers: Spanish Immigrants in Buenos Aires, 1850–1940*. Berkeley and Los Angeles: University of California Press, 1998.

Muñoz, Gabriel T. *Kitakaze: Los japoneses en Baja California*. Mexicali: Editorial Larva, 1997.

Nagata, Mary L. "Labour Migration, Family and Community in Early Modern Japan." In *Women, Gender, and Labour Migration: Historical and Global Perspectives*, edited by Pamela Sharpe. London: Routledge, 2001.

Okamura, Jonathan. *Imagining the Filipino American Diaspora: Transnational Relations, Identities, and Communities*. New York: Garland, 1998.

Ong, Aihwa, and Donald M. Nonini, eds. *Ungrounded Empires: The Cultural Politics of Modern Chinese Transnationalism*. New York: Routledge, 1997.

Pan, Lynn. *Sons of the Yellow Emperor*. Boston: Little, Brown, 1990.

Pastor, Rodriguez. *Herederos del dragón : Historia de la comunidad China en el Perú*. Lima: Fondo Editorial del Congreso del Perú, 2000.

Puig, Juan. *Entre el río Perla y el Nazas: La China decimonónica y sus braceros emigrantes, la colonia china de Torreón y la matanza de 1911*. Mexico City: Consejo Nacional para la Cultura y las Artes, 1993.

Purcell, Victor. *The Chinese in Southeast Asia*. London: Oxford University Press, 1951.

Reid, Anthony, ed. *Sojourners and Settlers: Histories of Southeast Asia and the Chinese*. Australia: Allen & Unwin, 1996.

Renique, Gerardo. "Anti-Chinese Racism, Nationalism and State Formation in Post-Revolutionary Mexico, 1920s–1930s." *Political Power and Social Theory* 14 (2000): 91–140.

———. "Race, Region, and Nation: Sonora's Anti-Chinese Racism and Mexico's Postrevolutionary Nationalism, 1920s–1930s." In *Race and Nation in Modern Latin America*, edited by Nancy Applebaum, Anne S. MacPherson, and Karin Alejandra Rosemblatt, 211–37. Chapel Hill: University of North Carolina Press.

Romero, Robert Chao. "'El destierro de los chinos': Popular Perspectives on Chinese-Mexican Intermarriage in the Early Twentieth Century." *Aztlan: A Journal of Chicano Studies* 32, no. 1 (Spring 2007): 113–44.

———. "Transnational Chinese Immigrant Smuggling to the United States via Mexico and Cuba, 1882–1916." *Amerasia Journal* 30, no. 3 (2004–2005): 1–16.

———. "Transnational Commercial Orbits." In *A Companion to California History*, edited by William Deverell and David Igler, 230–46. Malden, Mass.: Blackwell, 2008.

Ropp, Steven M. "Japanese Ethnicity and Peruvian Nationalism in the 1990s: Transnational Imaginaries and Alternative Hegemonies." PhD diss., UCLA, 2003.

Rouse, Roger. "Mexican Migration and the Social Space of Postmodernism." *Diaspora* 1, no. 1 (Spring 1991): 8–23.

Safran, William. "Diasporas in Modern Societies: Myths of Homeland and Return." *Diaspora* 1, no. 1 (Spring 1991): 83–99.

Salyer, Lucy. *Laws Harsh as Tigers: Chinese Immigrants and the Shaping of Modern Immigration Law.* Chapel Hill: University of North Carolina Press, 1995.

Saxton, Alexander. *The Indispensable Enemy.* Berkeley and Los Angeles: University of California Press, 1971.

Schirokauer, Conrad. *A Brief History of Chinese Civilization.* San Diego: Harcourt Brace Gap College, 1991.

Schurz, William. *The Manila Galleon.* New York: E. P. Dutton, 1939.

Skidmore, Thomas E., and Peter H. Smith. *Modern Latin America.* New York: Oxford University Press, 1997.

Skinner, G. William. *Chinese Society in Thailand: An Analytical History.* Ithaca, N.Y.: Cornell University Press, 1957.

Taylor, Lawrence D. "Chinese Smuggling across the United States–Mexico Border, 1882–1916." In *Annual Proceedings from the Rocky Mountain Council for Latin American Studies,* edited by Theo R. Crevenna, 93–107. Albuquerque: Latin American Institute of the University of New Mexico, 1992.

Tololyan, Khachig. "The Nation-State and Its Others: In Lieu of a Preface." *Diaspora* 1, no. 1 (Spring 1991): 3–7.

Trueba Lara, José Luis. *Los chinos en Sonora: Una historia olvidada* Hermosillo: Instituto de Investigaciones Historicas, Universidad de Sonora, 1990.

Tsai, Shih-shan Henry. *China and the Overseas Chinese in the United States, 1868–1911.* Fayetteville: University of Arkansas Press, 1983.

Turner, Mary. "Chinese Contract Labor in Cuba, 1847–1874." *Caribbean Studies* 14, no. 2 (July 1974): 66–78.

Vasconcelos, José. *La raza cosmica.* Translated by Didier T. Jaen (Baltimore: Johns Hopkins University Press, 1997).

Walker, Townsend. "Gold Mountain Guests: Chinese Migration to the United States, 1848–1882." PhD diss., Stanford University, 1976.

Wang, L. Ling-Chi. "The Structure of Dual Domination: Toward a Paradigm for the Study of the Chinese Diaspora in the United States." *Amerasia* 21, no. 1–2 (1995): 149–60.

Watson, James L. *Emigration and the Chinese Lineage: The Mans in Hong Kong and London.* Berkeley and Los Angeles: University of California Press, 1975.

Wickberg, Edgar. *The Chinese in Philippine Life, 1850–1898.* New Haven: Yale University Press, 1965.

Wilcox, Walter F., ed. *International Migrations.* Vol. 1, *Statistics, Compiled on Behalf of the International Labour Office, Geneva.* New York: National Bureau of Economic Research, 1929.

Wong, Bernard. "A Comparative Study of the Assimilation of the Chinese in New York City and Lima, Peru." *Comparative Studies in Society and History* 20 (1978): 335–58.

Woon, Yuen-fong. *Social Organization in South China, 1911–1949: The Case of the Kuan Lineage in K'aip'ing County.* Ann Arbor: Center for Chinese Studies, University of Michigan, 1984.

Yamawaki, Chikako. *Estrategias de vida de los inmigrantes asiáticos en el Perú.* Lima: Instituto de Estudios Peruanos, the Japan Center for Area Studies, 2002.

Yu, Renqiu. "Chinese American Contributions to the Educational Development of Toisan, 1910–1940." *Amerasia* 10, no. 1 (1983): 47–72.

Yung, Judy. *Unbound Feet: A Social History of Chinese Women in San Francisco.* Berkeley and Los Angeles: University of California Press, 1995.

Zhenman, Zheng. *Family Lineage Organization and Social Change in Ming and Qing Fujian.* Honolulu: University of Hawaii Press, 2001.

Zhou, Min. *Chinatown: The Socioeconomic Potential of an Urban Enclave.* Philadelphia: Temple University Press, 1992.

Index

About the Author

Robert Chao Romero is Assistant Professor in the UCLA César E. Chávez Department of Chicana/o Studies. He received his Juris Doctor from U.C. Berkeley and his PhD in Latin American History from UCLA. He is a former Ford Foundation and U.C. President's Postdoctoral Fellow and currently serves on the editorial boards of *Law and Society Review* and *Revista Meyibó: Instituto de Investigaciones Históricas UABC–Tijuana*.

Romero's research examines Asian immigration to Latin America and historical and contemporary relations between Asians and Latinos in the Americas. In addition to the present book, he has published several articles on the Chinese of Mexico, including: "'El destierro de los chinos': Popular Perspectives on Chinese-Mexican Intermarriage in the Early Twentieth Century," *Aztlán: A Journal of Chicano Studies* 32, no. 1 (Spring 2007); "Transnational Chinese Immigrant Smuggling to the United States via Mexico and Cuba, 1882–1916," *Amerasia Journal* 30, no. 3 (2004–2005): 1–16; and, "Transnational Commercial Orbits," in *A Companion to California History*, ed. William Deverell and David Igler (Malden, Mass.: Blackwell, 2008).